"Chris Hillman has been a well-kept secret in the history of rock. Yeah, we all know how great he was in The Byrds, but his contributions go well beyond that. Chris was a true innovator—the man who invented country rock. Sorry, Gram, Chris got there first! Every time The Eagles board their private jet, Chris at least paid for the fuel."

—*Tom Petty*

"Before I met Chris Hillman, I imagined him to be a larger-than-life musical adventurer who had been to the moon and back, lived to tell about it, and was the keeper of a thousand songs and stories. After I got to know Chris Hillman, I learned that he is, indeed, a larger-than-life character—a fearless musical adventurer who has been to the moon and back more than once, and brought back a lifetime's worth of colorful stories to tell, many of which are within the pages of this book.

I also came to understand that Chris Hillman is a bona fide pioneering godfather to generations of musical souls who've sought inspiration at that divine crossroads where rock & roll, country, bluegrass, folk, honky tonk, and gospel music intersect and harmonize. Chris sings like a Byrd, his is the soul of a poet, he's the only guy in the world that can properly play 'Eight Miles High' on the mandolin, and his bass playing is the essence of great American rock & roll. Chris Hillman is a national treasure, truly a statesman. He's my brother, and I dearly love him."

—*Marty Stuart*

"This book brought back a lot of great memories! Chris covers the humorous origins of The Byrds and subsequent adventures, from meeting our heroes the Beatles in 1965 to going on tour together with Marty Stuart and his Fabulous Superlatives in 2018."

—*Roger McGuinn*

"Reading this book reminds me how much fun it was to be in the Byrds. We didn't really have a clue about the music biz, but we did love the music and we had such a blast when we were actually doing it. Wish I had known more and done better, but we did create some wonderful art together, and I will always be proud to have been a part of it and to be friends with Chris."

—*David Crosby*

"I always loved Chris Hillman's bass playing in The Byrds—really muscular, yet surprisingly nuanced. Never given to flash or anything showy, he concentrated on keeping a death grip on the groove. So, when he would come around the Whisky a Go Go to catch a set or two of our band, The Buffalo Springfield, I was always thrilled. We'd lurk about at the back of the Whisky a Go Go, cracking each other up with flinty-eyed observations regarding the predatory titans of the music business. Chris taught me that it was "all about the songs," and we agreed that the best thing to do was to write them yourself and publish them yourself. Own the copyright.

We had a great time putting the Manassas band together in England and creating that telepathic bond that develops playing live onstage or writing songs—open enough to let the other get inside your head and embrace the magic. It was all made possible by the fact that we started out as friends. We had an epic musical partnership for a while, and that Manassas band made some incredible music."

—*Stephen Stills*

"Chris Hillman emerged from the ashes of The Byrds a seasoned and prolific songwriter. His compositions infusing folk, country, and rock have always been lyrically substantial and melodically memorable. That standard of excellence has never wavered, making him the unvarnished gem of every band he has inhabited. It's time to applaud his legacy and salute the hands that rocked the cradle."

—*Bernie Taupin*

# TIME BETWEEN

# TIME BETWEEN

MY LIFE AS A BYRD, BURRITO BROTHER, AND BEYOND

## CHRIS HILLMAN

BMG

Time Between
My Life as a Byrd, Burrito Brother, and Beyond

Book production by Adept Content Solutions.

Cover design by Patrick Crowley
Cover photo courtesy of Sony Music Archives

Library of Congress Cataloging-in-Publication Data available upon request.

Hardback ISBN: 9781947026353
Ebook ISBN: 9781947026384

Second Printing.

Published by BMG
www.bmg.com

www.chrishillman.com

*For Connie, I'll love you until time passes me by.*

*For Catherine, Nick, and my grandchildren,*
*and for Nicky and Annie, you are all more precious than gold.*

# CONTENTS

# FOREWORD
# OUT OF A CALIFORNIA SKY

The iconic cover photo of *Time Between* captures, with the snap of a camera's shutter, everything about the moment in American musical history when a quintessentially seminal California band forever changed pop culture throughout the world. That band, The Byrds, which would come to be known as "America's Beatles," not only reintroduced Bob Dylan as a rock-and-roll songwriting giant with the release of their indelibly cinematic recording of "Mr. Tambourine Man," but planted a sonic victory flag foretelling the Golden State's imminent conquests, reshaping, and shared dominance of modern popular music.

With everything that photo of The Byrds' founding member Chris Hillman says about the cultural moment in which it was taken, it's only upon reading here Chris's telling of his life's journey and musical evolution that the image fully conveys everything else about the "times" between that moment and the collective moments that led up to it and beyond. In reading his book, I have come to conclude that a very strong argument can be made that Chris Hillman was, in fact, the very soul of The Byrds, always pushing himself and those around him in the band to see the possibilities of, not just what their music *was,* but what their music could become.

In the spectrum of California cultural expressions, if James Ellroy's viscerally tragic scat-jazz autobiographic history, *My Dark Places,* embodies the antithesis of the world's "Ozzie and Harriet" vision of post-war 1940s, '50s, and early '60s Southern California, then Chris Hillman's self-penned story unfolds as a parallel universe version of the same time and place that is disarmingly compelling in its succinct directness and profoundly innocent emotional candor. The window he opens onto his and his family members' lives reveals the California that existed beneath the hazy shimmering mirage that was often viewed from the distance by those of us in the rest of America as an idealized sunlit Hockney-like daydream illusion that we believed existed. Unlike Ellroy's seductively glamorous seedy tomes that often strut around in gilded counterpoint to the citrus crate bucolic perfection of the Nelsons' TV world, Hillman's book resonates in a realm of unaffected honesty, never attempting verbose grandeur, but with every page, paragraph, sentence, and word disclosing a sublime reality.

That cover photo moment of Chris embodies, simultaneously, the worldly awareness, cultural coolness, and ricocheting angst-riddled earnestness that is uniquely and specifically embedded in the Tom Joad-cum-James Dean/Steve McQueen DNA of California's versions of rock, pop, country, and, ultimately, the LA-born genre of country-rock music. As I remarked in a previous foreword for the book *Hot Burritos: The True Story of the Flying Burrito Brothers,* and have now reaffirmed after reading the telling of his own story in the following pages, Chris Hillman proved to be a Kit Carson-like California musical frontiersman and pathfinder that all of us who have subsequently followed in modern country and country-rock music used as a crucial navigational beacon to track toward our own musical destinies. In spite of Chris's varying degrees of chagrin through the years at being given the title, to me and millions of other fans, he will remain forever immortal as one of the principal architects and a founding father of country-rock.

Dwight Yoakam
Los Angeles, California, May 2020

# INTRODUCTION
## HEAVENLY FIRE

It was December 4, 2017, the night of my seventy-third birthday. I was celebrating with my wife Connie, our daughter Catherine, our son-in-law Nick, and our granddaughter at a restaurant near our home in Ventura, California. Nick, a firefighter, received a text at the dinner table around 7:00 p.m. alerting him that a strong brush fire had broken out in Santa Paula, California, an inland city about twenty miles east. There was no indication of an immediate problem.

As the evening wound down, Connie and I said our goodbyes and made the short drive home. We noticed that the wind had picked up. By the time we pulled into our driveway it was blowing at least seventy-five miles per hour. We went to bed around 9:30 p.m., just after the power had gone out as a result of the high winds—or so we assumed. We went to sleep, but Connie was later awakened at around 11:00 p.m. by the smell of smoke. She ran to the window and saw an angry red glow covering the whole skyline. The entire ridge across the street from us was on fire.

We had no advance warning to prepare, but we knew we had to evacuate immediately. Having no electrical power, we propped open the garage door with a broom handle and backed out one of the cars. We loaded it up with important papers, our passports, family photos, and icons we had brought home with us from a pilgrimage to Jerusalem, and two of my prized instruments: a Lloyd Loar mandolin that Stephen Stills gave me many years ago and a Martin D-28 guitar that was gifted to me by the widow of Bill Smith, who had been one of my earliest musical mentors. We kept returning to the house for more things until I realized time was running out and we were in danger. The fire was gaining on us, and we could be trapped if we didn't get moving. We grabbed our dog Daisy, started up the car, and headed down the hill.

Having grown up in California, I was used to brush fires and their destructive potential when combined with powerful Santa Ana winds. I could tell that what we were seeing around us as we descended from the neighborhood was serious. This was a firestorm, and it was moving quickly, destroying everything in its path. Our son, who is also named Nick, phoned from Napa County. He had seen the news and was calling to tell us that we needed to evacuate immediately. We assured him we were already headed for safety. My phone rang again. It was John Jorgenson, one of my longtime friends and musical collaborators who happened to live, with his wife Dixie, on one of the city streets down the hill from the fire. He urged us to come to their house. When we arrived, we stood outside their door where we could see the fire roaring across the hillside. Houses were literally exploding. We decided to evacuate to a hotel near the beach to avoid the danger zone. As we left, however, we hit complete gridlock. The county was evacuating families to the local fairgrounds for temporary shelter, and we got caught up in the traffic. The route was overwhelmed with thousands of people from all over western Ventura County heading there with their horses and livestock. I turned the car around to go the other direction, but we soon discovered that the only available hotels were in the San Fernando Valley, almost an hour away. We eventually gave up and headed back to John and Dixie's for the night.

I slept through the night, but Connie didn't. At about five in the morning she saw a fire battalion chief parked with a bank of engines, holding the line where the hillside neighborhoods met the flatland. She asked if it was possible for him to check his interactive map to see if our home was still standing. He promised to do more than that. "I'll go up and check for you," he told her, "and I'll call you in twenty minutes." He kept his word. When Connie answered her phone, he said, "If I have the right place, I think your house made it, but everything around you is gone." When the sun rose, we decided to drive up the hill to check on our home. "It's possible," I told Connie as we got in the car, "that the house is gone. We might not have a home anymore." She squeezed my hand. "But we're alive," she responded, "and that's all that matters." Connie has always had a wonderful way of putting things in perspective.

As we rounded the last curve to our driveway, there stood our house. Fire had consumed two rooms of our home but, by the grace of God, it was still standing despite the total devastation all around us. The surrounding area was an eerie sight. Entire homes were reduced to rubble. It looked more like a bombed-out scene from war-torn Syria than the familiar neighborhood streets I drove every day. Smoke was still rising from the ground, gas lines were burning, and the wind was whipping up toxic ash that floated in the air all around us. I saw some strange and unfamiliar faces on our property. Possible looters. Our front door was smashed, and a number of windows were broken. With no way to secure the house, I decided to stay the night. With a mask over my face, a flashlight in one hand, and a Glock 26 nine-millimeter pistol in the other, I was prepared to take on whatever might come along. We were able to secure the property the next day, and I decided not to stay another night, with the air so toxic.

It was the next morning, when we were checking the damage, that we discovered what happened the night of the fire. Four Ventura County firefighters from Simi Valley Station 41 stopped by to check to see if there was anything still smoldering on our roof. They told us that after we evacuated and the worst of the firestorm had passed, they were checking on the homes that had survived so they could extinguish any remaining blazes that might threaten houses that hadn't yet burned. It was about three in the morning when they pulled up to our house just in time to see our neighbor's burning balcony collapse through our kitchen window, setting our kitchen and den on fire. The city generators weren't activated, which rendered the neighborhood fire hydrants useless. Hoses were left in the street as firefighters hooked up, only to discover that there was no water. But the crew of Station 41 calculated that they had just enough resources left on their engine to save our home. They broke down the front door, rushed in, and extinguished the flames. Fire had already consumed the two rooms, but their quick action saved the rest of the house from total destruction. We are eternally grateful to that team of first responders who saved our home, led by Captains Lance Austin and Jon Jelle.

Hotel rooms were difficult to come by for a few days, but our insurance agent came through with a hotel at the harbor. That became our home for several weeks until we could relocate to a large and comfortable furnished house near the beach for the next eight months. Everything from our home that was not destroyed would be moved into storage at a restoration company while repairs were undertaken on our battered home. It was bad, but it could have been much worse. The Thomas Fire, as it was named, burned over 280,000 acres and was the largest wildfire in modern state history until it was surpassed by an even bigger blaze the following summer. Many around us lost everything. As the fire moved north, mudslides completely overran the city of Montecito and twenty-three people lost their lives, as their homes and neighborhoods were swallowed up by a torrent of flowing mud and boulders. We were affected but, as Connie reminded me, we were alive. We'd survived it.

The Thomas Fire wasn't the first fire I ever faced. In fact, it was the third time that a blazing inferno drove me from a home. And, over the course of my life, I have faced down and survived plenty of metaphorical fires too. I've been confronted by personal struggles, and I've lost people I loved deeply. I've overcome the ravages of disease. I lost an earthly father too young and found a heavenly Father that I only wish I'd found sooner. I've experienced the highs, lows, temptations, and triumphs of life as a professional musician. I was blessed to have been a member of The Byrds, The Flying Burrito Brothers, Manassas, Souther-Hillman-Furay, and The Desert Rose Band, where I survived countless miles of endless highway pursuing my dreams. I was honored to be inducted into the Rock & Roll Hall of Fame, but my greatest honor is being a husband to Connie, a father to Catherine and Nick, a father-in-law to their spouses, Nick and Annie, and "Papa" to my granddaughter and grandson. I've lived a very full life, and God has blessed me abundantly.

I was born on December 4, 1944. One day, when my time on earth is finished, that date will be chiseled in stone. It will be followed by a dash and another date will be chiseled next to it. My faith teaches that we are only passing through this earthly realm, so that's when I will be reunited with my loved ones who have gone before me. But I *do* believe that what happens in the dash between those dates matters. That's why I want to tell you my story. As time moves on and history fades, those dates might become what's remembered about Chris Hillman. Let me tell you about the time between. At least so far.

# CHAPTER ONE
# IN ANOTHER LIFETIME

"**W**hat the hell's the matter with you?" the old man roared as he snatched the rifle from my hands. Whenever he used that voice I knew I was in trouble. "Dad, Dad," I protested. "I didn't mean to! He ran right in front of me just when I was pulling the trigger!" I had just shot our family beagle in the rear end with my Daisy Red Rider BB gun. My father shook his head and stomped off, getting about forty feet away before abruptly spinning on his heels to face me once again. "That was one hell of an excuse," he shouted back in my direction. I could detect the faintest hint of a smile, but he managed to maintain his parental composure. Our ever-faithful beagle was fine, but I wasn't. Sure, I was feeling a little guilty for what I'd done to the dog, but the real reason was because I knew I wouldn't see that rifle again for a long time.

I was eight years old, and it was 1952 in Rancho Santa Fe, California. The population of the San Diego County town at the time was approximately 750. We lived on an acre of land on a street called Las Planideras, which loosely translates "the wailing women." There was something magical about growing up in post-World War II small-town America—particularly at the furthest point west, in the "Golden State." I've always been in love with this unique part of Southern California and feel fortunate to have grown up in such a rural environment that was also socioeconomically diverse at the time.

1

My mother, Betty Ann Charlton, married my father, David Sidney Hillman, in Los Angeles in 1935. By the time I came along—on December 4, 1944—my folks already had two kids: my brother Dick, who was six years older than me, and my sister Susan, who was nine years older. My little sister Cathy would come along about three years after I was born.

My dad had a successful advertising agency called Hillman-Shane in downtown L.A. that he started in 1935. As far as I know, my parents never had any plans to move from the house they built on Cordell Drive above the Sunset Strip. But then they stumbled upon their dream house in Rancho Santa Fe on one of their frequent weekend trips down south. It was a one-story California ranch house with a big fireplace, four bedrooms, three bathrooms, and huge support pillars in the front living area. We relocated to our new home in 1946, when I was all of two years old. Upon our arrival, I was quickly confined to my high chair and given half a bagel to keep me occupied while the rest of the family members unloaded the car.

The roots of Rancho Santa Fe—roughly translated "Ranch of the Saint's Faith"—stretch back to a Mexican land grant called Rancho San Dieguito that was given to the first mayor of San Diego, Juan Maria Osuna, by Don Pio Pico, the last Mexican governor of California, sometime in the 1840s. The grant was well over 8,000 acres and, upon Osuna taking possession, he began building two adobe houses for his family. Both structures still stand today and have been designated as historical landmarks.

In 1906, the Santa Fe Railway bought most of the Osuna family's holdings. The idea was to import and plant eucalyptus trees from Australia to eventually be harvested for use as railroad track ties. As it turned out, the wood was too green. It would have had to age for decades to be of any value to the Santa Fe company, so the original idea was abandoned. But the beautiful leafy trees remained and grew in abundance over the entire Rancho San Dieguito tract. Out of one failed experiment, another far more successful idea began to bloom.

The railroad, looking to recoup its losses, formed the Santa Fe Land Improvement Company for the express purpose of developing an agricultural and residential community. With the hiring of noted architect Lillian J. Rice, agronomist A.R. Sprague, and landscape architect Glenn A. Moore, the team was in place to create the village of Rancho Santa Fe.

Ms. Rice designed the homes to look like an early Mexican settlement. She also designed the town center—a mix of commercial and residential buildings—as well as the first elementary school and the La Morada guesthouse, which later became the Inn, a noted hotel that's still there today. It took no time for the town to grow as more people discovered the hidden beauty in the rural backdrop of San Diego County.

By the time our family came along decades later, the unincorporated town of Rancho Santa Fe still had strict guidelines set down by the town overseers. The covenants kept the architectural style within the established boundaries to preserve the area's quaint beauty. Unfortunately, there were also rules firmly stating that people of color couldn't reside anywhere within the town limits. And keep in mind this was progressive California, not Mississippi. Sure, a small-town body could establish a set of covenants to preserve a town's image and character, but this was blatant racism, pure and simple—an embarrassing stain on an otherwise idyllic environment for a kid to grow up in.

Though my father was Jewish, I suppose he managed to find a way to slip through the community's bigoted restrictions. Perhaps it was the fact that he virtually ignored his heritage and identity. Yes, he was a Jew by birth, but there was no religious dimension to his life. My dad was a committed atheist.

The only time our family personally felt the sting of the town's discriminatory guidelines happened when I was three years old. It's actually my earliest memory. I'm wrapped up in a blanket in the back of our Pontiac station wagon. It's late at night, and I'm looking out the window of the car at our house. Our house is on fire! My father is on the roof, furiously chopping away at the shingles with an axe. It's still a vivid snapshot in my mind. Fortunately, the fire truck finally arrived and got everything under control. The damage was minimal, and life eventually resumed after the house was repaired, but not before we felt that sting I mentioned.

In the main part of town was that beautiful hotel called the Inn, which had been designed by Lillian J. Rice all those years ago. The night of the fire, my father drove us over to the hotel so we could stay there until it was safe to return home. When he went to check in, he was turned away at the front desk. "I'm sorry, sir," the clerk told him, "but this is a restricted hotel." "Restricted" meant no Blacks, no Mexicans, no Asians, and no Jews. We were actually friendly with the manager of the hotel and his family, which made the rejection even more difficult to understand.

That very night, after being told there was no room in the Inn, Mom and Dad managed to find some wonderful friends, the Dunns, who agreed to take us kids in. I'm not positive where my parents ended up staying that night, but I do know that, at three o'clock in the morning, my father woke up, bolted out of bed, and told my mom, "I'll be right back. I have to take care of something."

Dad drove over to the hotel manager's house, knocked on the door, and when the gentleman answered, landed a right hook to his jaw. It was a true Rocky Marciano moment, sending the hotel manager sprawling across the floor. That was my dad's sense of justice. His family had been disparaged, and he wasn't going to allow it to stand. Amazingly, after many apologies, the manager of the Inn and his family remained friends with the Hillmans through the years.

Even after moving down to San Diego County, my father maintained his advertising business one hundred miles away in downtown Los Angeles. While my mom and siblings and I lived in Rancho Santa Fe all the time, my father spent his weeknights at an apartment he kept in the city. Every Monday morning, he would catch the northbound Union Pacific at the Del Mar train station. It was a classic turn-of-century depot that had one ticket window and a small waiting room. Outside, there was a big handcart for luggage and an old vending machine that dispensed a piece of gum for a penny.

It was always an adventure waiting for my dad's train to arrive on Friday evenings, when he'd finally return home for the weekend. I would carefully place a penny on the tracks when my mother wasn't looking. Then, hiding behind the corner of the station, I'd keep a close watch for the southbound Union Pacific to start slowing down to make its stop. Once it ground to a halt, I'd search for my lucky flattened penny while carefully dodging my mother's watchful eye.

My father's weekly return wasn't always a joyous occasion, however—especially if I had done something wrong while he was away. In those instances, my mother would patiently wait until he was settled in and had his first martini before telling him about the mischief I had gotten into. Even when he had to discipline us kids for the various ways we'd managed to turn the place upside down in his absence, however, my dad was always glad to return home. The gentleman rancher, back in command of his personal Utopia.

While he was certainly great at his job, the ranch was where my dad felt most fulfilled. He built all kinds of interesting things: a walk-in tool shed, a large wishing well made out of river rock, a full flagstone patio, and a barbeque with a waist-high brick wall that wrapped around the whole patio area. He even built beautiful white wooden corrals all around our property, giving it the look of a proper ranch. But just because he loved undertaking projects didn't mean there weren't a few funny mishaps along the way. One day, for example, my father decided to replace the tile in the shower. He did a magnificent job. Standing back and surveying his handiwork, he decided to go ahead and tile the ceiling, too. It looked great until he took his third shower. Most of the tiles came loose and fell on his head. But he was able to laugh at the misadventures and move on to his next project.

I have many warm memories of wonderful summer evenings out on our patio, Mom cooking on the barbeque, Dad knocking back a martini, and all us kids running around the back lawn. We had an incredible view of the valley below and there was a certain wildness to the place that was enchanting to a kid. The street we lived on, Las Planideras, was bordered on both sides by huge eucalyptus trees, all left over from the railroad experiment. I always thought a koala bear would magically appear high up in the branches someday, but I guess they didn't make the trip over with the Australian saplings in 1900.

The mighty eucalyptus trees' thick branches were perfect for building forts and tree houses. Pieces of bark would become our imaginary weapons of choice: swords, rifles, clubs, and anything else we could come up with to fight off the "bad guys." When I got a little older, my dad took me down to the army surplus store and let me get an old World War II M1 rifle with a plugged barrel, plus a canteen and web belt. Most of my friends had the same equipment, which allowed for hours of fantasy and adventure. Once I got to be about ten, I inherited my brother Dick's old 0.22 single-shot rifle. My father taught me about guns and gun safety, and more adventures ensued. There was so much space and so many mysterious places to explore in our little corner of the universe; this was a boys' paradise, and we were all allowed to play outdoors with (mostly) free reign.

Rancho Santa Fe itself was built in the old Mission Style; the buildings were adobe with mostly red tile roofs. The Village, as we often called the town center, was our version of idyllic Main Street Americana. Like most other small towns, we had one gas station, Bob Francisco's Mobil station. We had one grocery store called Ashley's market. Then we had a post office and the curious distinction of hosting more real estate offices in one square mile than any other city in Southern California. Finally, there was a restaurant called Bill and Emma's Fountain Lunch, which was the central meeting place for all the town's residents.

Bill Apperance cooked at the café, while his wife Emma waited on customers. Bill was quite a character. He had jet-black hair slicked back and parted in the middle and a long handlebar mustache. Bill looked (and acted) like an 1890s bartender. He loved to bet the ponies and all manner of things one could wager money on. One of the regulars at Bill and Emma's was Paul Wilson. He had long red hair (quite a rare sight at the time), wore boots and a jean jacket, and gave off a Marlboro Man vibe that qualified him as possibly the coolest guy in town. Paul was always sitting at the counter, smoking a cigarette and drinking coffee. I'm pretty sure he did some ranch work for some of the locals, but he always remained a mystery. Everyone in our family referred to him as the Red Cowboy.

There might have been a total of eight homes on Las Planideras Street back in the early '50s, stretching out a mile or more. The remote location attracted well-known Hollywood performers who were drawn to the rural setting as a refuge from the limelight. About a quarter mile down from our house lived Madame Amelita Galli-Curci, a famous singer who toured the world before joining the Metropolitan Opera in 1921. But I never actually saw Madame Galli-Curci in my time living on Las Planideras. If you knocked on her door, it would creak open ever so slightly. All you would see were the two dark eyes of her housekeeper or assistant peering through the tiny crack in the door. That only added to the mystery. Sometimes I would stop my bike in front of her house and just stare, wondering what was going on inside.

At the top of Las Planideras, on one of the side streets, lived well-known character actor Robert Keith. Like others, he saw our town as an oasis from the chaos of the Hollywood scene. Mr. Keith was well remembered for the role of the small-town sheriff in the Marlon Brando film *Wild One*. Robert's son, Brian Keith, was equally famous, having a long and successful career in television and movies. Mr. Keith the elder was rarely seen but for occasional forays into town where you could spot him nursing a Bromo seltzer at Bill and Emma's café.

Mr. Keith and Madame Galli-Curci certainly weren't the first to escape Hollywood and seek solace on the Ranch. In a much earlier time, Douglas Fairbanks and Mary Pickford discovered the pristine beauty of the San Dieguito tract, buying 3,000 acres of prime land in 1926, just as the ranch properties were being marketed and sold. In the '30s, Bing Crosby bought up the original Osuna Adobe and most of the surrounding land. He restored and added to the existing ranch house, creating a true Spanish paradise as a summer home. Other notable actors such as Victor Mature and Robert Young made their second homes in Rancho Santa Fe, as well. We would always see Victor Mature cruising around town in his red Cadillac convertible; a nice man who was very generous with his charitable contributions and made a point of being involved in the everyday life of the Ranch. He became a close friend of my father's.

George J. Lewis was also seen a lot around the center and became a friend to our family. Though he appeared in hundreds of films as a character actor, he became best known for the role of Don Diego, Zorro's father on the Walt Disney weekly television series *The Adventures of Zorro*. When not working in Hollywood, he had one of the many real estate businesses in town. These were some of the more interesting neighbors we had nearby, and their notoriety made for wonderful legends and strange tales.

One of those great Rancho Santa Fe characters was later immortalized in a song I wrote when I was in my twenties. There was a prominent older gentleman, John Robertson, who made the rounds of the Village when I was a kid. Mr. Robertson had enjoyed a successful movie career as an actor and director. Most of his work was in the silent picture era, but he ended up directing one of Shirley Temple's movies in the '30s before he finally retired to the Ranch. Mr. Robertson wore a silver belly Stetson hat, riding jodhpurs, and boots. With his long, white handlebar mustache, he resembled a sheriff out of the Old West. Robertson was never without his wife Jo by his side. He was a wonderful man who knew everyone by name and was so very kind to all of us kids. I always loved running into him. In 1967, as a member of The Byrds, I wrote "Old John Robertson" with Roger McGuinn in tribute to my childhood memories of him. Legend has it that John Robertson could never properly drive a car because he couldn't drive in reverse. Instead, he would just saddle up his horse and ride into town to get his mail. My kind of man! A man I looked up to and never forgot for the rest of my life.

Though it might seem a bit odd to think about people riding horses around town in that era, it wasn't particularly unusual. In fact, old John Robertson started the Rancho Santa Fe Riding Club, which was exactly the kind of place I wanted to be. My dad was an accomplished horseman and made sure my brother Dick and I learned to ride at a very early age. Dad would frequently take us to a stable outside of town that was run by a man named Leo Sides. I don't know why I remember his name after all these years, but he must have left a great impression on me. I even remember the first horse I ever rode: Peanut Brittle. I was only about three or four when I first got on him. I was already living the childhood dream with my cowboy hat, boots, and everything.

Dick never quite caught the bug like I did, and as he grew older, he started to lose interest. He finally called it quits. But I was on a mission to someday get a horse of my own. When I was around six years old, my dad and I would rent horses from a man named Tex Weimer who had a small outfit just outside of town. Tex was an older fella who didn't have much to say, but when he did speak, it stuck with you. He was an important teacher who continued the lessons I'd begun with Mr. Sides. Often, my dad and I would get a couple of horses from Tex and take off for a few hours, riding around Rancho.

As I got older, there was another man I took riding lessons from named Jess McMillin. Jess was a big part of the Rancho Santa Fe Riding Club with John Robertson, and he was as tough as they come. Under no circumstances would he ever allow you to surrender to the horse. His wise words saved me from many scary encounters. Horses are big animals, and when they get rattled, you have to control them. You can't show any fear—even if you're scared for your life.

By the time I was six or seven, I was focused on becoming a real cowboy and getting a horse of my own. All of us kids were assigned various chores around the house and were paid one dollar per week for doing our different jobs. No, we weren't indentured servants; that was actually a decent wage back in very early 1950s. Still fairly young at the time, my responsibilities included sweeping, raking, watering, and any extra little projects my folks would come up with. Once I caught horse fever around the age of six, I started saving my money with a vengeance. Within a year, I had sixty dollars to my name.

My father was reading the newspaper one evening when I slipped in with my small fortune. "Dad," I asked, "do you think I could find a good horse for sixty dollars?" He smiled and turned to the classifieds to see if anyone had one for sale. Soon, we were checking the want ads every day and started driving around to some of the smaller ranches in the county to see if we could find anything. After a week or two of searching, we hadn't come up with any options. But I knew we would eventually find the right horse.

Then, late one afternoon, my mother, father, and sister Cathy and I were pulling into the driveway of our house. As my dad stopped the car and turned off the engine, he leaned over the seat and said, "Chris, go out in the corral and pick up some boxes I left this morning." I slowly got out of the car and reluctantly headed for the corral, not really wanting to pick up any boxes. When I got to the end of the driveway, I opened the gate and there, standing ever so proud and handsome, was a horse. *My* horse! My *palomino* horse! I was speechless; I couldn't believe this was happening! *Where did he come from? Was he really mine?* Mom and Dad walked over. "What do you think, son?" my dad asked. "Do you like him?" Like him? I *loved* him!

"Dad, is he really mine to keep?" I said when I was finally able to find some words.

"He's all yours," my father nodded. "But there's one rule you must learn: the day you forget to feed him is the day he'll go back where he came from." I got the message loud and clear. I immediately fed him and began grooming him. That very night I decided to call him Ranger. I was so excited that, after I finally fell asleep that night, I dreamed of all the great adventures Ranger and I would have together.

As soon as dawn broke the next morning I jumped out of bed and ran down to the corral to feed Ranger. But my horse was *gone!* And the corrals were in shambles. I already mentioned that my dad had built corrals all around the property, and I mentioned that sometimes his little projects didn't work out exactly as planned. Well, when he built those corrals—with the help of my older brother and a man named Adolph, who worked for us at the ranch—he ran into some problems. While digging holes for the posts they were only able to go about a foot-and-a-half before hitting solid clay. Southern California soil is perfect if you're building an adobe house or a mission, but if you're trying to dig a hole, it can be virtually impossible. Dad decided to shortcut the process by just sinking the posts in eighteen inches, laying in lots of concrete, and hoping for the best. To finish off the project, they laid the cross bars on the outside of the fence. That design looks great but is completely useless if you have any plans to keep horses or cattle inside. Sometime during the night, Ranger had simply walked through the crossbars and knocked over the posts.

Talk about extreme heartbreak. I was in tears and truly felt like my world had just ended. I think my father must have heard me because he suddenly appeared, putting his arm around my shoulder. "We'll get him back," Dad whispered. "He's probably just run home to the ranch where we got him from." A quick phone call confirmed that that's exactly where he'd ended up. We got Ranger back that day, and my dad soon went to work repairing the corrals.

With Ranger back home, I was ready to ride. But there was just one problem: I didn't have a saddle, bridle, halter, or even a blanket. This was a major obstacle, so I went to my dad and asked if there was anything else I could do to earn enough money for some basic tack.

"Let me see what I can come up with," he replied. "Hang on a minute." He disappeared into his tool shed. A few moments later he reappeared with a saddle, bridle, blanket, and a halter. "I figured since you worked hard for the horse," he smiled, "I would look out for a good used saddle to help you get started."

I ran down to the corral, put the halter on Ranger, and brought him up to the post to saddle him for the first time. My heart was beating fast. After all the wishing and dreaming, it was finally coming true: my own horse and saddle. All went well until I slipped the bridle over his head and went to put the bit in his mouth. That was the day I learned the term *bit shy*. Ranger did not want that bit in his mouth and was ready to fight me until the end. Of course, I called out to my father for help. "He's your horse," Dad shouted back. "Let him know you're the boss!" A life lesson. I got that bit in Ranger's mouth with patience I never knew I possessed. Finally, Ranger and I rode off into the unknown with only the fading words in my ears, "Be back before dark!"

Ranger was a good old boy and usually behaved himself. But there were more than a few unpleasant times when he would catch me off guard and throw me off his back. By the time he learned that trick, he already knew where his new home was. He would go tearing off for the house, followed by one mad seven-year-old, vowing to never let that happen again. Ranger also had moments of greatness. I entered local horse shows and rode in what was called a Western Gymkhana event. This was where Ranger shined. It was as if he knew he was in the spotlight and, even though he sometimes acted like the all-time demon horse on some of our trail rides, in the ring he became Champion, Gene Autry's famed horse. He cantered around in perfect cadence, looking sharp and (pretty much) obeying all of my commands. Ranger and I took home some ribbons after those horse shows and, despite his sometimes-contrary nature, he remained my closest childhood pal.

When I was eight, I joined the California Rangers, a group for boys in Rancho Santa Fe that was started by one of my early riding instructors, Jess McMillen, and a younger guy named Bruce Oxley. We would meet every Saturday morning in the summer for a day of riding, working with our horses, and basically just having a great time with each other. There were only about four or five guys in the Rangers that summer, but we got to take two multiday trips in the back country between the towns of Escondido and Rancho Santa Fe. Those experiences were incredible. In the late afternoons, we would unsaddle, brush our horses, tie them, and settle in for the evening. Sure, we could only carry so much food, so sometimes a

Ford or Chevy station wagon would come lumbering up a dirt road with someone's mom behind the wheel with additional provisions, but it was fun to pretend we were in the middle of nowhere. Cooking our own food and lying in our sleeping bags looking up at the stars were picture-perfect moments. As the evening grew later, you couldn't hear anything but the horses and whatever wild critters were out and about. It was pure heaven for a horse-loving kid.

Of course, when it wasn't summer I had to go school, but would you believe that we kids could actually ride our horses to our little three-room school house and tie them up in the back? Not many kids did that on a regular basis, but you'd see it occasionally. I know I did it a few times. With that tiny school building and those horses, you could almost imagine you were attending class at the turn of the century. There were only two teachers, Mrs. Trethaway and Mrs. Ross, each of whom covered three grades. It was a very different experience for me than what happens now. The public school system in California in the early '50s worked very well. There was discipline when needed, and the teachers and parents took a collaborative role in raising a child. If you got in trouble in school, rest assured, your folks would get the phone call from the teacher and then all hell would break out at home. We were taught responsibility and a sense of morality and values. It was the same way our parents—the "greatest generation"—had been raised. Sadly, I don't think it's like that anymore.

# CHAPTER TWO
# THE COWBOY WAY

**M**rs. Trethaway became my first teacher when I started school in first grade. She taught me to read, to write properly, and to respect and embrace life and all it had to offer. Most kids from my generation had similar grade school experiences: Our mothers sent us out every morning with a sack lunch; we sat through class with forced resignation; and we played baseball, football, dodgeball, and all manner of sports. We got into fights, which were never fun, and we suffered being bullied. Sometimes, at least in my case, we experienced getting chosen near the very end of the process when teammates were selected for a game on the playground. But we persevered, and we learned important lessons about dealing with both acceptance and rejection.

As I alluded to, this was a time when parents, teachers, and students had more of a familial relationship, which heightened the overall educational experience. I remember playing outside with my friends at one of my birthday parties when Mrs. Trethaway showed up. Not only did she make an appearance, but she brought me the most amazing present—a genuine Hopalong Cassidy hat!

Like so many guys my age, I loved the cowboys who rode on the big screen and began showing up in our living room when television was still in its infancy. My dad bought a TV in 1950 or 1951, and we may have been the only family on our street to own one at the time. There were maybe three or four channels at best, with all the shows originating out of Los Angeles and, later, a few from San Diego. It was standard fare for the time period to have cartoons, live wrestling matches, movies, and—later into the mid-1950s—soap operas and game shows. I used to love the old movie serials that Channel 5 showed every weekend. They were part of the movie theater experience in the '30s and '40s: a newsreel, a chapter of a serial, a cartoon, and then the main feature. I watched *Flash Gordon, Don Winslow of the Navy, Ace Drummond,* and *Tim Tyler's Luck* about a boy searching for his lost father in Africa. But my very favorite were the cowboys. These guys were true heroes in every sense of the word, and they stayed true to character both on and off screen. I loved Roy Rogers, Gene Autry, Johnny Mack Brown, Tex Ritter and one of my favorites, Col. Tim McCoy, who was a former World War I cavalry officer. They filled my days with adventure.

My all time favorite cowboy was Hopalong Cassidy, whose real name was William Boyd. He dressed all in black, rode a white horse, wore two guns, and took care of any trouble that came along. Hoppy was different from the other gunslingers; he seemed to light up the scene with his smile and, even at such a young age, I knew that Hoppy would never fail. He was tough, but also gentle and kind. That's why I was so thrilled when Ms. Threthaway brought me that Hoppy hat for my birthday.

Emulating cowboys and having horses around were just a couple of the ways I was gaining an appreciation for rural living. Another was learning about life from the people I would meet in our community. Our neighbors directly north of us were two interesting guys, Bill Costello and Suell Bradley. Bill took care of Suell, who we all knew had some issues. Suell was a nice man but very shy. Looking back, he reminds me of Boo Radley from *To Kill a Mockingbird.* Bill was paid by the Bradley family to care for Suell. There was a family that lived in the small guesthouse on the Bradley property named the Trujillos. Mrs. Trujillo cooked for the boys, and Mr. Trujillo was the property manager. When I was small, I would often ride my little bike with training wheels over to visit Mr. Trujillo. I called him Gardener because he tended to the grounds. I think he missed having a young kid around, as his son Malcolm was pretty much grown up by then. We instantly formed a bond and I became like Gardner's adopted son by following him around on the property. I remember that he would often build a small fire and roast fresh corn over the flames. And he always had RC Cola in the old bottles with the camel and the pyramid on the outside. Together, we would share this magnificent feast. Every so often, Gardener would catch scorpions (which were in abundance), pinch their tails off, and toss them into the fire for the strange joy of watching them dance in the flames. "Son," he would say, "don't ever touch these scorpions. They bite you bad, and they can kill you." My conversations with Gardener around the fire were my first lessons in surviving the wilderness.

But just because I was learning didn't mean I was totally prepared for a real-life threat. Most of our house's exterior doors had a one- to two-inch gap above the sill, and we would occasionally have unannounced visitors find their way inside. My mother, who was from tough Texas stock, was never bothered by the snakes, spiders, or scorpions that occasionally appeared indoors. I think I was around seven when the first snake came to visit. He was stretched out on the floor next to an extension cord when I saw him, and I must have jumped three feet in the air! My brother came into the room and, at that point, we both scrambled up on the dining room table and began squealing as if were about to die. My mother walked in with her broom and casually swept the snake out the door, telling him, "Okay, mister, this isn't your house, so time to get moving." Once he was gone, she strolled past the table where we were still cowering and quipped, "My two brave sons rescuing their poor mother from the awful, dreadful snake." We never shied away from any critter after that.

Speaking of critters, my brother joined the 4-H Club when he was eleven. He raised two hogs, which he named Benny and Mike. We also had a chicken coop, complete with actual chickens. I remember my mom gathering their eggs every day when I was around four or five, but the chickens didn't last too long. The local coyotes and an occasional bobcat managed to wipe them out pretty quickly. As for Benny and Mike, their fates weren't much better. I remember hiding in the laundry room and watching through a crack in the door as my father and his friend Pete Hernandez were fighting to get those hogs into Pete's truck to take them to the market to be butchered. I think Benny and Mike knew their fate. They were screaming their heads off and eliminating every foul substance you can think of from their bodies. What a sight! I know I picked up some particularly colorful language from my dad that day while he was wrestling those pigs. After all that trauma, most of the meat was contaminated, with the exception of a small supply of bacon that was quite tasty. Unless my Grandma Hillman was visiting from the city, there was never any mention of the word *kosher* around our household.

The animals that made the greatest impression were the various family dogs. The first of many that I remember was a dalmatian named Patch. He would chase cars, which were usually few and far between on our road. Of course, lots of dogs do that, but Patch would actually try to leap up to the driver's window. The one time he succeeded, he hung on with his paws and managed to bite the driver on the arm. Unfortunately, that driver was Sheriff Albin Pelco, a nice older fella hired by the Rancho Santa Fe Association to patrol the town. Patch had to go away after that, but I want to believe he was given to another family that lived way far away from any roads.

Barney was the next dog to live with us. He was a very sweet and lovable beagle, so that's why I felt a little guilty after I lodged that BB in his hind end. Like all beagles, Barney loved to roam. Sometimes he would be gone for hours, and we could often hear a faint howl in the distance as he was on the "chase." As Barney grew older, he rarely strayed far from home, but the coyotes would taunt him and try to lure him out. As a young fella, he knew better than to heed the coyotes' cry, but they did manage to coax him out one night in his later years. He didn't show up until the next morning, badly beaten and chewed up by the pack. We rushed him to the vet. Barney, who was a member of the family, died later that night. It was the first time I had ever seen my mother cry.

Somehow, on farms and ranches, a new dog always manages to come along. One night, while we were having dinner, we detected a quiet whimper at the side door. My dad opened it and, sitting outside, was a frightened and wounded female boxer. It appeared her ear had been damaged, as she was bleeding pretty badly. We gave her some food, but she wasn't ready to come inside yet. My mom and brother cleaned her ear up and, for the next few nights, she would show up at the door for food. She finally trusted us enough to come inside and let us all pet her. We named her Gretchen, and she happily joined our family. My father thought somebody had shot her ear with a 0.22 round because she cowered when hearing any gunshots.

It didn't take long for Gretchen to get comfortable at the ranch. There was a family named the Fleetwoods who lived next door, and Gretchen thought chasing their poodle was an especially exciting challenge. Not surprisingly, this resulted in some problems with the neighbors. After many complaints about Gretchen from Mr. Fleetwood, my father came up with one of his more bizarre schemes. It was decided that Dad would wait until midnight and then hide in the Fleetwoods' bushes in full disguise, including a trench coat and hat. He had a pistol with him and figured that when Gretchen came by to mess with the poodle he'd fire a couple of rounds in the air to scare her off. Right on time, Gretchen came over, ready to do battle with the poodle. When my father jumped out of the bushes and fired off a few shots, Gretchen took off running toward home. The plan worked! Well, almost. Mr. Fleetwood, a man who enjoyed his libations, had completely forgotten about the undercover operation. The local sheriff was called, but "the case of the mysterious armed man in the trench coat" was quickly closed after an awkward but simple explanation from my father.

As long as there weren't any gunshots, Gretchen was a bold and protective dog. One late night we suddenly heard a loud commotion outside. Gretchen was savagely barking, and a man was frantically yelling in Spanish. She had pinned this poor guy against the side of the house and was on full attack mode. Here was this poor fella who had obviously just crossed the border—lost, hungry, and scared out of his mind—with a large angry dog pinning him with her front paws, ready to take him down. My mother and father pulled Gretchen off the man and calmed him down. Mom fed him and gave him some sandwiches to take for later. Dad slipped some money into his palm. That night I learned what true kindness is. The love and respect I felt for my parents only grew in that moment.

There were other dogs I remember fondly, but one of the more unique family pets was a burro named Chiquita. He was given to us by the Dunn family, our dear friends who so graciously helped the family way back when we had our house fire. I remember the Dunn boys, Tommy and

George, walking five or six miles from their house, leading Chiquita while Mr. Dunn followed in his pickup truck. Chiquita was actually our first guest in my father's corrals, though she managed not to wreak havoc as Ranger did on his first night with us. Cathy, my younger sister, who was now around six or seven, was the only one small enough to ride Chiquita. That little burro became a true member of the Hillman family, just like the dogs. Whenever we drove home, she would start braying and would sometimes unlatch the corral gate and walk over to the front door. It was a divided door, where the top would open separately from the bottom. Chiquita would push the top section open and stick her head in the house to finish her greeting.

Every year in Rancho Santa Fe, we had a "pet parade," but for the life of me, I can't recall if it was linked to some special holiday or feast day or something. Every year, like clockwork, all the kids brought out their pets and paraded them through the center of town. There were mostly dogs, cats, and birds. One year there was even a coyote pup in a little cage that someone had caught in their backyard. There were also horses, ponies, even a raccoon or a possum. Chiquita made the parade one year. There was *always* a dog pulling a wagon and, to me, that was the best part of the pet parade—a dog pulling a wagon with another animal or a doll riding behind. This classic annual event was right out of William Inge's play, *Picnic,* which captured the small-town Americana way of life so well.

Growing up on the ranch not only sparked my love for animals but also was where I first became attracted to interesting cars. The first thing a man needs on a ranch, even if it is only an acre or two, is a good truck or jeep. One day my father came home behind the wheel of a World War II military Jeep. It had the big white star on the hood and was painted standard army green. He also managed to pick up a trailer to hook to the back of the jeep and, within a matter of days, the transformation began. My father recruited my older siblings Dick and Susan (I was still young enough to escape the work detail) to help him paint the Jeep and trailer bright yellow. Yellow! I couldn't believe it. The really cool army Jeep suddenly looked like a carnival attraction. All we lacked was a couple dozen clowns to come piling out of the trailer. Regardless of its looks, the Jeep proved to be a good asset for working around the ranch. And it was a lot of fun to ride in, too—especially on our trips to the beach. It never occurred to us that riding in an open cockpit without seatbelts might be a little dangerous.

My father's real love was exotic English cars, the ones first imported after World War II. One of his first roadsters was a black Austin sedan. He didn't keep the car but a month or two at best. Shortly thereafter he showed up with a Hillman Minx, certainly appropriately named but a mechanical nightmare. He quickly sold and replaced it with an even more exciting automobile, a 1950 light green Cadillac convertible, which was given to him to settle a long overdue gambling debt. I think the old man felt a bit out of place cruising the rural streets of Rancho Santa Fe in such a flamboyant set of wheels, so that car was quickly disposed of and replaced once again with an even better and classier model: a 1950 MG convertible. It was truly a work of art: black with red leather seats, spoke wheels, and just plain beautiful. As memory serves, it was one of a very few MGs imported into the US at that time. My father loved that car, and I was given the honored title of wash and wax attendant, which included caring for the exterior and sweeping and saddle-soaping the interior. For my efforts, I earned a full three dollars and the possibility of an extra tip for a job well done. I usually received it, too, my father being the generous man that he was.

Other than the yellow Jeep, my dad would show up with strange vehicles on a regular basis: Morris Minors, Sunbeams, Triumphs, Nash Ramblers, and another Hillman car thrown in for good measure. They were great looking rides and certainly fit my dad's character, but every hour on the road equaled an hour of shop time. The problems would involve the Lucas-designed electrical systems or a water pump or a carburetor or any manner of odd breakdown. But my father was persistent and always felt the next acquisition would be the best and last.

Fortunately, my mother held sway on her choice of cars, which was always a big, solid, dependable American station wagon. Those wagons remained our saving grace for getting around the county. I learned to drive stick shift in our 1953 Ford station wagon, and I had many adventures in that car when my folks were out on the town. Mind you, it was hard sitting on a phone book and trying to peek over the windshield, but I escaped many death-defying stunts when I "borrowed" that station wagon, always evading Sheriff Pelco's patrol car. I did manage to get the rear axle stuck on the edge of a cliff one night. My friends and I were terrified we would either go over the cliff or never get it loose to get home. Ultimately, we made it home that night and proceeded to lay low for a long time. But I would have a thing for interesting cars for many decades to come.

Maybe what I liked about cars was that they represented adventure and could literally take you to another place. Though I now think of my childhood as largely idyllic, there were two threatening shadows looming that every kid wanted to escape back then—unthinkable tragedies that could strike at any time: polio and the atomic bomb. Polio was the invisible killer. Though I wasn't aware of anyone in our little town who suffered from it, we were all instructed on how to avoid contracting the disease. The constant reminder of a photo of some poor child in an "iron lung" was enough to scare the daylights out of you. Amazing myths arose in daily conversations with classmates. It was bad enough for us kids, but the moms and dads were really scared too. A couple of pieces of crucial advice that were drilled into me: never cut your apple in two pieces using the side of your metal lunchbox and avoid public swimming pools because of the unknown bacteria lurking in the murky waters. This didn't make too much sense but, thank God, within a couple of years Dr. Salk invented his vaccine, which saved the world.

As kids, we figured if polio didn't get us, the atomic bomb just might do it instead. We had regular bomb drills at school that taught us to "duck and cover." The Atomic Age, as it came to be known, produced some interesting science fiction movies out of Hollywood that dealt with the possible after-effects of an atomic explosion: giant mutant ants in the movie *Them* and a giant reptilian monster in the Japanese classic *Godzilla*. While this was very entertaining for us kids, the specter of mass destruction in our weekly "duck and cover drills" was deeply implanted in our brains. Finally, the government realized many years later that this exercise wasn't very effective in surviving an atomic bomb attack. As for the bomb? We *still* haven't quite figured out how to deal with that issue yet.

Maybe those threats, and a need for escapism, also contributed to my love of Hopalong Cassidy and the other cowboys of the screen, both large and small. Soon my love for fantasy and adventure that was fueled by the television only deepened, as my imagination was sparked by a budding love of reading. Mrs. Trethaway, along with my mother and father, encouraged me, and I discovered it was something I really loved. I would practice every night with my father, who would have me read articles to him from the *Los Angeles Times*. It was great practice. Soon, my world expanded into fiction: The Hardy Boys, Edgar Rice Burroughs, Arthur Conan Doyle, Rudyard Kipling, and comics—the absolute greatest. I loved all the Action Comics, featuring heroes such as Superman and Batman, but I was also drawn to the Classic Comics, which published a series of condensed versions of classic literature, complete with illustrations.

Every kid who ever read comics in the '50s will now remember that the inside back cover of so many of them featured full-page ads for Charles Atlas's bodybuilding program. There was the man himself, in leopard-print bikini briefs, flexing his mighty arms. The standard sales tool was a cartoon showing a skinny guy with his girlfriend on the beach. Then, of course, a big bully would come along, kick sand in his face, and humiliate him in front of his girl. But not to worry. Charles Atlas could easily remedy this problem if you sent in your money and diligently followed his workout instructions. These ads were mighty convincing, and every kid entering adolescence wanted to become an unstoppable muscleman. You just knew no one would ever mess with you again if you could end up looking like Charles Atlas!

I must have seen those ads a million times, and they finally got to me when I was around twelve years old. Along with many of my peers around the country, I sent away for the official Charles Atlas Bodybuilding Course. The wait was unbearable. Each time we would go into town to pick up our mail, I would hunt through the stack of envelopes to see if Mr. Atlas had responded. Finally, one day the mysterious plain-wrapped envelope arrived. All the secrets to becoming an impressive physical specimen lay inside, just waiting for me to apply them. I tore open the package that contained the complete instructions, along with photographs and everything I would need to become a guy to be feared and respected. No one was ever going to kick sand in my face or "pound me," which was our term back then for getting beat up.

I must have stuck with the course for maybe two or three months, practicing in my room every day with an occasional eye toward my mirror to see if anything miraculous had occurred yet. No such luck. To this day I have never met anyone my age who benefited from Mr. Atlas's instruction, but it was a relatively inexpensive way to seek out a better life for a skinny kid.

Those were the days when you sent away for all kinds of cool things that were advertised on the backs of cereal packages or in magazines like *Popular Mechanics, Police Gazette,* and *True Adventure.* These publications had the greatest artwork on the covers: big tough guys with machine guns saving buxom blondes and holding off the Japanese army with one hand. Inside you'd see things like, "Only $14.95! Send away today for the 'Wolf Killer,' genuine Italian push-button stiletto!" The picture of the "Wolf Killer" was more than enough to motivate me to gather up the necessary funding. Of course, I sent away for one and it arrived approximately three weeks later, all the way from the exotic land of Florida. Wow! It was just like the knife in the movie *Blackboard Jungle.* Somehow, that knife disappeared soon after. It probably ending up in my dad's secret drawer, where so much of my good stuff was locked away after getting confiscated.

The really exciting reading material, however, was at the barber shop, where one could gaze on all sorts of publications that were of particular interest to boys and young men. My father took me to see Cliff, the town barber, every two weeks. I would get lost perusing all those magazines, and there were rumors that there were other, more exotic magazines stashed in the back for the older folks.

My dad always instructed Cliff to "leave the sideburns on" (whatever that meant), but all us boys wore crewcuts or buzz cuts then, like you'd see a guy get on his first day of bootcamp. It was the end of the Korean War, and that was the prevailing fashion for guys my age. Some of the older high school boys, however, were starting to wear ducktails or pachuco hairstyles, thanks to a popular young singer named Elvis Presley. To certain girls, this was a major attraction. But to us, it didn't matter. Girls were still an alien species yet to be discovered. But that was all about to change. In fact, a lot of things were about to change.

# CHAPTER THREE
# CARRY ME HOME

It's easy to describe what my life was like in Rancho Santa Fe back in the 1950s, but it's a little harder to pinpoint *who* I was as an individual in terms of my values, beliefs, and understanding of the world around me. I mentioned that my father was Jewish by birth but atheist in practice. My mother, on the other hand, was baptized in the Presbyterian Church as a child. She embraced a hazy sort of Christian faith that wasn't really discussed. Her cousin, Joe Broadley, was a Presbyterian minister, and she would take us to his church every now and then. We certainly rarely attended formal services with any kind of consistency, however, so church wasn't a big part of my experience when I was young.

Rancho Santa Fe, for one reason or another, had a sizeable population of Christian Scientists. Founded by Mary Baker Eddy in Boston at the turn of the century, the group was described as a "new thought metaphysical faith." Christian Science was based on something like "mind over matter." In other words, all matter was an illusion, while the perfect being was the *spiritual* being. One was never *really* physically sick and only made the choice to be out of balance. Those who embraced the philosophy claimed they could, through prayer, conquer all disease and misfortune. Unfortunately, it was a theology that resulted in worsening illnesses and sometimes premature deaths.

By the time my little sister Cathy and I were getting a bit older, my mother was suddenly struck with the impulse that somebody in the family should get some religious training. Since it was a popular religious community in our town, she took us to a Christian Science Sunday school for a time. It wasn't bad, but it ended up not being something we committed to for more than a brief time. With the exception of singing "Onward Christian Soldiers," I barely remember anything about my church education.

I suffered from asthma as a kid, which could be very frightening but was generally controlled with medication. One night, while sleeping over at a friend's home whose family were Christian Scientists, I had a terrifying asthma attack. Being away from home—and away from my medicine—I tried to tough it out, gasping for every breath. Hubert Brooke, my friend's dad, eventually came into the bedroom and handed me what looked like a clove lifesaver. "Chris," he said, "take this and your asthma will go away in five minutes." And in five minutes it went away! Truly amazed, I went home the next day and told my mother we needed to get some of those magic remedies for ourselves. Cathy and I still weren't on any sort of conscious search for spiritual enlightenment, but we sure stocked up on those clove lifesavers.

Another source I looked to as I tried to understand my own identity was my grandparents. As a kid, I was blessed to have two grandmothers in my life. My grandmother on my father's side, Lillian Greenburg, was born in England sometime in the 1880s. She grew up, got married, and had a son named Alex. Lillian ultimately divorced her first husband, however, and immigrated with her young son to America soon after the turn of the century. Ending up in Washington, DC, she met and married Joseph Hillman, a recent immigrant from Russia. They soon had a child—my father, David—and not long after, they packed up and moved out west to begin a new life in Los Angeles.

My grandfather was a tailor, so they set up shop in Boyle Heights, which was originally the Jewish section of Los Angeles. Since he passed away in the late '30s, the details of Joseph's history still remain somewhat of a mystery. Apparently, he was a very quiet and polite man who worked hard to support his new family. I can't imagine how he got the name "Hillman," having immigrated from Russia. It's hardly a Russian name, so the Ellis Island immigration people must have had an interesting time providing shortened and Americanized names to the new arrivals.

My father's half-brother, Alex, was, by all accounts, a professional thief who served time in jail. I remember visiting my grandma when I was young and seeing his framed picture on her table. He looked like the actor Paul Muni with black, wavy hair and a pencil-thin mustache that was so popular among men in the '30s. His story was one of those mysterious family secrets, the kind that all families keep hidden away. My dad was the hardworking, straight ahead, and focused son who, growing up poor, worked his way over to Hawaii and back on a tramp steamer in the early '20s. His adventure was right out of a Kipling or Jack London story; my father the adventurer, the world traveler. These early experiences added to his creative genius; which helped him flourish in the coming years. After earning enough money as an able seaman, he put himself through UCLA, graduating with honors and a bachelor's degree in journalism. Alex, however, was certainly the proverbial "black sheep" of the family. He had died by the time I was born, so I'll likely never really know where the two brothers diverged.

My paternal grandmother was my only window into the world of Jewish ethnicity. Between 1950 and 1955, I would sometimes visit her in her apartment near Fairfax Avenue in Los Angeles. It was as if I was transported into another country and another century. There were wonderful things cooking on the stove, strange and new cuisine that I soon got used to and loved to eat. We would walk hand-in-hand down to the old Farmers Market on Third Street. Occasionally, we'd ride the bus there, which was even more of an adventure for a kid from the country. Grandma Hillman knew everyone in the Farmer's Market and made it a point to always take me to see the talking Mynah bird that occupied one of the spaces. I was mesmerized; here was a bird looking me in the eye and talking!

Every now and then my grandmother would come down to the Ranch and stay with us. That's where I would become the bad grandson, sneaking up on her in the kitchen when she was cooking and yelling, "Mouse!" at the top of my lungs. She nearly had a heart attack when I pulled that stunt and would point her finger at me and scream, "Meshugge," which means "crazy" in Yiddish. We would watch television together, and whenever any footage of Hitler came on the screen, she would throw something at the TV and scream some Yiddish curse words. I dearly loved my grandmother, and I remember telling her, when I grew up, I was going to make a lot of money and buy her a Cadillac. When I was in sixth grade, however, she quietly fell asleep and had a heart attack at the age of seventy-six.

In terms of character and background, my grandmothers were as different as fire and water. My mother's mother, Catherine Charlton, was born in Georgetown, Texas, in the 1880s and came from an old established family called the Cheshires. At the turn of the century, she visited Los Angeles with her father. While there, she met my grandfather, Everett Charlton, a native of the city. His father—my great grandfather, Charlie Charlton—moved to Los Angeles in 1884, traveling across the country from Newton, Massachusetts, by train, wagon and horseback. Charlie was a musician in the LA Shriner band and a member in good standing with the Musicians Union, Local 47. For his part, my grandpa Everett was a good tenor in the church choir. Catherine and Everett had a long courtship, which was quite the normal affair in those days, and were married in Los Angeles in the early 1900s.

My grandfather ran a successful insurance agency in downtown Los Angeles and, after building up his business, was able to start a family and build their home on Doheny Drive in what later came to be known as Beverly Hills. My mother was born in 1914, the middle sister of three girls: Doris, the oldest; Elizabeth Ann (my mother); and Catherine, the youngest. Grandma Charlton was hellfire on wheels, a tough Texas gal who ran a tight ship. Grandpa was a quiet and patient man, and I remember him very fondly.

My visits to Grandma and Grandpa Charlton were a completely different experience than my times with my paternal grandmother. The Charltons were classic white Anglo-Saxon Protestants and, unfortunately, they harbored a bit of a racist worldview. Grandma was brought up in East Texas, and anyone who wasn't white and Christian was someone to be wary of. The Charltons did not want their daughter marrying a Jewish man, so my poor mom and dad ended up getting married at the Justice of the Peace in downtown Los Angeles. This was a thorn in the family's side while she was alive, but I still loved Grandma Charlton just as much as I loved Grandma Hillman.

When I came up to Los Angeles as a boy to visit Grandma Hillman, I would often visit Grandma Charlton too. Grandma Hillman did not drive, so I would usually stay with her for a few days and then Grandma Charlton would pick me up and drive me over to the west side of town. When it was time to drop me off or pick me up, they would hardly look at one another. This was never explained to me and only added to my confusion about my heritage. I thought all grandmas and grandpas were like the Charltons. But even though Grandma Hillman's ethnic heritage seemed "different" to me, she still seemed like just as much of a grandma too. Nobody ever explained to me that her being Jewish was, indeed, different from my Gentile grandparents.

Looking back, the religious tension between the grandmothers seems odd. The Charltons were Presbyterian and all the girls were baptized, but the family seldom attended church. Grandma Hillman may have attended services on Friday evenings at the synagogue, but if she did, I never really knew anything about it. Honestly, it seemed that neither side of the family was actively attending services, so I'm still trying to figure that all out. If it wasn't important enough for them to actively participate in, then why was it important enough to cause divisions? I'll probably never fully understand, but what I do know is they were all wonderful people in my life. If Grandpa Joe Hillman had still been alive at the time, he probably would have straightened out the whole problem in no time flat.

Though I never got the opportunity to know my father's father, I did enjoy my time with Grandpa Charlton. Their house on Doheny was built in early California mission style with a tile roof and a big wrought-iron door leading into a small outdoor alcove with a big oak door in the front. They had an actual icebox they used up until the mid-1950s, and I recall the Union Ice Company delivering ice to the house. Every night after dinner, my grandfather, still wearing his three-piece suit, would say to me, "Let's go into the parlor and have a cigar." I would follow him in to the other room where he would pull a cigar out of his breast pocket. Then he'd produce a big piece of licorice for me. When I was up to visit, he always stopped on his way home from work to get my licorice "cigar." In the parlor, which was a small, cozy sitting room in the front of the house, we would discuss all manner of important things that only a grandfather and a young boy could understand. Not having a son, I think he looked upon me as his own boy.

Not long after Grandma Hillman passed, both of my maternal grandparents developed diabetes. Grandma Charlton faced up to this new challenge in her life and followed her doctor's advice, but Grandpa just wouldn't acknowledge the disease and refused to listen to the medical professionals. He became very ill, and other issues soon developed with his health in his declining years. The last time I saw him, he was in bed, unable to move or say very much. I went into his room, and he took hold of my hand. He held it so tight, looking into my eyes with a silence so loud as to say, "It's time, but I love you, and I'll always be with you." I was quickly learning about mortality. He died a few weeks later. My friend had gone away. I secretly hoped there really was a heaven because, if there was, I would try and go there someday and see my grandparents again.

Grandma Charlton lived into the early 1960s. I remember visiting her in her room occasionally when I was a young man starting my career in music. She would have her little television on, usually tuned to a Dodgers game. She had been a smoker but wasn't allowed to smoke anymore, given her health condition. She would always say, "Chrissie, come in and lock the door behind you. Do you have a cigarette on you?" We would light up together and talk. She said to me one day, "I like that long hair. Men used to wear their hair long until World War I. After that, they cut it all off short; I never liked that look." She was probably the only person next to my mother who didn't have a problem with my long hair at the time. Grandma Charlton died while I was off on tour in late 1965. The last pioneer in the family. With her passing, I lost my one true link to old Texas and the West.

Though I had no real spiritual or ethnic identity to call my own, I did recognize that—as we moved into the late 1950s—times were changing. My body was changing, too. I was moving from boyhood to adolescence and was developing new interests. By the time I reached twelve or so, my interest in horses was waning. I stopped riding, and we sold Ranger to a good family.

It was time for a new hobby. When my brother Dick was twelve, he had acquired a Cushman Pacemaker motor scooter. It was a big, long-bodied, fat-tired, straight-handled scooter with a top speed of fifty miles per hour. It had a transmission with the gear shifter sticking out of the left side of the body, which meant that you drove with one hand. You'd have to step on the clutch with your right foot as your left hand shifted gears. I loved that rig and always knew that someday I would have one of my own. When I reached the right age, I became aware of an even cooler scooter—a used Italian Vespa that an older gentleman in town owned and wanted to sell. At the time, Sears Roebuck was selling it under the Allstate label. This would be like having a Porsche next to my brother's Nash Rambler. It was fast and far more sophisticated, having three speeds and a design so elegant it made people stop and stare.

Like my dad's English cars, Italian motor scooters were rare in the States in the '50s. The downside was that it had a two-cycle engine, which meant you had to mix the oil with the gasoline. Otherwise, they were fast, dependable, and offered up real freedom—a huge step up from my bicycle or even a horse. I worked hard that summer to earn the money for the scooter. By that time, Dick had moved on to working as a car wash attendant at Bob Francisco's Mobil gas station, so I inherited his old one-man car washing business. I advertised my services around town and, when a client called, I would ride my bike over to their house to wash their car, clean the interior, and then chamois the exterior for $1.75. Of course, everyone had huge American cars, but it was a job. Plus, $1.75 was a lot of money. I also did yard work and any other odd jobs I could find until I finally had enough to buy that Vespa.

Some of my pals on the Ranch had scooters, too, which made for some serious mischief. One of my friends managed to get a Cushman Eagle, which was their "top of the line" scooter and actually looked like a motorcycle. A different guy had a Lambretta, which was another Italian-style scooter. And then there were a couple of Pacemakers like my brother's. Since there was no official law enforcement within the boundaries of the Ranch, and since we all had great parents who trusted us, we cruised up and down the deserted roads and trails all over Rancho Santa Fe. The unwritten rule was to never venture beyond the Ranch borders for fear of immediate arrest and confiscation of our metal steeds. It was the greatest feeling but fraught with occasional danger when one of us would get a little cocky and end up laying our "bikes" down, sliding end-over-end, and winding up with a bent frame and skinned-up legs. I can't recall anyone breaking any bones, at least.

Things were changing for my father in the late 1950s, too. Several years prior, he sold his Hillman-Shane advertising firm in Los Angeles and gave up the weekly commute. My parents ran a successful mail-order side business out of our garage, selling what was commonly referred to as "bric-a-brac": drinking glasses, novelty items, dishware, Western-themed stuff, and all sorts of exotic items. The mail-order operation eventually morphed into a real shop in the center of town, and the offerings expanded to household items, toys, and antiques. Dad never wanted to sell any "sketchy" merchandise, so he always kept an eye toward high-quality items. The shop was a success but, always ambitious, my father decided to further expand on his entrepreneurial impulses.

As soon as the shop was established, my dad began formulating *The Rancho Santa Fe Times,* a weekly newspaper for the residents of Rancho Santa Fe and the neighboring towns of San Diego County. Having run a successful advertising agency for the better part of twenty-five years, he had a flair for writing and design. In fact, prior to starting up his ad agency in the mid-1930s, he had been a reporter for the *Los Angeles Herald Express,* later called the *Herald Examiner. The Rancho Santa Fe Times* started out as a monthly newspaper and eventually grew into a weekly edition. It was printed on high-gloss paper in a magazine format, a bit different from the other neighboring towns' local newspapers. He wrote about local events and covered regional news.

*The Rancho Santa Fe Times* had some competition in the weekly *Coast Dispatch,* which was published in Solana Beach, as well as another small paper out of Del Mar. *The Times* beat them all in journalistic style and format. My father was an impassioned editor who often wrote scathing pieces about anything and everything he felt was unfair or took advantage of the voiceless. He loved to make light of the local gentry and managed to upset a few residents in the process. He unleashed his wrath on the "covenants" that ostensibly governed the town rules about architectural style and upkeep but which also included sly restrictions against people of color. As a result of their prevailing bigoted mindset, the Rancho Santa Fe Board of Directors and the RSF Association were also frequent targets of my dad's biting editorials. My father being Jewish only fueled their growing resentment of an *outsider* coming in where he wasn't wanted and trying to change things. At the same time, he had loyal friends and followers who rallied around him, so the cheerleaders balanced out the naysayers.

In his various editorials, my father would assume the roles of different characters. Sometimes there was a picture of him in a Stetson hat and fake whiskers with the byline "Wild Dave Hillman." At other times he would be "Canvasback Dave Hillman," which was a variation on the gentleman Jim Corbett of modern times, and sometimes he would use a stock photo of a well-known comical figure. His playfulness added a little levity to his editorials, injecting just enough silliness to soften the blow of his attacks enough that it tempered the vitriol in his opponents' responses. For a kid just starting his teen years, this didn't exactly seem like particularly cool behavior, but I loved and respected the old man despite his strange sense of humor. Plus, he was one great writer. *The Times* won several awards for a weekly newspaper of that size, which brightened the overall mood around the Ranch.

The Rancho Santa Fe Times proved to be a family affair. My sister Cathy had a weekly column about goings-on at Rancho Elementary; my mother wrote a fashion column; and my job was basically menial labor— helping assemble and mail the newspaper. As the publication grew, my dad introduced a twice-a-year special edition that was bigger and usually focused on a particular theme (e.g., fashion, the start of the racing season in Del Mar, etc.). In the early '60s he expanded the newspaper by opening his own printing plant in neighboring Solana Beach, suitably named the Rancho Press. The Rancho Press did outside work for other clients but was mainly focused on the weekly *Times*. Now my dad had an in-house operation and soon brought in an old pal from Los Angeles named George Laws, who became a very close and dear friend to our family.

When I started junior high school in 1957 it was a big adjustment from my elementary school experiences in Rancho Santa Fe. I began attending Earl Warren Jr. High School, which was a little frightening at first. After spending my days in a single room with a single teacher, I felt lost when I was expected to switch from class to class while getting used to all the unfamiliar faces from other northern San Diego County towns such as Del Mar, Solana Beach, Cardiff, and Encinitas. I was accustomed to a fairly homogenous upper middle-class environment. Sure, we had fights in grammar school, but nothing more serious than an occasional wrestling match. But now the kids were bigger, and they were coming from a variety socioeconomic backgrounds and experiences.

The fights between guys—and sometimes even girls—in junior high were way beyond the grammar school wrestling matches. Guys would choose each other off and meet up behind the gym after school. On their own, kids can present an angelic countenance, but sometimes, when they gather in groups of three or more, the "pack mentality" takes over and the individual who's not part of the pack becomes easy prey. It seemed as if the school bully would purposely challenge the weaker kid. Crowds of students would stand around cheering like animals as the two combatants fought to a standstill. Once in a great while, the smaller kid would triumph, which made for a good ending. I was always the smaller kid, but I usually lost, which was embarrassing and emotionally devastating for a sensitive young man. The Hispanic boys were kind of the cool guys on campus. I'm grateful that some of the bigger ones among them took a liking to me and made sure to look out for me so I didn't have to experience getting my ass kicked too often.

Maybe one of the reasons for the fighting was that we were all a mess of raging hormones as our bodies transitioned from those of children to those of adults. It was in seventh grade that I discovered girls and experienced my first kiss. For the first time, being around girls felt like an electric charge, and I started keeping company with some nice young ladies. These, of course, were "proper" times, so relationships didn't venture further than a hot and heavy make-out session at a party or at the movies. Of course, I was too young to drive, so whenever I dated I'd have to get one of my parents to drive me to the theater. I'd make them drop me off blocks away so nobody would see us and find out that I had—gasp—a real father and mother! That would have been very uncool.

The best part of that era was rock and roll, which changed our whole culture. Our hormones weren't only firing off in every direction, but we even had our own soundtrack for it. Nothing was safe anymore, and perhaps we were the first generation of Americans to have a unifying musical revolution. My parents loved music, so I'd grown up in a house filled with records by Count Basie, Duke Ellington, Louis Armstrong, Peggy Lee,

Frank Sinatra, Benny Goodman, and that kind of thing. I loved it all, but rock and roll felt like it belonged to us kids. You could dance to it, but it also felt a little dangerous. When Elvis hit in my last year of grammar school in 1956, it was monumental. My teacher, Mrs. Ross, actually let some of us bring Elvis records into class and dance; truly amazing that this encouraging teacher—probably in her mid-fifties at the time—was so open to this new music that must have seemed very strange to her.

My older brother had an RCA 45 record player, which only played singles. After graduating from high school the same day that Grandma Hillman passed away in 1956, he was accepted into the Air Force Academy, which was only in its second year of existence. The previous year, my father had started taking flying lessons at the old Del Mar airport in exchange for an ad he ran in his newspaper. He soon tired of the process and let Dick finish off the remaining lessons. My brother definitely caught the flying bug and within weeks knew he wanted to join the Air Force and fly jets. When he left for the Academy in Colorado Springs I inherited his little record player and began buying every new single I could find. This was the era of Chuck Berry, Little Richard, Fats Domino, The Everly Brothers, and a host of others who completely turned the world upside down. I was in heaven!

Different kids at the junior high would throw parties where we'd dance to those classic records from the absolute best period in rock and roll history. My parents even let me host a party one night. I pulled the rugs back in the living room and cranked up the hi fi in preparation for the evening. As the cars started arriving to drop off other kids, my heart was racing. *The party was about to start! Would it be cool? Would everyone have fun?* As the festivities kicked off, my parents hid out in their bedroom while we danced the night away and made out on the couch. Around 11 p.m., the station wagons began arriving with weary parents behind their wheels. They quickly retrieved their kids and disappeared into the night. We were all so young, but I felt a bit older after that event. My one and only party was a big success.

When I was in ninth grade, I tried out for the basketball team and actually made the final cut. Just barely. The coach was our science teacher, a good guy who gave everyone on the team the opportunity to get in the game. Otherwise, I would have just been a lowly bench warmer. Winning was important, but it wasn't the only thing. Coach was a rare example of a kind but firm leader who believed in building up the kids instead of tearing them down when mistakes were made. My brother was a great athlete. Not only did he excel at basketball, but he was also the quarterback of the San Dieguito Mustangs. I always looked up to my brother and tried to follow in his footsteps, but team sports didn't come as naturally to me. Nevertheless, I enjoyed being on the team that year. I even spent a month or so on the junior varsity football team in high school, but I got hammered so badly I actually developed a small crack in one of my vertebrae. That one proved to be a physical challenge for the next forty-five years. High school sports weren't my greatest area of strength, so my athletic career soon came to an inglorious end.

In high school, however, I developed a new passion that fit me better than team sports when I became enamored with surfing. Our house was only about five miles from Del Mar, and I loved the ocean. Our favorite family haunt was 25th Street, which boasted a perfect beach break and was part of the long stretch of coastline claimed by Rancho Santa Fe residents. My older sister Susan and her friends had built a palm-frond beach hut there, which served as their unofficial "club house" during her time in high school. Since Susan was nine years older than me, she went off to college when I was still in third grade. She was a fearless adventurer, independent, and always on the lookout for new and exciting places to explore. She was a bohemian free spirit who, during college, moved to Mexico for a year. I remember when she returned to the airport, she stepped off the plane with her flowing jet-black hair and brightly colored dress. She had learned to speak fluent Spanish and was full of stories of her adventures. Upon her return, she reconnected with Hugh Curtis, a boyfriend she'd met at the University of Colorado. They were married in 1957 at our family home in Rancho.

When Susan was gone, my brother Dick and his friend, Dick Clotfelter, taught me to body surf one summer. By the time my brother was entering his second year at the Air Force Academy, Susan and Hugh had settled in San Diego, where she resumed her schooling, and he found work building furniture and working as a lifeguard. Hugh's college roommate, Buzzy, had grown up in California and had learned to ski with Hugh in Colorado. It was only a matter of time before Buzzy returned the favor by teaching Hugh to surf. With Dick away at school, Hugh became like a surrogate big brother to me. In 1959, during my ninth-grade year at Earl Warren Jr. High school, Hugh had gotten pretty proficient on the board and shared his knowledge with me. It took a while for me to finally get the feel of his old balsa wood surfboard, but once I finally caught that first ride standing up, I was hooked. I traded something for a used ten-foot board, which became my training tool as I learned how to ride. As I improved, I knew I needed a better board—and not just any board. I needed a Hobie surfboard, which had to be ordered from Hobie's shop in Dana Point, about seventy-five miles up the coast from where we lived. The new boards were made out of foam. They were lighter, stronger, and more maneuverable. I longed for that Hobie the way I had longed for a horse when I was younger. Horses, scooters, cars, and surfboards all represented freedom.

By the summer, Solana Beach became my regular haunt. My pals and I would paddle out on a daily basis when we weren't at our respective summer jobs. These were the "glory days" of California surfing when we would get out of the water, build a bonfire on the beach, and sometimes even sleep on the nearby cliffs overnight to catch the morning "glass-off." Sadly, that kind of stuff is now illegal in the Golden State.

After a few months, I finally had the money to order my new board from Hobie. I called up the shop in Dana Point and placed my order. Six weeks later, it was ready to be picked up. It was a beautiful nine-foot squaretail with an abstract motif of red and blue painted on the underside. My dad was driving back from one of his Los Angeles business trips, so he picked it up for me and brought it home. I was still only fourteen years old so, not being able to drive the five miles to the beach, transportation was a challenge. Some of my buddies and I built trailers for our bicycles so we could carry our boards to the shore. We were determined to get in that water.

Swami's was a reef point break, which would break big in the winter. Named for the Self-Realization faith, which was started by Paramahansa Yogananda, the "temple" was built on the cliffs above the beach. I'm not sure who came up with the name "Swami's" but with these East Indian

Mystics living right above the beach, it was the perfect name for that particular break. Steep, twisting stairs led down to the beach. The live-in members of this mysterious sect were fine with us guys using their stairs to get down to the water.

Perhaps it's fitting that my first real experience of God occurred at Swami's one very foggy, cold morning in the late fall of 1959. I paddled out with Bob Kramer, an older guy from school. The fog was so thick that we only had maybe four or five feet of visibility. I could hear the waves breaking as we stroked through the set, but it was difficult to see much of what was going on. I thought we had made it past the swell. I knew it was breaking bigger than I had ever attempted to ride before, but I felt we were safely beyond the set and would be able to catch our breath. I heard it before I saw it; we both heard it coming and instinctively turned our boards around and paddled like there was a herd of elephants chasing us down. The wave was cresting as I turned to Bob, who yelled, "We're screwed!"

The wave was topping ten or twelve feet. These were the early years when everyone rode long boards without a leash, or even a decent wetsuit. When the wave hit, I rolled under and immediately lost my board. I couldn't even see it as it disappeared into the fog. I was scared; I could swim, but it was cold and I was swimming blind. I started heading for what I thought was the shore but got caught in a small rip current. In desperation, I finally just floated on my back and asked God to help me. I believe He did. I managed to get oriented and worked my way back to shore, where I found my Hobie board washed up on the sand. To some, the surf probably wasn't that threatening on that particular day, but to me, it was like the devil's wrath churning me around and ripping my lungs apart. It rattled me, but that experience of reaching for God was like a small awakening of my spirit. It would be years before I fully understood the real meaning of spiritual awakening, but another awakening was just beginning that would set me on a new path and transform the rest of my life.

# CHAPTER FOUR
# RUNNING

While girls and surfing certainly electrified the summer of '59, the music of the day didn't really do it for me. The real rock and roll of Little Richard and Chuck Berry was suddenly replaced by sappy crooners—well-coifed guys from the East Coast with perfect hair. Beneath the commercial surface, however, the Beat movement was giving the world Kerouac and Ginsberg, bongos, poetry, guitars, and coffee houses. Folk music and jazz were filling the void left by rock's comatose state. All of a sudden, The Kingston Trio were on the *Billboard* Top 40 music charts, and I liked them. It seemed like they had something to say.

My eyes were really opened to an exciting new world of meaningful music when my sister Susan, ever the artist and intellectual, came home from college with a stack of albums under her arm. She played me Woody Guthrie, Pete Seeger, The Weavers, and Lead Belly. This stuff felt like the real deal. Suddenly, The Kingston Trio took a back seat as I completely devoured Susan's record collection. I soon discovered The New Lost City Ramblers, which introduced me to old-time string band music. After that, I was a goner. Music had its hooks in me, and there was no turning back.

After pleading with my mom to buy me a guitar, she finally relented. On one of our shopping trips down to Tijuana, she bought me a ten-dollar gut-string model. Believe it or not, it was actually a pretty good little guitar. My mother made me a promise that if I stuck with the instrument for a full year, she would help me buy a better guitar. "Help me" meant that if I saved up half the money, she'd kick in the other half. I think she was hedging her bets since my brother had taken up the instrument several years earlier but quickly abandoned it.

I was fifteen years old, indestructible, and knew everything about life. Of course I would just become an instant guitar virtuoso! Or maybe not. I hovered over my record player for hours trying to figure out every nuance and every note that these strange and gifted people were playing. *How did they do that?* I slowed the records down and tried to stay focused. Having the patience of a mosquito, I did the best I could to decipher what I has hearing and translate it to the guitar, but it wasn't easy. At first, I played rhythm with my fingers on the right hand, while carefully forming the chords with my left. Eventually I was able to clumsily play along with the record on the turntable. In less than a year, I had actually learned enough to go back to my mother to see if she would honor our original agreement for a better instrument. She did. After working out a budget—my savings from working all summer at local hotels and a bit of help from Mom—we took off in search of a proper music store in San Diego.

I had heard of a guitar made by a company called Goya. It was a medium-sized nylon string model, a suitable instrument for the folk songs I was beginning to sing and play. We found a new Goya for about $100.00, and I counted out my bills. And just in time. My Tijuana guitar was about ready to explode. Good as it was for my needs in the beginning, it was undoubtedly time to move up a notch. The Goya played great, but as I got further into bluegrass and old-time string music in the following months, I realized it wasn't the right instrument for the music I was increasingly gravitating to. Not understanding the workings of a fine instrument, one day I decided to change out my nylon strings for a set of steel strings. The next morning, I opened my guitar case and saw what the tension of the new strings had done. The neck looked like somebody had bent it into a bow and was ready to fire off an arrow. It was that bad. I'd singlehandedly destroyed my Goya, and now I needed another instrument—quick. I started searching for a used dreadnaught like Lester Flatt or Carter Stanley played. I knew I couldn't afford a Martin or a Gibson, but I knew I would eventually find another instrument.

One day while my brother-in-law Hugh and I were down in San Diego, we stumbled upon a dusty antique shop that also dealt in musical instruments. It was owned by a guy named Frank, and he had some rare and beautiful things. Hugh was refinishing antique furniture at the time and would pick up items to be worked on from different antique stores around San Diego County. That particular day that I was riding around with Hugh, I asked Frank what acoustic guitars he had in stock. The first one he pulled out was a 0–45 Martin "New York" model, very old with beautiful inlay and in excellent condition. He said, "I can let this go for $125.00." $125.00! That was a huge amount of money! Had I known anything about that guitar back then, I would have done whatever it took to get a hold of it. It would easily be worth six figures today. That was the first "one that got away."

There would be many more through the years. I told Frank I couldn't afford the Martin and asked what else he had. He retreated way back into his shop, pulled out an old case, opened it up, and took out an Epiphone dreadnaught guitar. It wasn't a brand I was familiar with, but once I sat down and played a few chords, I knew I had to have that guitar. It was a really fantastic instrument. When Frank said I could buy it for fifty dollars, I couldn't believe it. I left fifteen bucks with him that day and promised to come back in a week to pay it off. Several days later, I returned and collected the instrument that would unlock the next phase of my musical growth. I loved that guitar. It's been more than half a century, but sometimes I wish I still owned it. It was that good.

Now that I had the right equipment, I was on my way. Listening to The New Lost City Ramblers, Flatt and Scruggs, The Stanley Brothers, and all the other great bands I was discovering energized me in a way I couldn't explain. It was a combination of the singing and the instrumentation: hillbilly jazz, fiery solos, and soulful vocals. Then, when I discovered Bill Monroe and the mandolin that really did me in. The mandolin hit a nerve like nothing else I had experienced in my life before. I *had* to learn how to play. I was still working on my guitar, having moved to a flat pick instead of using my fingers to play rhythm, but I couldn't stop myself from adding another instrument to the mix. I started out with a few rudimentary chords on an old Italian bowl-back mandolin I'd picked up somewhere. At least I had something to get me started, but the real prize was staring at me from a shop window of a small music store in Encinitas called Singing Strings. It was a brand-new Kay mandolin that slightly resembled the high-end Gibson F models that would remain years away from my grasp.

As I'd done with my first two guitars, I started to work on a plan to get that instrument as soon as I could come up with the money. The total was $55.00 out the door. The store had recently been opened by a man named Ed, a nice older guy who had retired and moved down to San Diego County from Los Angeles. Ed was very understanding about my financial situation; I was still in high school and, although working after school at the local hotel, $55.00 was a lot of money in 1960. Ed offered an extended layaway plan for the Kay mandolin but wisely held onto the instrument until I had paid it off in full. He knew I wasn't going to flee the country, but, as I look back, I think he was trying to teach me patience and responsibility.

After I finally paid off Ed and had my new mandolin in hand, it was time to practice and, once again, try to decipher what these guys on my records were doing to make those wonderful sounds. There wasn't anyone in the county I was aware of who played or gave mandolin lessons; heck, it was hard enough finding bluegrass records in the music shops.

At San Dieguito High there were maybe two other guys who played guitar or banjo, but there were no mandolin players yet. Finally, I met up with a guy named John McLaren, who was about a year older than me and shared my obsession with bluegrass and folk music. John had a Martin D-18. Nobody had a Martin guitar, especially not a D-18 dreadnaught! This guy was serious. In addition to being an outstanding player, he was also a really good singer. We immediately hit it off and started playing music together. John would sing tenor harmony to my lead vocals. We were having fun, learning, and exploring old music that was completely new to us. John's parents were immigrants from Scotland, wonderful people who always welcomed me into their home. John's older brother Scotty was also a great guy and an incredible surfer. Scotty encouraged our musical pursuits and welcomed us into his surfing crowd. All the older surfers who were out of high school and starting college were big folk and jazz fans, so John and I were always invited to their parties where we would play a few tunes and get handsomely compensated in beer. Honestly, John and I weren't that good, but we made up for our inexperience with a lot of enthusiasm.

Soon thereafter, I was at school one day when a friend of mine mentioned, "I think the janitor plays guitar, and I think he plays bluegrass." I immediately sought out San Dieguito High School custodian Bill Smith who, I found out, was originally from Arkansas. I told him I was trying to learn guitar and mandolin, and we became instant friends. He invited me over to his house that weekend, marking the start of my formal education in country music. Bill was my window on authenticity. This guy was the real deal. In addition to his day job at the school, he worked every weekend in a local bar, playing and singing with a small band.

Bill became my mentor as he patiently showed me all he'd learned over the years. On my very first visit, he set me straight on my rhythm and chord approach, and he encouraged me to sing more. One time he pulled out a new record he'd just bought by a new artist I'd never heard of named Buck Owens. "Someday this guy will be a huge star," Bill assured me. He played me the album, and I really liked it, though I was years away from really appreciating country music. It was bluegrass I was chasing, and Bill Smith was my guru.

While music was igniting a new burning passion in my soul, the world around me seemed full of promise and opportunity. It was 1960, and I was a sophomore in high school. John Kennedy would soon be sworn into office, and there was a sense of optimism among young people around the country. Just as I was cluing into the outside world, however, life at home was beginning to feel more strained. Something was "off" when it came to our family life, and I noticed that my dad was acting differently. He was often nervous and could be short-tempered, which wasn't his typical demeanor. I noticed he wasn't keeping his usual routine, instead coming home later each night and drinking a lot more. One night he announced to the family that we were going to sell the house and move closer to town. I had a feeling that money was becoming an issue, but, being a naïve and self-absorbed sixteen-year-old, I didn't really grasp the gravity of the developing situation.

My mother and father eventually had to close down their Corral Shop; they just couldn't balance running a weekly newspaper with operating a retail shop at the same time. Though the two businesses were only within a block of one another, both required a daily presence and full-time attention. Small towns—always noted for their intimacy, quaintness, and beauty—are not the best settings for privacy. As the old saying goes, "bad news travels fast." It wasn't long before most of the residents of Rancho Santa Fe were aware that the Hillman family was having financial difficulties. These weren't minor issues, as I later found out, but serious money problems. When the house finally sold, we moved into the top floor of a new home that had just been built by the local restaurant owners, Bill and Emma. I'm sure it was devastating to my parents to rent a portion of a house in a town that would quickly become one of the wealthiest enclaves in America.

It was a big change, but I didn't have the emotional capacity to deal with the various feelings swirling inside. When my beloved childhood tree house was torn down by the new owner of our old property, I felt betrayed. When he began building his new house, I took my BB gun and shot out some of his brand-new windows. Unfortunately, I got caught, so I got grounded, temporarily lost the use of my trusty rifle, and had to pay for every single window I destroyed. It wasn't a good time for us Hillmans.

I found out later just how bad things had gotten for my father, a proud man who was forced to scrape by any way he could to keep us fed and clothed. He kept the newspaper open, though it was struggling. I spent the summer of 1960 working for my dad and his partner, George Laws, as well as doing some other odd jobs on the side when I wasn't working to master the guitar and mandolin.

My friend Pebble Smith, who I'd known since elementary school, worked part time with me at the paper, too. We enjoyed hanging out together after work, which usually consisted of spending Friday nights at the corner liquor store that was two doors down from the Rancho Press. When we got lucky, an older guy or a willing migrant worker would come along and we'd ask them if they'd buy a couple of big bottles of Pabst Blue Ribbon for us. It usually worked out, but if it didn't, there was always Frank's Market in Eden Gardens. Frank would sell beer to anyone who had the money. Underage drinking was plenty of fun, but we conjured up a grand scheme one day that would take our beer acquisition skills to the next level. The Rancho Press had what was called an offset printing system. We figured out a way to change the date of birth on a driver's license by crudely typing over the real date and reprinting or copying it. Why embark on a life of crime with our fake ID scam? Because it was dangerous territory, and like most young guys, we never stopped to think about the potential consequences.

After creating our first masterpiece, we tried it out at the aforementioned corner liquor store. No more loitering in the parking lot waiting for an accomplice. We just walked in, bought the beer, showed the altered driver's license, and walked out with our prizes in hand. It was a rush! Not wanting to draw too much attention to our new business venture, we were very selective about our clientele. Only a few close surfing pals were eligible to receive a carefully-doctored Hillman/Smith ID.

Everything was working out fine until one day when I was at work at the presses. George Laws appeared next to me. "Chris, step into my office, please," he said flatly. I followed him down the hallway, wondering why he was so stern. He sat down at his desk and motioned for me to take a seat across from him. He was silent for what seemed like an eternity. "Chris," he finally spoke, "we had some gentlemen from the FBI stop by here yesterday. They were very concerned about a possible false identification card that they believe was manufactured at this printing plant. Do you know anything about that?"

George locked eyes with me. I could feel my palms get clammy. My first thought was, *Who ratted us out?* I knew I was busted, so I 'fessed up. I told George everything. He didn't break his gaze or even blink. "Do you think your dad needs this right now?" he asked. I felt my heart sink.

"No," I mumbled, as I hung my head in shame.

"I don't think so, either," he replied. "I'll take care of it, but don't you ever do anything that stupid again, do you understand?" I nodded.

"Yessir," I said. "It won't happen again." By the grace of God, George Laws convinced the FBI agents that we were just dumb kids and that we were already doing heavy penance. The two agents let it slide. I doubt if anyone else could have handled this other than George—a newspaper reporter, professional gambler, savvy "street guy," and a gentlemanly survivor who was another of my important mentors.

My days of making counterfeit driver's licenses were behind me, but I can't say I became an angel. By the start of 1961, I was a music-obsessed mediocre student with no interest in school and no real life goals other than some vague notion of one day becoming a rambling folksinger. Every year, in the early spring months, San Dieguito High held its annual Sadie Hawkins dance where the girls asked the boys to the dance, and we all dressed up like something out of Al Capp's *Li'l Abner* comic strip. The night of the dance, some of my criminal surfing pals and I met up at the vacant lot on the bluffs overlooking Solana Beach. Someone in our group made a big score, a full unopened bottle of Vodka and a can of tomato juice. Bloody Marys for all! At some point during our predance party ritual, I spilled a glass of tomato juice on my light-colored pants. There was really nothing I could do about it but continue to get loose with my pals, knocking back our jury-rigged Bloody Marys. We all finally got in our cars and, by the grace of God, made it safely to the dance. But then things got real interesting.

The school was too small to hire a live band, so the music for the dance was provided by a small turntable. My friend Tim—who stood six feet, four inches and played varsity football, basketball, and surfed—decided he wanted to play a Muddy Waters album. Only problem was, there was already a Frankie Avalon record on the turntable. Tim, feeling no pain after a few Bloody Marys, strolled over and pulled the needle off, scratching the Frankie Avalon record in the process. He plunked down the Muddy Waters LP and dropped the needle. As soon as the strains of "Tell Me Baby" roared from the speakers, one of the teacher-chaperones came running over and ripped Tim's record off the player. Tim shoved the teacher, and the fireworks began. "Don't even think about it, son!" the teacher screamed. Suddenly, another teacher appeared by his side, took one look at my tomato juice-stained pants and demanded, "You boys have been drinking, haven't you?"

Tim and I were both immediately sent to the office along with another guy. The vice principal, who was a real hard ass, told us that we were all going to juvenile hall for our underage drinking and disorderly conduct.

He called each of our parents, and my mother arrived shortly thereafter. My mom was the disciplinarian of the family and was known to deal with behavioral issues in a harsh and decisive manner. I dreaded seeing her come through the door.

"Your son is going to juvenile hall in San Diego," the vice principal informed her as soon as she walked in.

My mother squared up and looked him in the eye. "Over my dead body," she shot back. She looked over at me. "Get in the car," she yelled. "You're in big trouble."

I stood up and started walking out slowly. I longed to turn back to the vice principal and ask, "Is that juvenile hall offer still good?" I knew every step toward my mother's car was one step closer to the hell that awaited me.

After I headed to the car, our beloved vice principal explained to my mother that Tim and I would both be suspended for three weeks. This wouldn't affect Tim too much because he was a sports star who was graduating in a matter of months anyway. For me, however, it was a far worse fate. Missing that much school when I already wasn't a great student meant I would miss preparing for the final exams of my junior year.

My mom gave me a piece of her mind in the car that night, but I dreaded going home to tell my father what had happened. I knew my dad wasn't in a good place. He was coasting along, but it was clear he was hiding from something. There was something chasing him; his own self-doubt and paranoia were taking a toll. I knew he was struggling, but it wasn't until later that I knew the extent of what he was going through. He had been trying to tread water with the newspaper, but a lot of bad debt had been piling up for a couple of years. He had taken on an additional job editing and publishing a city weekly in San Diego while keeping his own weekly going in Rancho Santa Fe. That would have been enough to severely test a man's spirit, but I later found out that the partner in my dad's new venture in San Diego had talked him into backing the project. Then the guy skipped town and disappeared to Europe. He left my father with even more debt. My dad had already borrowed against everything he owned up to that point, and it was clear he was getting desperate.

My father, though suffering, didn't get as mad as I thought he would about my drunken school dance escapade. "You made a really bad choice," he said, "and I think you know that. We'll get through this, but let's not create any more problems for your mother and me right now." That was all he said. I couldn't understand why he didn't just blow up and let fly with all manner of yelling, but there wasn't much drama. I was grounded for a month, which meant that, other than driving to work, I could not use my car or go anywhere.

Once my home detention period had ended and I was back to normal life, I went out surfing one afternoon with my buddies. It was daylight savings time, so we had plenty of light and were still out on the water around 5:30 p.m. It was one of those picturesque California afternoons with perfect conditions on the water. All of a sudden, my mellow bliss was interrupted when a friend shouted over to me, "Hey, Hillman, your dad's on the beach, and he doesn't look very happy." I looked back toward the shore and there he was, frantically waving for me to come in. I thought something horrible must have happened at home, so I quickly paddled in and jogged up the beach toward my dad.

"What the hell is the *matter* with you?" my father hissed. I hadn't heard him say that since I was a young beagle hunter. "You don't have a brain in your head, do you? You couldn't even think beyond yourself to call your mother and tell her you weren't going to be home for dinner? Unacceptable!" With that, he turned and stormed off. I had never heard him express that much frustration toward me in my life. He handled it pretty well when I was suspended from school, but now he was losing it over missing one dinner? I didn't get it. After a few days, it dawned on me why he was so angry. It was all about responsibility, manners, and being considerate of others. Those values were in short supply for a selfish sixteen-year-old. My dad was trying to help me grow up and be a responsible man.

By that summer of 1961, I was increasingly spending more and more time bent over my guitar or mandolin than I was spending on the surfboard. With Susan and her husband Hugh enjoying their lives in Del Mar, and my brother Dick finishing off his flight training in Colorado, my little sister Cathy and I were the only ones at home. We were each doing our own thing as my dad struggled with what we now know was stress and depression. We didn't see much of him that summer. My mother, meanwhile, had been diagnosed with diabetes—just like both her parents before her—and was caught up in making some serious changes to her life. The various members of the Hillman family were just doing our own thing and plodding through daily life.

July 2 was a beautiful day. It was a Sunday and I was standing in the living room in the midmorning when my father walked in. He stood in front of me, and I was struck by the sadness in his eyes. There was such a weary countenance on his face that it caught me off guard. "I'm leaving for a while," he finally said. "I love you very much." It was unsettling. I just stood there looking into his eyes. Finally, his gaze left mine as he slowly turned, walked out the front door, and drove away. In that moment, I knew in my heart that I would never see my father again.

The next day I was supposed to drive down to Solana Beach to meet up with some friends. I was rushing out the door when the phone rang. Typically, I would have ignored it, but something made me stop and pick up the receiver. It was my sister, Susan.

"Daddy's dead," she sobbed.

*This isn't real. This isn't happening.* I couldn't move. "What do you mean?" I stammered. "Dad is fine. I just saw him yesterday!"

Silence. "Chris," she finally replied. "He's gone. Daddy is dead." I gently set the phone down and stood there motionless. I was numb—no tears, no feelings. Just numb.

I finally came-to enough to jump in my car and drive to Susan's house. I later found out that Hugh was the first to get the news from the police. He had gone searching for my mother, who was enjoying a day at the beach with friends. When he finally located her on the shore, he calmly told her that he needed to speak with her in private. It must have been the most difficult conversation of either of their lives. By the time I pulled up in their driveway, they were all standing outside the house—Hugh, Susan, and Mom. It was surreal. I didn't know what to say. I don't think I even hugged my mother that day. I just didn't know how to react.

I slipped out of Susan and Hugh's house that night, disappearing on the empty streets of Del Mar. After three hours of stumbling around aimlessly, my tears finally came. I tried to grasp the meaning of it all, still secretly hoping that my sister was somehow mistaken and it wasn't really true. Hugh was waiting up for me when I finally made it back to their house in the early morning. Again, no words. None of us knew how we were supposed to behave in that kind of situation. A crippling sadness permeated the house.

The following day we learned that my dad had driven up to San Clemente and checked into a motel. We all thought he had probably had a heart attack in his sleep. He was stressed out with work, and perhaps it was just too much for his body. Dick was summoned home from Colorado and, while awaiting his arrival, Hugh and I drove up to San Clemente to retrieve the death certificate from the coroner's office. The man who waited on us went out of his way to avoid saying anything about the cause of death, simply referring to it as a pulmonary problem. I think he was probably evasive for my benefit. It wasn't a heart attack or emphysema. My father had committed suicide. After checking into the motel, he took his own life with a handful of sleeping pills.

In the early 1960s, psychiatric therapy was still fairly uncommon. Having abandoned his upbringing in the Jewish faith, and without the resources of a good mental health professional, my father simply lost hope. I can only imagine the pain he must have been in. We held a very brief and very sad memorial for my father at the mortuary in Encinitas. My mother's cousin, Presbyterian minister Joe Broadley, presided over the ceremony. I can hardly remember any of the details.

Suicide—that dark abyss where the inner demons take hold of the mind and all rational thought and logic disappear; the destroyer of the family. How could this loving, affectionate, talented, sweet man who brought us up to believe in ourselves—to make a life marked by morals and values, to be responsible and caring toward others—have taken his own life and, in doing so, left us alone and destitute? Somehow, my mother began gathering up the scattered remnants of her sanity. The following days, weeks, and months are a bit of a blur, but my mom demonstrated great resiliency in the wake of my father's death. She found the will to carry on, determined to keep the family together. Dick Blackledge, the agent who had sold my dad his life insurance policy, fought like hell to try to get a settlement for my mother. Unfortunately, my father hadn't been paying his premiums, and the insurance company wouldn't pay out on a suicide anyway. We were on our own. But my mom singlehandedly and heroically managed to deal with the aftermath of financial ruin and all the collateral damage that was left behind.

The long-term ramifications of a suicide in a close-knit family can never be erased. My father's death affected each of us in different ways. While my mother rolled up her sleeves and fought for her family, I grew angry and self-destructive—patterns that would linger well into my adult life. In fact, it would take me almost forty years to finally forgive my father, realizing that he was sick and that he grew overwhelmed with the voice of failure ringing constantly in his head. In his pride, he surrendered. Yes, we each carried scars with us, but we also carried the memories of a man—an incredible man—my father, David Sidney Hillman.

# CHAPTER FIVE
# RESTLESS

As if the summer of 1961 wasn't tumultuous enough, when September rolled around, I still had the consequences of my bad behavior from the previous year lingering over me. As it turned out, I had failed most of my final exams as a result of having missed so much school during my suspension after the Bloody Mary incident. I had to repeat most of eleventh grade, which was not fun. I made the decision to make a fresh start by enrolling in La Jolla High School. Nobody would know me, and I could quietly slip in under the radar without having to answer a bunch of questions about my dad or about flunking so many classes. Fortunately, I didn't have to forego all social support. Two of my friends from San Dieguito decided to change schools, too.

We lasted a total of three months before returning to San Dieguito in defeat. It was beyond humiliating to have to go back again. I dreaded having to face my friends after all that had happened—not to mention suffering the indignity of attending classes with kids that were younger than me.

Meanwhile, my mother stayed with *The Rancho Santa Fe Times* for a while longer. Then, we moved to a small house in Del Mar, near where Susan and Hugh lived. Not really knowing how to cope, Cathy and I continued to struggle with our friends and with school. I didn't qualify with enough credits to graduate in the following spring so, that summer, I enrolled in Oceanside Junior College, hoping to get enough credits to earn my diploma. I signed up for the first class that held any interest, political science, and received a D minus on my first test. I was walking around in a fog, wondering if I would ever get beyond age seventeen, much less actually earn a high school diploma.

One day, Edward Covey showed up at our door. Edward was the son of my parents' best friends and would go on to become Dick's brother-in-law. He was a nonconformist in the truest sense of the word, having broken most of his family's rules and boundaries as a young man. He was in his late twenties and had such a positive effect on all of us with his contagious smile and amazing energy. He stayed with the three of us for a week or two, cheering up my mom and Cathy, and, most importantly, sitting down with me as an all-caring surrogate big brother. I told him about my first test score from junior college, and he just smiled. "Let's see if we can work this out together," he replied. Every day, Edward worked with me, showing me how to study, how to read more effectively, and how to retain information. I took my next test and got a B plus!

Edward led a very reclusive and mysterious life. Nobody really seemed to know much about him, and his family was always vague on his activities after he graduated from college. I always suspected that he spoke three or four languages and probably did clandestine work for the government—ours or some other country's. Even though my brother married Edward's sister, Midge, I didn't see him many times after that summer. But he certainly came into my life at a critical juncture and helped get my academic pursuits back on track.

The summer of 1962 was abruptly interrupted when my mother announced that she was moving us to Los Angeles. It seemed like the best option for her to move away from the sadness and despair that haunted her in San Diego County. At first, we stayed at Grandma Charlton's home on Doheny Drive in Beverly Hills until we could find a suitable apartment nearby.

Once we arrived in Los Angeles, things started happening at a rapid pace. Cathy enrolled in Beverly Hills High School, and Mom got a job downtown working at a fashion magazine that was published and edited by an old friend of my father's. Meanwhile, I went looking for a job of my own. I applied at the May Company on Wilshire and Fairfax in midtown.

You had to be eighteen to qualify for a job there, and I was still two months shy of my birthday. God was surely with me the day the nice young lady who interviewed me pointed out the age problem, but then proceeded to change the numbers and hire me on the spot. A truly kind and understanding person had again entered my life.

My job required me to be at work every day at 8:00 a.m. working as a "stock boy" in the men's clothing department, where I kept the shelves and arranged displays. It was a real "punch the clock" kind of gig from 8:00 to 5:00 on weekdays, with Saturdays and Sundays off. Still lacking enough credits for my diploma, I enrolled in night school at Beverly Hills High. I took typing and reported for class three times a week, which would give me the credits needed to finally finish.

In addition to the three of us finding new work and school situations, we quickly moved into a nice little two-bedroom apartment on Robbins Drive across from the high school. It was small but comfortable. In just two months we'd gone from Rancho Santa Fe to Del Mar to an unfamiliar metropolitan city. Life was changing so rapidly that we didn't even have time to process the extreme culture shock.

My daily regimen consisted of waking at dawn, grabbing some breakfast, and walking to the city bus stop for my twenty-minute ride down Wilshire Boulevard to the May Company. I put in my eight-hour workday, then arrived home by 5:30 p.m. to get ready for my 6:00 p.m. night class. My net take-home pay was $80.00 per week, half of which I gave to my mom. It was an adjustment to get used to the May Company job and all the faces and experiences that came along with it. And I know it was scary for Cathy to adjust to her new school. She had been an excellent student at San Dieguito High and now had to catch up at Beverly Hills High, which had a much more advanced curriculum and a huge student body. Most of the students came from very wealthy backgrounds, and many were the sons and daughters of Hollywood actors. But we both managed. Our family was picking up the pieces, and the three of us managed to keep moving forward in the face of some big changes. None of us complained; we just did what we had to do.

It was music that really helped me get through that time of transition. I was listening to and learning from every resource I could find. Fortunately, the Ash Grove was mere minutes away from our new apartment. It was an amazing club that was known for presenting traditional folk, blues, and bluegrass. In fact, I was well aware of the Ash Grove before we even moved to Los Angeles. I used to make the trip up with my friends Kenny Wertz and Gary Carr to see Flatt and Scruggs, The Stanley Brothers, and Bill Monroe—all of whom we saw within a six-month period. That's also where we saw The Kentucky Colonels, who were then called The Country Boys. The last time we saw them, their mandolin player Roland White was in the Army, stationed in Germany, so a Berkeley student named Scott Hambly was filling in on mandolin and vocals.

He was so good that I went up to him after their first set and asked if he gave lessons. "I do," he responded, "and if you can get up to Berkeley, I would happy to teach you some basics." All of sixteen years old—with just a change of clothes, my mandolin, and a round-trip ticket, I took the train up from Del Mar. Fortunately, my sister Susan had moved to Berkeley, so I had a place to stay. Arriving in the early evening, I called Scott and arranged for our first lesson, which would be the next morning. What a great guy Scott was. He showed me the right pick to use, how to play scales, all the chords I would need to know, and how to develop a good strong tremolo with my right hand. After two days of lessons he said, "Now you're on your own. Practice, learn off your records, and practice some more." The next time I got together with Kenny and Gary, I was able to hold my own.

Once I moved to LA, I became an Ash Grove regular on most week-end nights. I also managed to meet some guys from Pasadena who were bluegrass players. I'd been playing with Kenny and Gary some down south, which I missed, so when those Pasadena guys occasionally invited me out to play with them, it was a much-needed boost. By that point, I'd finally gotten a much-coveted Gibson F2 mandolin, and my skills had improved considerably.

After a few months, I realized I needed new wheels. The bus was all fine and good, but I needed some real transportation—a way to physically escape when not burdened with the daily drudgery of the May Company. By that point I'd finished night school and had finally gathered the credits for my diploma. In celebration, I started saving some cash to buy a new

Honda 305cc Super Hawk motorcycle. Amazingly, my mother gave me permission and even co-signed a small loan so I could buy the magnificent machine. It was black and looked like an English Café Racer. Now that I had my cool bike, the door was open for many exciting adventures.

By the end of the year, things were getting better. I had met a sweet young lady who worked in the May Company's cosmetics department. We became fast friends, and she offered just the right amount of affection to soothe my wounds. I can't even recall her name now, but she made settling into a new life much more bearable. Cathy, too, adjusted to the rigid atmosphere of Beverly Hills High, and even Mom grew happier than I had seen her in months. Feeling that we'd stabilized, and having just turned eighteen, I decided perhaps it was time for me to move out and begin my adult life.

In January of 1963 my bluegrass pals Kenny and Gary invited me to move back down to San Diego and join their new band, The Scottsville Squirrel Barkers. I sat down with my mom to explain how I was feeling and to discuss the new opportunity. I didn't want her to feel like I was abandoning her, and it was important for me to have her blessing. Thankfully, she was very encouraging and believed in me enough to let me go.

I gave notice to the May Company, and probably right in the nick of time. I'd been shoplifting Levi's on the job. Fortunately, a very kind fellow employee, who was also a floor walker, took me aside one day and told me I was being watched. Had he not done that, I probably would have been arrested. I'll never forget his kindness in not turning me into the authorities.

With my mother's blessing and the May Company behind me, I stuffed a few pieces of clothing into a duffle bag with my mandolin, strapped it all down on the back of my motorcycle, and hit the highway. I was excited and scared to be embarking on a new and unknown path.

Kenny and Gary's bandmates in The Scottsville Squirrel Barkers were Ed Douglas and Larry Murray, who ran a place called the Blue Guitar shop. It was Ed who was responsible for the group's memorable name. He had been born in Scottsville, Kentucky, and used to talk about "squirrel barking" back home. The way it worked was that a fella out hunting for his supper would run a squirrel up a tree. Once it froze, he'd take careful aim and shoot at the bark of the tree just below where the squirrel was perched, knocking it out of the tree and onto the ground in a semi-conscious state to be picked up completely intact and ready to become that night's meal.

The first step upon arriving down south was to figure out where I was going to stay. Ed had a little tiny shack out behind the Blue Guitar that had no furniture, no hot water for showering, and no amenities other than a broken-down little cot for sleeping. Sometimes I'd crash with one of the guys, but I usually stayed out in the shack in those terrible conditions, trying to figure out how to find a proper place to live.

The Squirrel Barkers rehearsed every day and played every Saturday night at the Blue Guitar. Ed and Larry worked it out to have intimate shows every weekend. In addition to our group, they'd bring in local folksingers, a couple of Flamenco guitarists, plus an occasional Flamenco dance troupe. The Blue Guitar stage is where we really learned how to play. It was a great time of musical growth, but living behind the guitar shop and having limited funds wasn't exactly the best situation. Other than our shows on stage, it was a tough haul. I was rapidly becoming a burden to my friends as I was a functional borderline panhandler in those lean times.

I was finally saved from my shack after a couple months when I moved in with a guy named Juan Martin, which I think was actually just a stage name. Juan was Cuban and had been a member of The Jose Greco Flamenco Dance Troupe. Known throughout the world, Jose Greco brought the art of Flamenco to America. Juan had grown up in Cuba and barely escaped with his life the day Castro rode into Havana. On his way to the Havana Harbor to make his escape, some of Castro's troops opened fire on the car Juan was riding in, killing his best friend. He managed to get to the harbor and to a safe passage on the next boat leaving for Miami.

When I met him, Juan was actually living across the Mexican border in an apartment in Tijuana. Since he wasn't a citizen but occasionally worked in the US, Juan had a day pass to come across the border, but it was only valid until sundown. I had gotten to know Juan through a guy named Yuris Zeltins, who was a Flamenco guitarist and instrument repairman—as well as Ed and Larry's third partner in the Blue Guitar. They shared the Tijuana apartment, which happened to have a spare bedroom. Three stranger people never rode across the Mexican border every night:

a Cuban dancer, a Latvian Flamenco guitarist, and a half-Jewish teenage bluegrass mandolin player. But, hey, I didn't mind. I had upgraded to the luxury of heat and a decent bed to sleep in. Juan took Yuris and I around to the nice parts of the city to the good restaurants and clubs that featured the best Flamenco music. He also taught me enough Spanish to navigate the streets of Tijuana on my own.

My living situation had improved a bit, but I was still living for those Saturday nights at the Blue Guitar. Just getting up to play was a thrill. If we made any money, that was an extra treat. Our reputation began to grow around San Diego, and soon we started booking some other gigs. Ed played bass but also handled all our business and served as the manager. Larry was our emcee on stage, played the dobro, and sang baritone. Gary played rhythm guitar and sang lead, while Kenny sang tenor and played banjo. Gary Carr was a great guitar player and an exceptional singer, as was Kenny; they had the Stanley Brothers duet harmony down. I, of course, handled the mandolin. Being the youngest and still extremely shy, I only sang occasionally.

As our reputation grew, we even got the chance to perform on live television. It was a local morning show hosted by a very young Regis Philbin. One of his other guests on the show the day we appeared was Frankie Avalon, whom I distinctly remember standing in front of us while we were warming up and just staring, transfixed at what we were doing. I'm guessing he'd never encountered bluegrass music in his hometown of Philadelphia.

The band was starting to sound really good. We began branching out, not confining our activities to San Diego County but venturing up to Los Angeles, too. The Troubadour in West Hollywood, right up the street from my old haunt, The Ash Grove, was the premier folk club in LA. Every Monday night was the "Hoot," which was basically an open mic night. This was the place to be seen and possibly move up a rung on the ladder. We would pile into Ed's Volkswagen van and make the 130-mile trip up to LA to play the Monday night "Hoots."

This was around the time Herb Pedersen entered my life. Herb was in a bluegrass band called The Pine Valley Boys that had moved down to LA from Berkeley. We immediately hit it off and became fast friends. Herb would later become a very important figure in my musical life.

Everyone we met who was anybody in the burgeoning folk music scene told us we had to have an album to get any real work. So, during one of The Squirrel Barkers trips, we all decided it was time to focus on getting some kind of a record deal. Ed had seen the name Jim Dickson listed as the engineer and producer on the back of an album by The Dillards, who had recently moved out to Los Angeles from Salem, Missouri. Ed called up World Pacific Studios in West LA, where Jim worked, and it just so happened he was in the building at that particular moment. Jim invited us to come down and play him a few songs. He liked what he heard, but Jim wasn't ready to take on The Scottsville Squirrel Barkers just yet. He was, however, very encouraging and steered us toward Crown Records, which he said might be another possibility. He called up Crown and arranged for us to drive over and audition right then.

Crown Records consisted of a very small office and tiny recording studio, but we played a few songs and they loved us. In fact, they wanted to start recording an album right away. This was exciting stuff, but Crown was a very small independent label. Their distribution network wasn't even record stores, but supermarkets and five-and-dime shops. A deal with Crown Records meant you got to make one album, and all the songs had to be public domain material so there were no song royalties to be paid. Plus, we had to record the entire album live, with no overdubs. We literally set up—right then and there—and cut the whole record in four hours. They even mixed it straight to two-track tape as we recorded it. To top off the day, we headed out to Griffith Park right after the recording session for a photo shoot for the album. We were all dressed in matching vests and boots, looking every bit the part of a proper Kentucky bluegrass outfit. Talk about streamlined! We had a complete, fully mixed album, including the cover art, within a total of eight hours. The album was titled *Bluegrass Favorites*.

Within a few weeks we had actual copies, a box of ten albums for each band member plus a small stipend for each of us. I still hold up this record, my very first, as one of the best I've ever been a part of. We played without fear, just pure unbridled passion. I even got to sing lead vocals on one song, "Reuben." That's the earliest recording of my vocals. It would be a few years before I'd get the chance to do it again.

We were still making our weekly appearances at The Blue Guitar, but on one of our trips to LA to play the Troubadour Hoot we met a man named Tom Campbell who worked at Disneyland, booking talent around the park. Tom offered us a three-week summer showcase in front of the Mine Ride, taking over for a band called The Mad Mountain Ramblers. Every afternoon we would dress in our stage clothes, which resembled miner's outfits—boots, scarves, suspenders, and hats like the one worn by famous cowboy sidekick Gabby Hayes. We got to play music, meet girls, and get free passes to the Disneyland rides. As soon as our engagement was over, Herb Pedersen's band, The Pine Valley Boys, came in and took over the gig.

Another big opportunity for the Squirrel Barkers was the chance to play the Sunday afternoon show at Smokey Rogers's Bostonia Ballroom in El Cajon, just south of San Diego. Smokey was a local country singer who'd had a few regional hits. He performed at the Bostonia on Friday and Saturday nights, but the Sunday show featured guest acts, and Ed managed to get us the booking. It was a big deal because The Bostonia Ballroom, along with The Palamino Club in North Hollywood and The Foothill Club in Long Beach, was part of the Southern California touring circuit for a lot of the bigger country acts.

The day came for our appearance at Smokey's club, and I was sitting outside in the back of the main stage practicing my mandolin to warm up for our portion of the show. All of a sudden, I felt a hand on my shoulder as a huge shadow descend over me. "You sound real good, son," said a deeply resonant voice. "Keep playing, work hard, and you may find what you're looking for someday." I looked up. It was Tex Ritter. *The* Tex Ritter, the cool singing cowboy whose movies I'd watched as a kid. Receiving a dose of approval and encouragement from a childhood hero meant the world to me.

In the fall of 1963, Kenny and Gary got their draft notices and, not wasting any time waiting to be called up by the army, decided to join the air force. So much for The Scottsville Squirrel Barkers. We still had a few shows booked that we had to honor, so Doug Jeffords, an active navy officer, filled in for Gary Carr on guitar. We invited Bernie Leadon, who was still in high school at the time, to fill Kenny's spot. In fact, Bernie, who I had met a few months earlier, was a Squirrel Barkers fan and was really inspired by Kenny's style on the banjo. It looked like we might even be able to figure out a way to carry on beyond the dates we'd booked.

Bernie was an incredible banjo and guitar player, but his family soon moved on to Gainesville, Florida, where he continued his music. It was there that he met Tom Petty, who was just beginning his own musical journey at the time. Fortunately, Bernie and I kept a close friendship and reunited a few years later in The Flying Burrito Brothers before he left to form The Eagles with Glenn Frey, Don Henley, and Randy Meisner. Without Kenny, Gary, or Bernie in the Squirrel Barkers, however, our group splintered. I eventually got back on my Honda Super Hawk and headed back to LA the same way I'd headed down to San Diego six months earlier—with nothing more than duffel bag of clothes and a mandolin. I was on the hunt for my next musical adventure.

I wasn't back home but a short time when I ran into Ross Blackledge, an old pal I'd grown up with in Rancho Santa Fe. His father was the insurance agent who had fought for my family after my dad's death, so I thought a lot of Ross and his family. Ross was working driving trucks— big trucks—and I found out he was taking a load on a flatbed rig to San Francisco in the next few days. I managed to hitch a ride. We met up at 10 p.m. off the Golden State Freeway, loaded my Honda on the flatbed trailer, tied it down, and headed north. I didn't know what I was looking for—let alone what I was doing—but now, as I look back, it was as if I was wandering down a long road full of blind corners, just trying to figure myself out. We arrived in the Bay Area very early the next morning, where Ross unloaded his truck at the freight receiving area in Oakland. We pulled the motorcycle off the bed of the truck, cranked it up, and took off for San Francisco. Ross was a big guy, so him riding behind me on my Honda must have been quite an interesting sight for other travelers on the road.

Ross went on his way the next morning, while I stayed several days with some high school friends. My next mission was to find a job—any job. I applied at Swift's Packing Plant in South San Francisco but failed the math test and wasn't hired. Good thing because that wasn't meant to be. Somehow Ed Douglas from the Squirrel Barkers found out where I was and sent me a telegram telling me that Don Parmley, the leader of The

Golden State Boys, was trying to find me. They needed a mandolin player and he thought of me. Having watched different variations of The Golden State Boys on the weekly *Cal's Corral* TV show on Channel 13 when I was in high school gave me a pretty good idea of the band's sound. Cal was Cal Worthington, a famous car dealer who let the bands on his show use a new Dodge station wagon. I immediately called Don who asked if I could come to his house to audition. Don lived in Norwalk, all the way down in Los Angeles County, where I'd just come from.

But this was The Golden State Boys! I was on a plane for LA within the next six hours. I left the Honda with another old high school pal who swore he would take care of it for me. The next day I showed up at Don's garage with my mandolin, hardly any clothes, and definitely no money. He introduced me to his bandmates, brothers Vern and Rex Gosdin. We huddled in Don's garage to begin our first rehearsal, which went fine. It was mostly bluegrass songs I knew and some others I learned very quickly. The band's manager, a man named Bob Flowers, stopped by to let us know we had been scheduled to play in Jackpot, Nevada, for two weeks. That was a place in the northeastern part of the state, on the Idaho border, that neither I, nor any sane human, had ever heard of before. I guess that meant I passed the audition. The best thing I heard that day was when Bob Flowers asked, "Chris, do you need any money? I can advance you a little." Boy, did I need some money. I took him up on his offer and bought some decent clothes and basic necessities for the trip to Jackpot.

The very next day, we all piled into the Dodge station wagon from Cal Worthington and made the long drive up to Jackpot, Nevada. I got to know the guys during that road trip and, being the youngest, managed to survive their ribbing. Vern and Rex were very open and friendly, while Don was also really nice, but guarded. When we arrived, we discovered that Jackpot had one gas station, one medium-sized casino, a small market, and one pretty suspicious-looking motel. We were shown to a cramped trailer behind the casino, which would be our home for the next two weeks.

The Golden State Boys played three to four shows a night for the next two weeks, and it was fantastic. All the guys were really good singers. Vern sang lead and Rex sang tenor, with the pair handling all the classic duet material and sounding just as good as The Louvin Brothers. Don added his baritone on several songs and was quite skilled, as well. That short engagement in Jackpot helped us really gel together as a group, and it went by really fast.

Back home in California, we played Friday and Saturday nights at places called The Harem Lounge, The Foothill Club, The Leilani Club and other hillbilly clubs in Los Angeles County. Along with our club work and our usual appearances on *Cal's Corral,* we also played a live radio show in Long Beach on Sundays called *The Squeakin' Deacon Show.* We were busy. In fact, that Honda motorcycle I left with the buddy in San Francisco who swore he'd take care of it for me? I never saw it again. I was way too wrapped up in the music to ever have a chance to retrieve it.

In order to work so steadily with The Golden State Boys I had to figure out how to get beyond one obvious hurdle. Since I was still underage, I needed an ID to work the clubs. I certainly wasn't going to manufacture one myself, since I'd learned my lesson on that front. Somehow, I managed to acquire one from the DMV in Napa, California, that wasn't *exactly* accurate. I told them my birthday was December 4, 1942—exactly two years before my actual birthdate. I also told them my name was Christopher Hardin. I borrowed that last name from Glen Dee Hardin, who played piano on *Cal's Corral* and in the house band at the Palomino Club in North Hollywood before going on to become a member of Elvis Presley's TCB Band. I just thought his name sounded cool and would look believable on a driver's license. God only knows how I got away with that stunt. There wasn't a bartender in all of LA County who believed I was twenty-one. I looked fourteen on a good day.

I had kept in touch with Jim Dickson after our brief meeting with The Scottsville Squirrel Barkers when he referred us to Crown Records. One day I called him up at World Pacific Studios and told him about the new group I was in, how good the Gosdin Brothers sang, and how tight the band was. He agreed to come down and see us at the next Monday Hoot Night at the Troubadour. Recognizing that our playing and singing was a huge step up from the Squirrel Barkers, Jim was knocked out when he heard us. He asked us to come down to the studio to record some tunes.

My maternal grandmother, Catherine Cheshire (on the left), with her friends
in Georgetown, Texas, in 1885. They're all riding side saddle, and you can
see a horse and buggy in the background. (Hillman Archives)

The main street of my hometown of Rancho Santa Fe, California, in the 1940s, known as The Center
or The Village by the locals. (Photo courtesy of the Rancho Santa Fe Historical Society)

Our home in Rancho Santa Fe, 1949: (L-R) My big brother Dick, our beagle Barney, me (age 4), my little sister Cathy, and my older sister Susan. (Hillman Archives)

The house where I grew up, on Las Planideras in Rancho. Every summer my brother and I had to paint the rocks in the driveway. (Hillman Archives)

One of my favorite photos: my brother Dick and me with Dad.  Mom bought us
those cool leather jackets at Sears Roebuck. (Hillman Archives)

(L) I was out for a trail ride with my dad in 1949, riding Peanut Brittle. (R) At the Rancho Santa Fe Horse Show in 1954, My mom holds the reigns of my Palomino, Ranger. (Hillman Archives)

"Old John Robertson" as I remember him when I was growing up in the early 1950s. The photo on the right shows him and his wife Jo having tea at their home in Rancho Santa Fe. (Photos courtesy of the Rancho Santa Fe Historical Society)

(L) In 1957 I joined the Earl Warren Jr. High School band. You can see my mother and my sister Cathy in the background, as well as our '53 Ford station wagon. I never got comfortable with playing the trumpet! (Hillman Archives). (R) My dear friend Bill Smith, my first mentor, in 1961. During the week he was the head custodian at my high school; on the weekends he played with his band at the navy base in San Diego. It was Bill who showed me the way. (Courtesy of the family of Bill Smith)

The Scottsville Squirrel Barkers: (L) Rehearsing at the Blue Guitar in San Diego, with Kenny Wertz playing guitar in the background, 1962. (R) Tearing it up in front of the Mine Train ride at Disneyland in the summer of 1963. Whenever you worked at Disneyland, you were outfitted by their costume department. (L-R) Kenny Wertz looking like a character from *F Troop*, me, Larry Murray, Ed Douglas, and Gary Carr holding down the rhythm guitar with a cool hat. (Hillman Archives)

The Scottsville Squirrel Barkers, looking like we just came out of Kentucky, on stage at the Disneyland Theatre, 1963. Unlike my bandmates, I wasn't able to grow a mustache yet. (L-R) me, Kenny Wertz, Larry Murray, Gary Carr, and Ed Douglas. (Hillman Archives)

The Golden State Boys, later to be known as The Hillmen, in Los Angeles, 1963. (L-R) me, Don Parmley, Rex Gosdin, Vern Gosdin. (Photo by Jim Dickson, from The Henry Diltz Archives)

Early Byrds photo taken at Columbia Recording Studio in Hollywood, with those fabulous suits from Mr. Parker's Closet. I'm playing the bass I used for my audition. (L-R) Jim, me, Gene, David, and Michael. (Getty Images)

Sound check at Jane Fonda and Roger Vadim's 4th of July party in Malibu, California. Jane's brother Peter got us the gig. (Photo by Dennis Hopper, courtesy of The Hopper Trust)

The legendary Von Dutch putting the finishing touches on Michael's bass drum, San Fernando Valley, California, 1965. (L-R) Me, Von Dutch, a friend of Michael's, Michael, and David. (Photograph by Barry Feinstein. © Barry Feinstein Photography, Inc. 2020. All Rights Reserved.)

Walking to the backstage stage door wth my bass during The Byrds summer tour of the Midwest, 1965. (Photograph by Barry Feinstein. © Barry Feinstein Photography, Inc. 2020. All Rights Reserved.)

The Byrds, walking by Radio City Music Hall in the rain on a very cold and blustery day during our first trip to New York City, 1965. (Don Hunstein, © Sony Music Entertainment)

Jumping in the "Big Apple," 1965.
(Don Hunstein, © Sony Music Entertainment)

Looking extremely happy and squeezed tightly on a couch for a photo in
someone's office at Columbia Records in New York. (Getty Images)

Jim, David, and me at LaGuardia Airport, early 1965, checking in for our flight back home after performing on the *Hullabaloo* TV show in New York City. Always interesting hair. (Don Hunstein, © Sony Music Entertainment)

With my borrowed Guild Starfire II bass. My first Guild Starfire had recently been stolen. I was very happy when Guild reissued this model in 2015. (Getty Images)

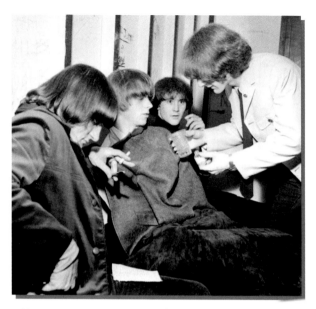

Dr. Jim, assisted by Gene and David, tends to me backstage in England in 1965. I was the the first of us to get sick on that tour. Extreme fatigue and illness caught every one of us. (Hillman Archives)

The Byrds sit down with some fans: (L-R) Columbia Records publicist Billy James (standing), me, Jim, Mike, Byrds' publicist Derek Taylor (standing), Gene, and David (partially obscured). (Hillman Archives)

The Byrds onstage at *The Ed Sullivan Show*, 1965.
(Photo by Jim Dickson, from The Henry Diltz Archives)

(L) Backstage with The Dillards in 1966. I'm playing Dean Webb's mandolin with Doug Dillard on banjo, Rodney Dillard on guitar, and Dean looking over my shoulder. (R) On stage shortly after Gene left the band and I was promoted to the front line as a singer. (Courtesy of Sony Music Archives)

The Byrds land in London as Jim continues filming, February of 1967.
(Getty Images)

The Byrds in 1967, a very good year for us:
Jim, me, David, and Michael. (Hillman Archives)

Mt. Tamalpais Music Festival, June 1967. Hugh Masekela joins us on stage for a rousing
version of "So You Want To Be A Rock 'n' Roll Star." (Photo by Henry Diltz)

At the Los Angeles County Museum of Art with our friend Dennis Hopper behind the camera, 1967.
(Photo by Dennis Hopper, Courtesy of The Hopper Art Trust)

Me and Jim, now known as Roger, contemplating the future . . .
and then there were two. (Photo by Henry Diltz)

His idea was to complete an entire album of ten or twelve songs and then shop it to Elektra or Vanguard, which were the big folk labels at the time. The first night, we ran through the usual bluegrass fare: Flatt and Scruggs, Bill Monroe, The Stanley Brothers, Jim and Jesse, and that kind of thing. Dickson listened patiently but, at some point, stopped the take. "Listen, you guys," he said. "You're a great group, but do you want to cover other peoples' songs like all the other bluegrass bands, or do you want to find songs from other kinds of artists that would lend themselves to a bluegrass treatment?"

We all sort of just looked at one another. We didn't really understand where Jim was going with this but, not having too many options and wanting to make a good record, we listened to his ideas. He wanted to help us find material, which was exactly what a good A&R (artist and repertoire) man was supposed to do in the music business. Vern and Rex were already writing some pretty good songs, a couple of which—"Roll on Muddy River" and "Going Up"—made the final cut. Jim was bringing in Bob Dylan and Woody Guthrie material and, when we started learning those songs, it worked. We preserved a couple of bluegrass tunes, "Brown Mountain Light," "Fair and Tender Ladies," as well as including our own arrangement of Bill Monroe's "Wheel Hoss." It was a worthy project with some fine singing. I was still figuring out the mandolin, but Don, Vern, and Rex more than made up for my learning curve. I'm still not entirely sure how I got that job, but obviously it was meant to be.

Jim Dickson had a friend who was an agent at the William Morris Agency who handed us a wonderful opportunity to play a couple of folk festivals: the Monterey Folk Festival in Monterey, California, and, prior to that, the Honolulu Folk Festival, which was a three-night weekend event at the Waikiki Shell (kind of like a smaller version of The Hollywood Bowl in a park right off Waikiki beach). Judy Collins was on the bill with us in Honolulu, and she was so kind to me. She looked out for me like a big sister, even reminding me to eat dinner and take care of myself. She was already well-known in folk circles, so it was really sweet of her to take an interest in us.

Despite Jim's involvement and encouragement, however, no record deal materialized for The Golden State Boys. Without that extra boost we needed, we just weren't earning enough money to keep it going. I was struggling as a single person, but the other guys had families and staying in the band would have been a true hardship for them. Sadly, The Golden State Boys ultimately broke up. Don found work as a driver for Continental Trailways, while the Godsin brothers found jobs in construction while continuing to sing and write songs.

Fortunately things would eventually work out for all of us. Don later formed the highly successful band The Bluegrass Cardinals with his son David, who grew into a fine lead singer, and Rex became a prolific songwriter. Vern and I remained very close throughout his life, and it was a thrill when we both started having hits on the *Billboard* country chart years later—me with The Desert Rose Band, and Vern with his huge catalog of radio hits that resulted in nearly twenty Top 10 singles. I hosted an episode of a TV show called *American Music Shop* in the 1990s, and Vern was one of my guests. It was the last time we performed together. Vern, Don, and Rex have all passed on now, but I'll always be grateful for my time with them. I learned a lot, and they truly helped prepare me for the next musical venture that awaited me.

# CHAPTER SIX
## SO YOU WANT TO BE A
## ROCK 'N' ROLL STAR

===========

After The Golden State Boys disbanded, I moved back up to Hollywood from Norwalk. I was flat broke and living with two other guys in an apartment on Fountain Avenue. Herb Pedersen lived right down the street from me and was in the same financial situation, as his band was struggling to survive. I had to get some kind of a job, so I went to an employment agency and was handed a couple of leads. The first was for a job at a machine shop, which was located back down the freeway near Norwalk, where I'd just moved from. I applied for a job as an apprentice machinist, but I was totally unsuited for that kind of work. The gentleman who interviewed me knew it and advised me to look for another line of work.

Next, I walked into the La Brea Carwash located on La Brea Boulevard between Sunset and Melrose. I applied for a job as a washer, but the manager, an older guy, just looked me up and down. "I can't hire you, son," he said slowly. "Take a look out the window at all the guys I've got working for me out there. Those guys'll eat you for lunch." Everyone working out there was Black or Latino. It didn't bother me, but this was still 1963, and the manager knew that those guys wouldn't take kindly to some dumb white boy working alongside them.

Fortunately, I soon ran into my old Squirrel Barkers bandmate Larry Murray. He told me about a band Randy Sparks was putting together to perform in his folk club, Ledbetter's, near the UCLA campus in the Westwood neighborhood. Sparks was the guy who had created The New Christy Minstrels folk group, which was a very successful touring and recording act at the time. He sold the Minstrels to a management firm and opened Ledbetter's as a venue to showcase his new groups. His latest creation, which was similar to the Minstrels, was called The Backporch Majority. And now he was hoping to assemble a bluegrass-oriented group, too. Larry advised me to come down to the club and try out; if I made it, I'd have steady work—and Randy was even providing a place for the musicians to live. Though the whole thing sounded way too manufactured for my tastes, as a broke and newly unemployed musician, I jumped at the chance to put a little money in my pocket.

The next day, I showed up to Ledbetter's with my mandolin and was hired on the spot. The band was named The Green Grass Group and featured Larry Murray on dobro and lead vocals; two old San Diego pals, Pete Socksie on guitar and Marilyn Powell on dulcimer; a stand-up bassist named Bob; and a very talented English woman named Patty Hill who played banjo. Patty could really play and, with her cockney accent and wonderful attitude, she made the whole experience bearable. The final member, who would become a good pal of mine, was Dwayne Story, the nephew of gospel singer Carl Story. Dwayne was a great bluegrass guitarist and singer/songwriter. In fact, he was way too good to have been in that band. Dwayne had a wife and young daughter and, like me, needed the money and stability until something legitimate came along.

The music was dreadful, to say the least. All the songs were written by Randy Sparks and sounded like they were right out of a bad *Lil' Abner* script. One lyric from that period in my life is still stuck in my brain to this day: "Billy's mule can tote a wagon, he can pull a plow." That was the opening line to "Billy's Mule" and pretty well gives you a sense of The Green Grass Group. But, hey, it was work, and we were each paid $100 per week, which was big money in late 1963. The lodging we were offered was in a very nice ranch-style home in Encino, in the San Fernando Valley. At least I had money in my pocket and a roof over my head at a time when I really needed both. To this day, I'm grateful to Larry Murray for tipping me off to the opportunity.

By early 1964 I was working steadily with The Green Grass Group. Then, on February 9, my life changed. Actually, *everyone's* life changed. It was a Sunday night and I just happened to pop into my mother's apartment. She was watching *The Ed Sullivan Show,* along with the many millions of other Americans who faithfully tuned in each week. Just as I sat down on the couch, I heard Ed say, "Ladies and gentlemen, The Beatles. Let's bring them on!" I had heard of these guys, but hadn't actually heard their songs yet. They burst into "All My Loving," and I was transfixed. *Who are these guys? What is happening here?* It felt like that moment in *The Wizard of Oz* when everything goes from black and white to color. The look, the hair, the songs! It was incredible. It was as if these guys were ending the nightmare of the Kennedy assassination from a few short months earlier and ushering our entire culture into a new era. It was that powerful.

By the time I reported for duty at Ledbetter's on Tuesday night, my head was still spinning from seeing The Beatles on the Sullivan show. I didn't know how or why, but I intuitively knew that something musically different and exciting was waiting for me right around the corner.

As taken as I was with The Beatles, they weren't darlings of the folk scene. Very few people from that world heard anything special in the group's blend of rock and roll, rhythm and blues, folk, pop, and light jazz. That didn't damper my enthusiasm for either folk music or The Beatles, however. Even though I wasn't playing Hoot Night at the Troubadour with The Golden State Boys anymore, I would still go down when I could just to visit friends and see what was going on. I couldn't really understand why a lot of my peers weren't as excited as I was about what this strange new British band was doing, but I was pleasantly surprised one night when a guy jumped up on the Troubadour stage and played "I Want to Hold Your Hand" on a twelve-string acoustic guitar. It sounds a little strange to describe it, but this guy was very good, and it really worked. I didn't get a chance to meet him that evening, but someone told me his name was Jim McGuinn, and I filed it away, hoping we would meet some day and share our mutual love for both folk music and the Beatles.

A few weeks later, Jim Dickson called and told me about a trio he was working with called The Jet Set. He was recording some demos in hopes of landing them a record deal, and he invited me down to World Pacific to hear them sing. He explained that one of them was a former member of Les Baxter's Balladeers named David Crosby, with whom Dickson had already done some recording in the past. David had been the third guy to come into the group after it began as a loose duo with Gene Clark, who had been a member of The New Christy Minstrels, and Jim McGuinn, who I'd seen play at the Troubadour Hoot Night. "Wait," I said. "Jim McGuinn? I think I saw him play at Hoot Night at the Troubadour a few weeks back!" Dickson confirmed it was the same guy, so I eagerly accepted his invitation to come hear them.

A few nights later, I went down to World Pacific after my last set at Ledbetter's. When I walked in, Jim McGuinn was playing a Gibson twelve-string acoustic guitar, while Gene and David were each playing six-string acoustics. They were singing one of Gene Clark's songs, and they sounded like angels, the way their three voices blended together. I knew something about good harmony vocals after having worked with the Gosdin brothers in The Golden State Boys, but this was something on a higher plane. David Crosby had one of the strongest, most beautiful tenor voices I had ever heard. I could tell he was approaching his parts from a different angle; his aesthetic didn't come from the church or from country music, but from a jazz-influenced harmony in the style of The Four Freshmen. Those three guys had the beginnings of a great blend and, needless to say, I was very impressed. I told Dickson that they had something really special going on.

I quickly discovered that The Jet Set was looking to hire a drummer to turn the three-man acoustic outfit into a proper quartet. They wanted to pattern themselves after The Beatles, with Jim and Gene on guitars and David on bass. I thought it could be something really special, but didn't think too much more about it once I was back to my nightly gigs with The Green Grass Group at Ledbetter's. Then, about two weeks later, Dickson called me and told me that the guys had recorded a couple of original songs, "Please Let Me Love You" and "Don't Be Long." They brought in a rhythm section of studio musicians to round out the session and, on the strength of those recordings, Dickson pitched Jac Holzman, head of Elektra Records, on the idea of releasing it as a single. Jac agreed, but wanted to call the group The Beefeaters, which had British implications but was a terrible name.

Unfortunately, The Beefeaters' debut didn't get any traction. Dickson, however, was undeterred. He believed in the group and was ready to continue developing the trio into a proper band. Then, one night at Ledbetter's, I was given a message when I got off stage. Dickson had called and asked that I call him back as soon as possible. I dialed him up that night, and he explained that David Crosby had met a guy named Michael Clarke in Big Sur, and they'd brought him on as the drummer. They thought they had their lineup, but Crosby wasn't comfortable playing bass and wanted to switch to guitar instead. Then Dickson asked me a question that would change the course of my life: "Can you play bass?" I replied, "Sure, I can handle it," lying through my teeth. I had never held a bass, let alone played one.

The race was on to find an electric bass guitar. I managed to locate a Japanese-made red bass with one pickup, but keep in mind that this was a good thirty years before they started making decent quality instruments in Japan. I didn't even have an amp. The night I showed up for the first rehearsal, I hoped I was going to be able to fake my way through it. When I arrived I met Michael Clarke, with whom I hit it off immediately. He was a great-looking guy with long blond hair, a dead ringer for Brian Jones from The Rolling Stones. He was sitting behind a makeshift drum kit of cardboard boxes and one cymbal.

As I looked around the studio, I noticed some beat-up gear and one tired old amplifier in the corner that Jim McGuinn was plugged into. *This is a pretty rag-tag outfit,* I thought to myself, but I was the new guy in the equation and was trying to keep an open mind. I walked over and plugged my bass into that lone amp alongside McGuinn. Since I was primarily a mandolin player—and sometime guitar player—I played the bass with a pick instead of my fingers. I figured nobody would mind since I'd noticed that Paul McCartney played with a pick and a lot of really good session guys used a flat pick on bass, too. I don't remember what we played that night, but my anxiety level quickly decreased as I realized the other guys were all scrambling to figure it out, too. McGuinn was undoubtedly the most seasoned player, having put in time as an accompanist with The Limelighters, The Chad Mitchell Trio, and Bobby Darin. He had the most experience, and the fact that he'd toured around the world made him the obvious choice to captain the ship of this still-nameless quintet.

Amazingly, I survived that first rehearsal and was offered the permanent gig, so I gave my notice to Randy Sparks and The Green Grass Group. I'll never forgot how hard Mr. Sparks laughed at the idea that I was leaving the stability of his group to work in a rock and roll band. I think he assumed I'd come crawling back in defeat. What he didn't know, however, was how determined I was to make this new situation work. Under Dickson's tutelage we began regular rehearsals. Dick Bock, who owned World Pacific Studios where Dickson worked as an engineer, was kind enough to give us access to the studio after midnight whenever there wasn't a session booked.

There was no money coming in at first, and we were all struggling just to stay alive. I was living in a one-bedroom garage apartment on Melrose, so Mike and Gene moved in with me. McGuinn and Crosby, meanwhile, would hustle enough money to stay at The Padre in Hollywood, which was a real fleabag hotel. We had to be clever to survive, which meant meeting sympathetic girls with cars and jobs and borrowing money from generous friends. Gene and I had checking accounts and checkbooks, but there were times we literally had a zero balance. Right down the street from our apartment was a small market where, at one time, Gene and I each had to knowingly write a bad check just to get some groceries. Dickson was generous and, when he had a little extra cash, would buy us all cheeseburgers at Norm's Restaurant on La Cienega Boulevard.

Though we still had nothing to show for our hard work, we spent almost every night rehearsing. Not only did we not have a dime, we didn't even have a name. Finally, it came to us when we were all over at Eddie Tickner's house for Thanksgiving dinner. Eddie was Dickson's business partner, as well as the business manager for the folk singer, Odetta. The subject of naming the group came up that afternoon and Jim McGuinn suggested The Birds. He thought that the sounds we were coming up with resembled a jet plane, which he associated with flight. Plus, he thought there was a certain magic to the letter B, since it had served The Beatles and the Beach Boys so well. We all agreed that we couldn't keep the normal spelling of the word "birds," since it was a British slang term for young girls. Plus, changing the "i" to a "y" gave it a little more mystery.

Our next step was securing some decent equipment, and Eddie Tickner came to the rescue. He had a business relationship with a lady named

Naomi Hirshhorn, a member of the famous Hirshhorn family whose members were known as major art collectors and philanthropists. Eddie persuaded Naomi to invest $5,000 into the band with a return of 2 percent of all future recording income from The Byrds. That probably turned out to be one of the best investments she ever made in her life.

With that $5,000 in hand, it was time to pick out our equipment. Around that same time, we all went to the Pix Theater on Hollywood Boulevard to watch *A Hard Day's Night*. It would prove to be enormously influential on our instrument choices. Jim McGuinn, already a twelve-string guitar player, saw George Harrison playing a Rickenbacker electric twelve string in the film and instantly knew where his destiny lay. That would become McGuinn's signature guitar. Meanwhile, Crosby fell in love with another guitar George was playing in the movie, a Gretsch "Chet Atkins" electric six string. Mike got some Ludwig drums, just like Ringo's set. Yes, we were desperately trying to emulate our favorite band, The Beatles. I was the only one who bucked the trend. Since I wasn't knocked out with Paul's Hofner bass, I chose a Fender Precision model, which I used briefly before switching to a Guild Starfire.

After spending most of Naomi's funds on our new instruments and amplifiers, we still had a little money left over. At Dickson and Tickner's direction, we were taken downtown to a men's clothing store called Mr. Parker's Closet that catered to young uptown African-American men. There, we bought matching stylish suits with Edwardian velvet collars while Eddie Tickner pranced around like a proud father whose sons were getting dressed for their Bar Mitzvahs. The next stop was Benson's Bootery on Melrose Avenue, where we all got cool black boots with Cuban heels that were very similar to those of our English heroes.

Since all five of us were coming out of the folk scene, we really didn't know anything about performing rock music. Dance steps and stage maneuvers? Forget it! We didn't have a clue. Dickson decided we needed to make the act more presentable on stage so, early one evening, a strange man showed up to the studio door at World Pacific. He wore a burgundy-colored suit and an ill-fitting toupee. Dickson introduced him to us and explained that this gentleman was from Las Vegas. He was there to show us some simple dance steps to incorporate into the act. It took all of ten minutes before we were snickering and calling him "Mr. Leather Hair" just out of earshot. Crosby finally blurted out what we were all thinking: "This is so lame! There's no way any of us are going to do this on stage." Dickson realized it was going nowhere and sent Mr. Leather Hair home in defeat. For the next few nights we would ask him, "Is Mr. Leather Hair coming down tonight?" Even Dickson was laughing by that point.

Finally, we were ready to make our public debut. We planned our first appearance for the next Hoot Night at our old haunt, The Troubadour. It was a hoot all right. Our folk pals got a big laugh seeing us in our matching suits stumbling through our three songs. I wouldn't call it a successful performance by any stretch of the imagination, but that clumsy first outing did give us some clarity on how to better structure the band. Gene Clark and Jim McGuinn both played guitars, while David Crosby just stood and sang. After the gig, David convinced Gene that they should switch. David would be the rhythm guitar player and Gene would be the non-guitar-playing vocalist. What could have been mildly traumatic for Gene wasn't at all. In fact, it really worked out for the best. Crosby was the better guitar player, and Gene turned into a striking front man and became a major focus of the group. He was the "Tambourine Man," playing percussion, singing lead, and playing the part of Prince Valiant with his good looks and great voice. From then on, the gaze of every woman in the audience was locked on his every move.

One of the best things The Byrds had going in the early days was the fact that we had access to World Pacific Studios on a nightly basis. That meant we could actually record our rehearsals and listen back right away. We could experiment with arrangements and analyze changes to the band's sound in real time. Plus, we had Dickson there, giving us feedback and offering advice about what we were hearing on the tapes. Such invaluable tools for rapid growth.

We never knew who might show up at World Pacific when we were working. One night we were out on the studio floor when I looked through the glass and saw Lenny Bruce and an odd assortment of his Hollywood minions hanging out in in the booth with Dickson. We were literally watching the cultural transition from the "beat era" of the 1950s—with all manner of Bohemian literary types, poets, and West Coast jazz artists—to a new paradigm that The Beatles had almost single-handedly created overnight.

Soon after the Troubadour debacle we began slowly booking some shows around Los Angeles. Sally Marr, who was Lenny Bruce's mother, booked us at LA City College for a noontime concert. Then we played Fairfax High School at a noontime assembly. There were a few other local, low-key shows that helped build a little buzz around town. As our reputation grew, we secured a one-week trial run at a club called Ciro's Le Disc on the Sunset Strip. The Strip was the centerpiece of Los Angeles nightlife throughout the 1930s, '40s, and '50s, but it was changing drastically by the time we came along. The classic-era clubs were slowly fading away as Las Vegas began to develop. As television took hold as the primary form of entertainment, most of the generation that once frequented the Sunset Strip was increasingly staying home. Even the jazz clubs were hitting hard times. Shelly's Manne-Hole was still going strong in Hollywood, but most of the other jazz clubs were suffering. The biggest change was the music you'd hear emanating from the nightspots on the Strip. Younger crowds were looking for a new kind of music, and the sounds were changing to reflect the tastes of a new generation.

Ciro's was one of the more famous nightclubs on the Strip. It was really jumping back in the '40s and '50s and was the place to see and be seen. Humphrey Bogart, Errol Flynn, and Spencer Tracy could all be spotted hanging out there. Supposedly, Judy Garland celebrated her eighteenth birthday at Ciro's in 1940. By the time we came along, it still had that classic nightclub décor with big red leather booths and beautiful waitresses wearing just enough to make you take a second look. Ciro's was no different, however, from the other old clubs on the Strip that had to adapt to changing times if they hoped to survive. Just down the street was The Whisky a Go Go, a newer establishment that featured commercial rock and roll bands and plenty of dancing for a younger clientele.

That forced Ciro's owner Frank Sennes Jr. to rethink the entertainment he brought in. He started booking acts like The Ike and Tina Turner Revue and a great local band, The Gauchos, which, at one time, counted actor Edward James Olmos among its members. The club quickly gained attention for the dancers who gathered there—total bohemian beatnik artists—who became nearly as important to the scene as the music. The Byrds and Ciro's became ground zero for a new era of the Sunset Strip.

There was electricity in the air as a California rock scene was forming all around us.

Despite the changes, the Ciro's name still carried particular weight with the previous generation. In fact, my mom and dad used to go there on dates all the time back in the 1940s. I think the first time my mother was truly impressed with my music career was when I told her The Byrds were booked at Ciro's for a week-long engagement. It was an important step for us, but not nearly as important as our first single, which would soon dramatically change the course of the band.

# CHAPTER SEVEN
# MR. TAMBOURINE MAN

J im Dickson burst through the control room door at World Pacific Studios one night when we were all gathered for rehearsals. He had an acetate under his arm and a huge grin on his face as he announced, "I've got a song!" As Dickson put the disc on the turntable, he explained that he was friends with Bob Dylan's manager, Albert Grossman. He'd told Grossman about his new project, The Byrds, and asked if Bob had anything the band could record. Once he dropped the needle on the disc, we heard a rough recording of Dylan and Ramblin' Jack Elliott running through "Mr. Tambourine Man." It went on for a few minutes with four very full verses and a repeated chorus after each one. When the tape ended, Dickson switched off the machine. "I love it," he exclaimed as he slapped the console. The rest of us just sort of looked at each another and shrugged. *How was that supposed to be a Byrds song?* Bob's demo was in 2/4 time, which is more of a country/bluegrass feel. I understood what he was going for because of my background in that world, but the song desperately needed some kind of arrangement if it was ever going to become anything approaching a rock record.

Noticing that we were less than enthused, Dickson shook his head and spun his chair around to fully face us. "You guys need to go for substance and depth," he said. "Make records you can be proud of—records that can hold up for all time. Are we making an artistic statement or just going for a quick buck?" It was a fair question. Being the shy nonsinging bass player, I didn't really have that much input. McGuinn went to work on "Mr. Tambourine Man" and rearranged it into a 4/4 groove. We were still a few years away from FM rock radio, and we knew there was no way the AM stations were going to play a single that was more than two-and-a-half to three minutes long. Figuring that there was really only enough time to include one of the verses, it was decided that the one that would work best was the one Dylan had written as the second verse, "Take me for a trip upon your magic swirling ship . . ."

Dean Webb from The Dillards stopped by one night and helped work out the vocal blend. It was decided that Jim and Gene would double the lead vocal on the chorus, with David singing the third harmony above them. The blending of Jim and Gene's voices was perfect and, with Crosby's harmony, they captured that angelic sound that I'd heard when they were first becoming familiar with each other's voices. Jim and Gene continued together on the verse with David coming back in again for the next chorus. It created a fantastic vocal blend and, most importantly, the recording came in at less than three minutes. We had made a decent demo of "Mr. Tambourine Man"—not slick enough for a radio release, but a good roadmap of what could be. When Dylan heard our version, he was impressed and told McGuinn, "Man, this is great; you can dance to it!"

We had the song, but now we needed the vehicle to get it heard—which meant a record company willing to take a chance on us. Since Dickson had already been active in the music scene for several years at that point, he had become good friends with important agents, managers, and artists. He started playing our demo for his various contacts in the industry, including Benny Shapiro, who owned a jazz nightclub on the Sunset Strip called The Renaissance. Jim and Benny were sitting in the living room listening when Benny's preteen daughter, who'd heard it from her upstairs bedroom, bolted down the steps to find out who the band was. She loved it. Benny might not have gotten it, but an enthusiastic response from a young girl was the ultimate stamp of approval when it came to the value of a rock band in the mid-1960s. Benny was close friends with Miles Davis, who recorded for Columbia Records. He talked to Miles about our demo and how his daughter reacted. Miles, having never heard a single note of our music, was kind enough to put in a call to Columbia president Goddard Lieberson, asking him to consider signing The Byrds to his label.

Whatever Miles Davis said obviously worked. Columbia offered us a singles deal, meaning we could record a couple of radio-friendly releases and, if there was any success, there would be an option to record an album. The paperwork was put in place, and Columbia assigned us to a staff producer named Terry Melcher, who was Doris Day's son. Terry had already had some minor success with some Beach Boys-flavored material, and he liked our stuff. It was decided that he would produce a new version of "Mr. Tambourine Man," along with a Gene Clark song called "I Knew I'd Want You" that would comprise the two sides of our first single.

All The Byrds members showed up for our first big recording session in January of 1965, knowing full well that Jim would be the only one playing on the session. Terry and Columbia felt that, since they were making a first impression in introducing a new group to the public, professional studio musicians should be brought into Columbia's studio in Hollywood to lay down the backing tracks. The label figured they had one shot to make The Byrds work, and they didn't want to risk any problems with tracking a great record. McGuinn, Crosby, and Clark each did their vocal parts, but Jim McGuinn was the only one of us who played anything. He had worked out a brilliant intro on his twelve-string electric guitar that that was almost Bach-like in its beautiful simplicity. The rest of the players were the top guys in the business: Hal Blaine on drums, Leon Russell on piano, Jerry Cole on guitar, and Larry Knechtel, who came up with that long slide on his bass for the song's intro. These were the same guys who would come to be known as The Wrecking Crew, and who played on thousands of recordings over the next thirty years. I don't know how the other guys felt, but it didn't bother me that I didn't get to play on that recording. For me, just getting to watch a master like Larry Knechtel made it all work—a great experience.

The spring of 1965 was a whirlwind for The Byrds. Columbia released "Mr. Tambourine Man" in April. It debuted on the *Billboard* pop chart in May and was sitting at number one by the end of June. Even before the single was released, the word was out that we were signed to a major label. We were creating great buzz over at Ciro's. The Byrds were a huge success, not only with the younger crowd who were starting to transform the Sunset Strip for a new era, but with other musicians, an assortment of aging beatnik artists and writers, and even several well-known actors. I was out in front of the club, smoking a cigarette, one night when I felt a hand on my shoulder. I turned around to see actor Lloyd Bridges standing next to me. "I love your music," he told me. "You guys have a great career ahead of you." Many years later, I told that story to his son, Jeff, who laughed and said, "Lucky my dad didn't grab that cigarette out of your mouth and stomp on it. He hated smoking."

It was during that era that we began experimenting with our onstage appearance. In fact, we had to figure it out quick after our matching velvet-collar suits disappeared in a perfect rock and roll moment. After the humiliation of our first Troubadour performance, we weren't so sure about those matching suits anyway. It was after our first or second night at Ciro's that we left them hanging in the dressing room. Little Richard and his band were booked there for a weekend show. As soon as we found out that one of my early idols was going to be playing, Mike Clarke and I made it down for opening night. Hearing Richard was unforgettable, but we were also blown away by his amazing lead guitar player who was over to the side of the stage. His name was Jimi Hendrix, and he possessed a magnetic presence that was irresistible. We ran into him again at the Monterey Pop Festival just as his solo career was exploding, and he remembered meeting us at Ciro's. As for our suits? Richard's band stole them. It was for the best. We all had a great laugh when providence intervened, saving us from convincing Dickson that the suits, along with the dance lessons, were not the direction The Byrds should be going.

I look back on that whole period now as a magical time. Bob Dylan came into Ciro's one night and played harmonica with us. Knowing how much he loved our rendition of "Mr. Tambourine Man" made it an incredible experience. I'm sure we may have been an inspiration for Bob to plug in with a band. In fact, I recall seeing Sonny and Cher sitting in one of the booths at Ciro's one night and grabbing everything they could from our performance—including our take on Dylan's "All I Really Want to Do," which was our follow-up single after "Mr. Tambourine Man." By the time Columbia released our version, however, Imperial Records had already put out a version by Cher. Both records hit the national charts on the same week, but she already had the head start on us and climbed higher up the rankings than we did in the US. It was the opposite in the UK, where ours became a Top 5 hit.

In addition to our shows at Ciro's, we started playing other cities around California, including a short tour on a bill with The Rolling Stones. Once we started getting known, The Byrds were occasionally hired to play at celebrity parties. We played a Fourth of July celebration in Malibu for Jane Fonda when she was still with French film director Roger Vadim. Guests included Steve McQueen, Lauren Bacall, Warren Beatty, Mia Farrow, and Sidney Poitier. It was all of twenty minutes into our set when I felt a tug on my pantleg. It was Henry Fonda who politely asked me if we wouldn't mind turning down the volume a bit. Fabulous! Here was the great Henry Fonda talking to the shy guy in The Byrds. We didn't turn down the volume. We also played a party for Lance Reventlow, heir to the Woolworth fortune and designer of the Scarab race car. The morning after the concert, he took us out on his racing catamaran, with Bob Dylan along for the ride.

We played a few more Hollywood star parties, all of which were very interesting, but nowhere near as interesting as another character who'd entered our lives—Derek Taylor. A very bright and hilariously dry-witted guy, Derek had been The Beatles' press agent and the right-hand man to their manager, Brian Epstein. In 1965, after severing ties with Epstein, Derek moved to California with his wife Joan and their children. He set up his own PR firm and started working with The Beach Boys. After Dickson and Tickner gave him a small percentage of their commission to work with us, he took on The Byrds as clients too. Derek was fantastic; he was our window on both The Beatles and the whole British music scene that we were enamored with at the time. Thanks to his hard work, we were all over the teen and preteen magazines, including cover stories in *Teen Beat* and similar publications. Derek was a madman at times; very funny, and if you got on the wrong side of him he would find a subtle way to get you back—usually in print. He was obviously a go-getter who would wake up each morning, have a drink and a cigarette, and fire up his one-man promotion machine. It didn't take long before he had us booked on all the Los Angeles-area TV outlets like *The Lloyd Thaxton Show,* Sam Riddle's *Hollywood A Go-Go,*

*Where the Action Is, 9th Street West,* and *American Bandstand.* Soon we were on network shows, too, including *Hullabaloo* and *Shindig.*

The summer of 1965 found us embarking on our first big tour across the Midwest. I was pretty excited. Other than the Nevada gig and the folk festival in Honolulu with The Golden State Boys, my travels outside California were pretty limited. At first, our inexperienced management team put us with a booking firm called the Willard Alexander Agency, which handled big bands and had no prior experience booking rock acts. We leased a bus—not a decked-out luxury tour bus, but a plain old passenger bus with a few sleeping cots—and away we went to conquer America in a month with Dickson's friend John Barrick along for the ride as our first road manager.

Dickson, Tickner, and Derek Taylor decided it would really add to the show to have a few of the dancers from Ciro's travel with us too. It was always a surreal moment when we would pull into a county fair in Iowa or some place, start the first show, and then watch the crowd reaction as the dancers came out, gyrating wildly in their full Sunset Strip regalia. Some of the local guys didn't take too kindly to these strange people dancing in their town and sometimes took so much offense that a fight would occasionally break out on the dance floor while we continued playing our show.

That wasn't the only challenge. I had never experienced a Midwest summer before, and it was hard to make my hair behave in that environment. I was a curly-headed boy, but I went to great lengths to get my hair straight to fit in with the band's look. This involved about forty-five minutes of styling, but it was all in vain. The heat and humidity would turn me right back into a curly-headed boy who looked like he'd been out shoveling sand in a windstorm.

Holiday Inns and hotel chains were still a relatively new thing in the mid-1960s. They'd just started building them a few years prior, so we were usually camped out in these old hotels in the middle of whatever town we were playing. They were nice enough, but they usually had no amenities except a radio—no air conditioning and no television. It was almost like traveling in the 1930s or '40s, but we handled it pretty well. For us, it was all a grand adventure.

As soon as he began working with us, Derek Taylor launched a campaign to convince Dickson and Tickner to book an English tour for the late summer. He thought we should go right after we finished our first big tour across America. Our managers thought it was too soon. They argued that we should wait until we had another couple of singles out, but Derek was persistent. There was certainly no argument from any of us in the band; we were more than ready to board a plane for London. It was finally agreed, and we were booked for a string of shows by Mervyn Conn, a notorious English promoter. Of course, we knew nothing about him, but he was the "go to" promoter in the UK at the time. We were all excited to be preparing for the next grand adventure—flying over the Atlantic.

When the Midwest tour was over, we departed out of Chicago on the first day of August. We didn't even get time off to go back home for a few days to rest. We just hopped onboard a Pan Am flight and off to London we went, with Derek leading the charge back to the motherland. We arrived around eight in the morning the next day—a Monday—to be greeted by lots of screaming fans and a very interesting man who promptly served us with a writ, demanding we change our band name. Apparently, there was another group in England called The Birds—in fact, one of their members was future Faces and Rolling Stones member Ronnie Wood. These guys didn't have a lot going with their career at the time, so their manager decided to drum up a little publicity by suing us. It was a waste of time, but at least it made for good copy in the musical press for a few days.

Between coming off a long tour and having just flown all night, we were exhausted when we checked into the Europa Hotel on Grosvenor Square. Derek, assuring us he'd take care of it, called up John Lennon. Within an hour a very strange gentleman showed up to the hotel lobby with a bag of purple hearts. These were the pills The Beatles used to help them keep going in the face of a grueling schedule. Most musicians relied on that kind of thing in those days, so John sent his guy over to help us out as we began the UK tour. Reinvigorated, McGuinn and Crosby immediately started doing press interviews. The rest of us were on the bench temporarily, but—being a little older and wiser in this area—they seemed to be the right ones to handle a somewhat hostile English press.

At day's end, the band went out to the Scotch club, a hip new hangout. I wasn't feeling well, so I didn't go out with the other guys that evening. The experience, however, helped Gene write one of his classic songs, "Set

You Free This Time." He finished it late that night, inspired by meeting Paul McCartney at the club. The Beatles became fast friends to The Byrds, thanks to the opportunity Derek created. He was in heaven coming back to his homeland with his new group. I suspect it was a way to show Brian Epstein what he had accomplished in America since leaving The Beatles.

The tour officially began on Tuesday, August 3, with an appearance on *Ready Steady Go!*, the biggest pop music TV show in England. We taped our performance of "Mr. Tambourine Man" and "All I Really Want to Do" before driving up to a small town called Nelson for our first concert. I mentioned I wasn't feeling well when everyone went out the night before, and I was feeling even worse by the time we arrived in Nelson. That was the night I collapsed in the dressing room with bronchitis. My memory is a little hazy, but I recall a turban-wearing East Indian physician leaning over me and giving me a huge shot of penicillin. I somehow managed to rally and play the show that evening. As it turned out, I just happened to be the first to fall. My bandmates would soon be navigating the same treacherous waters of bad health over the next week. Not a great time to get sick.

The English tour was a disaster as far as our live performances were concerned—bad sound, suspect equipment, and an English press that didn't make things any easier. Mervyn Conn, our English promoter who was one step shy of a circus carney, overhyped us to the press, calling us "America's Beatles." That may have bordered on sacrilege to a British audience. Nobody was more beloved than The Beatles, so the expectations he set weren't realistic. The critics seemed to almost enjoy watching us stumble through the tour. One of the more memorable of our decidedly uneven series of shows was at a tiny London club called Blaises. Curious to see what all the buzz was about, the audience was filled with a who's who of British musicians: John Lennon, George Harrison, Pete Townshend, Bill Wyman, Brian Jones, and Graham Nash turned out for yet another rough and very loose performance on a stage that was so small we couldn't even fit all our gear on it. I even managed to break a bass string that night—not fun.

I think it was after that gig that we all ended up at someone's house for an impromptu party with Brian Jones, John Lennon, and some other musicians. Everyone was having a great time, but I was so shy in those days that I usually tried to blend into the background. The last thing I ever wanted was to stand out in a crowd. Plus, I figured if Lennon noticed me, he'd probably get me with some sarcastic remark. At some point, during a lull in the conversation, John glanced over at me. He nodded his head in my direction and asked the others, "Does he talk?" Everybody erupted in laughter, and I could feel my face and ears get hot. I'm sure I must have turned bright red. Looking back, though, it *was* pretty funny. John made it all okay when he ordered Wimpy Burgers for everyone at the party. As a gesture, it was really nice. As a burger? Those must have been the worst burgers in the history of the Western Hemisphere. Nothing like topping off a questionable British tour with some questionable British food.

It turned out Tickner and Dickson were right; we should have waited, worked on our stage presence, and had a few more recognizable songs in our arsenal before trying to conquer Great Britain. After a punishing two weeks, we were ready to get out of there. But going home didn't seem that appealing, either. During our time away, Ciro's had closed down and then reopened as a new teen club called It's Boss. The scene The Byrds had created on the Sunset Strip had already started morphing into something unrecognizable. Meanwhile, Los Angeles was totally engulfed in the Watts riots. Reading about our city burning up was pretty strange, especially being so far away. As for "The Battle of Britain," we certainly weren't returning as triumphant heroes. Feeling defeated, we limped back to California, licking our wounds but determined to rebuild.

We arrived back in Los Angeles on Friday, August 20, but there wasn't much time for rest. Columbia wanted us to release another single and start planning for a second album, so it was time to return to the studio and get to work. Though we'd just seen them in London, The Beatles actually arrived in LA around the same time we returned. They rented a home in Benedict Canyon that I heard was owned by Burt Lancaster. We were all invited up to the house, and George and Paul came down to Columbia a few days later to watch us record "The Times They Are A-Changin'"— pretty exciting having The Beatles stop by your recording session. Of course, we didn't get much accomplished after they arrived because we were having too much fun. Of The Byrds members, David became the closest to The Beatles and was hanging around with them quite a bit during their West Coast stay.

Though our version of "All I Really Want to Do" was a Top 40 hit in the
US, it didn't make as big a splash as "Mr. Tambourine Man." The challenge
was on to come up with another undeniable hit during our summer recording sessions, and we had just the song. Jim McGuinn was a huge fan of Pete
Seeger and remembered one of Pete's greatest arrangements, "Turn! Turn!
Turn!," which had been covered by Judy Collins. Actually, McGuinn had
worked with her on the recording of the song. I remember one time he was
playing it on his acoustic guitar in the back of the bus during our Midwest
run earlier in the summer when he asked me what I thought of it. I loved it.
We all did, and we discussed recording it the next time we were in the studio.

Only problem was, Dickson was totally against us cutting the song.
In his eyes, the lyrics defined a sort of strict black-and-white philosophy.
There was no gray area in King Solomon's wisdom from the biblical book
of Ecclesiastes that described the cyclical nature of life. Dickson was adamant that if we insisted on recording the song and releasing it, that could
be the nail in the coffin of our career. We were unphased. We worked it
up, and McGuinn, once again, came up with a great intro arranged around
a descending syncopated bass and drum groove. There were a *lot* of takes
on the basic track, but we finally managed to record a stunning version,
and it was magic. This was not the slick Wrecking Crew session guys, this
was The Byrds! Something we could really call our own. It had the right
feel, and we knew it was a hit.

Columbia released the song, and it started up the *Billboard* charts in
October. In the meantime, we continued working on the second album
with Gene's great "Set You Free This Time," the song he had written
after meeting Paul McCartney in London. We even tackled our first true
country song, "Satisfied Mind," which was a big hit for Porter Wagoner
several years earlier. I'd heard it on the radio and thought it would be a
good tune for The Byrds to record. There were some other great tracks
we recorded for the second album, including McGuinn's song "It Won't
Be Wrong," another classic Gene Clark composition called "The World
Turns All around Her," and Bob Dylan's "Lay Down Your Weary Tune."

When we finished recording, Dickson and Tickner booked us on
another tour for November, which would prove to be our best live touring experience up to that point. Dick Clark's Winter Caravan of Stars was

like being on the road with one of the great package shows that toured the middle of the country during rock's early golden era. Our tour mates were Bo Diddley, Paul Revere and the Raiders, and We Five. All the acts were set up to ride in one bus together from town to town. The Byrds—being a little stranger than the other acts on the tour, and having a bit more power as the headliners, thanks to the success of "Mr. Tambourine Man" and "All I Really Want to Do"—opted for our own Clark Cortez Mobile Home, where we could engage in uninterrupted mischief.

The Caravan of Stars would roll into town, usually set up in the local high school gymnasium or theater, play the show, and then we were off to the next stop. Michael and I immediately gravitated to Bo Diddley, having loved his early records. He was a great guy with a rocking band that featured the Duchess. The Duchess was a very tall, very beautiful young lady that Bo told everyone was his sister, even though we found out years later she wasn't. That was his way of protecting her from other musicians. She played electric guitar and sang backup with his group without ever missing a dance step.

Whenever you passed by Bo's dressing room before a show you'd see all the guys sitting around a table wearing their "do rags" and dealing poker. We were mesmerized by them. One night, Mark Lindsey, the lead singer with The Raiders, tossed a firecracker into Bo's room and immediately ran off. I just happened to walk around the corner as Mark was disappearing down the other end of the hallway. I ran right into Calvin, Bo's drummer, and immediately realized he was holding a straight razor to my throat. "What the hell you think you doin,' boy?" he roared. I was shaking. Scared to death. I had no clue what was happening. I was five foot seven and one hundred forty-five pounds. And this *huge* guy is holding a razor and threatening to cut me up. *Where's this coming from?* Lindsey finally returned and confessed his guilt. Calvin released me without so much as an apology, but I figured that was fine, considering I was out of the life-flashing-before-my-eyes predicament I'd been in only minutes before.

I wondered why Calvin was so jumpy, but it became clearer to me when the Caravan played in Rome, Georgia. While walking around town before show time, I happened upon some of those old water fountain signs that read "whites only" and "colored only." I couldn't believe it. I was a middle-class California kid seeing something in person that I'd only read about before. That was a real eye opener for me. When Mark threw that firecracker, it sounded like a gunshot in the confines of that small dressing room—not a good thing for a black man in the South to hear in 1965. Mike Clarke and I, in all our naiveté, told Bo that we were going to go to The Apollo Theater when the tour wrapped up in New York at the end of the month. "No, no, no. You are not going there alone," he warned. "I'll take you boys; you can't just waltz into The Apollo looking like you do."

When we arrived in New York, we forgot all about Bo and The Apollo. With the last show of the tour behind us, our minds were on meeting girls, which was always foremost on the agenda. Michael was so much fun to hang out with—outgoing and always attracting interesting people. We visited an up-and-coming club called Arthur that was owned by Sybil Burton, ex-wife of Richard Burton who'd left her for Elizabeth Taylor. Mike managed to get us past the red velvet rope where we met the famous Mrs. Burton and were treated royally. We fulfilled our quest in a matter of minutes by meeting two beautiful young ladies. We brought them back to our hotel for drinks, where Mike and I were holding court in my room. Within an hour of settling in, just at the wrong time, there was a loud banging on the door. "Open up," someone barked. "Hotel security!" We opened the door to find a guy who looked like he'd just walked out of a 1940s crime drama, complete with a half-smoked cigar hanging from his mouth and a slouched fedora perched on his head. "You can't have girls in the room," he said matter-of-factly. "Pack your things; you're out of here, and I mean right now!" All of a sudden, we were outside in the middle of the night trying to hail a taxi. We ultimately ended up in a kinder, gentler hotel thanks to a friendly cab driver's tip.

The tour ended on November 28 and was a great success. "Turn! Turn! Turn!" hit number one on the *Billboard* chart on December 4, and two days later, the album of the same name was released. Everything had been restored to balance after the English debacle, and we were riding high. With two number one records under our belts, we were booked on *The Ed Sullivan Show*, so we immediately returned to New York. Not only was *Sullivan* the forum where I first saw The Beatles, but his show was the best of the old-fashioned live TV variety programs featuring music, juggling, acrobats, animal acts, and comedians all performing in front of millions of Americans. It was big!

The day of the show, we checked in at the studio for rehearsals. Things started well but quickly took a turn. Sullivan's producer, Bob Precht, was concerned that "Turn! Turn! Turn!" was a little long and asked us to cut the song down to a shorter version for the broadcast. David went ballistic. "Hey man, nobody tells The Byrds what we can and can't do with our art!" When Precht pushed back, David ramped up the vitriol, calling this guy some really nasty names and insulting his intelligence. Not only was Bob Precht the producer of *The Ed Sullivan Show,* he was also Ed's son-in-law! This was bad. Everything suddenly went silent and you could feel every bit of the tension in the air. Precht took a step closer to David. "Listen, you little punk, we've been doing this a long time, and we do it the way we do it, or it doesn't happen. You, my friend, are fired, and you guys won't *ever* be on this show again." The production guys in the sound booth literally broke into applause. This was *really* bad.

David Crosby was such a talent, but if he got nervous or scared, he would lash out. For whatever reason, he channeled his fear and intimidation into anger. I'm sure we were all a little intimidated simply being on the set of Sullivan's show, but David just totally lost control. To salvage a potential disaster, Dickson begged the Sullivan brass to reconsider. He pleaded with them, explaining that we'd flown all the way there from Los Angeles, and promising there would be no more problems from The Byrds. Fortunately, tempers cooled, and we were finally allowed to perform on the show that night. This was the platform that made Elvis Presley and The Beatles American superstars, and I was just relieved that we were able to remain on the show that night. Ed Sullivan introduced us, we did perform, and the audience loved it. The sound was not great. Were we sabotaged by the crew in retaliation for one of our members acting like a prima donna during the rehearsal? Who knows?

Whatever happened, it certainly wasn't a complete disaster. And it definitely raised our profile even further. When we got in a cab the next day, the driver looked in his rearview mirror. "Hey," he shouted, "weren't you guys on Sullivan last night?" It was always nice when people recognized us on the street after the broadcast, but—just as we were told—we were never asked back on the show. Regardless, the whirlwind of 1965 had been an unforgettable journey. Little did we know the flight would soon start hitting some more turbulence.

# CHAPTER EIGHT
# EIGHT MILES HIGH

In January of 1966 Columbia Records decided to record a promotional film for "Set You Free This Time," which they released as the follow-up single after "Turn! Turn! Turn!" Barry Feinstein, who shot the cover of the *Mr. Tambourine Man* album, brought his sixteen-millimeter camera up to the beach in Malibu where we would film something like an early music video (many years before the dawn of MTV). Barry got everything set up, and we began walking down the beach and miming the vocals, which would later be synched to the audio of the record.

Before long, Crosby decided that—for whatever reason—he didn't want to be there. Looking around for an accomplice, he zeroed in on Michael. "Hey man," he said. "This is stupid. Do you really wanna do this? Let's get out of here!" He managed to con Mike into agreeing to leave with him. "Mike and I are outta here," David announced. Dickson, who was a pretty tough guy and never shied away from using his fists if he felt like he had to, stepped in front of David and crossed his arms. "No, you're not," he said matter-of-factly. David fired some comment back at him and, almost immediately, the two of them were getting physical. The picture I have in my mind from that day is Gene—who was a big strong Kansas farm boy—pulling David off of Dickson. I yelled, "Barry, keep shooting! This is the video; *this* is The Byrds!"

Sadly, the confrontation put an end to our would-be music video. Feinstein packed up his camera, and we all trudged back up the sand to return to our cars. Nobody said much more about it. We all just drove back to our homes. We blew it, which certainly didn't endear us to Columbia. We were all young guys—basically kids—who didn't know how to handle ourselves, and interpersonal dysfunction would increasingly become a part of life as a Byrd.

In February of 1966, soon after the episode on the beach, The Byrds were on an airplane, preparing to take off from Los Angeles to fly to New York to appear on a television special hosted by deejay Murray the K. Jim McGuinn was the last one of us to arrive, appearing on the plane at the final moment before they shut the door behind him. To this day, none us really understands why, but Gene Clark began to panic as Jim approached his seat. Gene was having a nervous breakdown and he was begging to get off the flight. Jim tried to calm him down and reassure him that everything was fine, but Gene was beside himself. "Look, man," McGuinn said, "everything is fine. You've got nothing to be worried about. You can't be a Byrd if you can't fly." Ultimately, he made his choice. They opened the door of the aircraft, and Gene departed the plane and, effectively, The Byrds.

It was a bizarre moment. We'd never seen any indication that Gene was scared to fly, and there were no warning signs that he might have a nervous breakdown. In fact, it was so unusual that the rest of us were a little spooked. We were all secretly wondering if Gene had become psychic and knew that something horrible was going to happen during the flight. The pilot, a nice older gentleman, came out of the cockpit and talked with the passengers, calming everyone down before we finally departed for New York without incident.

When we reached the East Coast, I was recruited to join the front line to sing Gene's parts alongside David Crosby and Jim McGuinn for *Murray the K's All-Star Special*. As it turned out, we would remain a quartet for the rest of that year and into the next, despite my attempts to convince Gene to stick with us. When we returned to LA, I invited him over to my house in Laurel Canyon. I sat him down and told him, "Gene, you *need* to be in this band!" For whatever reason, though, he just couldn't handle the pressure. I think Dickson and Tickner were looking for an opportunity to make Gene into a solo artist, and maybe he had visions of solo grandeur—I don't know. Ultimately, I think he just couldn't handle Hollywood. He was a gentle soul. Of all the people who should've gone back to Kansas, gotten married, and had a normal life, it was Gene. I think the whole scene kind of chewed him up and spit him out. I didn't always get along with Gene, but—though our friendship was rocky at times—I'll always admire him as a great songwriter and a genuinely talented man.

Before Gene's untimely departure, we recorded what I thought was a major breakthrough song, "Eight Miles High," written by Jim, Gene, and David. During our time on the road with the Caravan of Stars, we listened to John Coltrane, Eric Dolphy, Ravi Shankar, and all kinds of eclectic sounds in our little Clark Cortez motor home that influenced us when we returned to the studio. Michael's drum work on the record is brilliant, and I think we all played our best. It was so free form, I seriously doubt if professional session players could have captured the vibe on tape as well as The Byrds did. Having gone from covering Bob Dylan songs to coming up with something like "Eight Miles High" in a little over a year was confirmation that we were turning into a great band. We all knew the song was our obvious next single.

"Eight Miles High" was released in March and started climbing up the charts the following month. It made it just shy of the Top 10 but stalled out following a radio ban that found many stations pulling it from the air. The controversy started when Bill Gavin, who published a broadcast industry tip sheet, warned stations around the country that the lyrics were about drugs. Not true. The idea for the song was hatched on our trip back home from England. The plane was flying at 37,000 feet, which is around seven miles. Jim planned to call the song "Seven Miles High," but Gene suggested using some poetic license and going with "Eight Miles High," which was a nod to The Beatles' "Eight Days a Week." I guess somebody at *Bill Gavin's Record Report* did the math and figured we couldn't be talking about an airplane because planes don't fly that high. So, we *must* have been talking about some other kind of high. The song vanished from the charts only because of misinformation and panic among the gatekeepers of AM radio. It was a setback, but it didn't stop the song from becoming a classic. Today, many people cite it as the first successful psychedelic rock song, though I always felt it was more of a jazz arrangement.

Undeterred by the controversy of "Eight Miles High" and the departure of Gene Clark, we continued on through 1966 with various television appearances and live shows. In fact, I think the best series of live shows The Byrds ever played happened in 1966. A new club called The Trip opened on the Sunset Strip, right down the street from Ciro's, and it became our off-and-on home base for a while. At one point, we were booked for a one-week engagement with The Paul Butterfield Blues Band as the opening act. That group, with lead guitarist Mike Bloomfield setting the pace, was nothing short of amazing. To this day, Mike is still one of the greatest guitarists I've ever seen. We rose to the occasion and played our finest. The Butterfield band was so good, there was simply no way we could get up on that stage after them and bring anything less than 100 percent.

Right after our last night at The Trip with Butterfield, Michael Clarke and I boarded a flight for Puerto Vallarta, Mexico. Our friend Alan Pariser, who loved the band and who often hosted us at his home in the Hollywood Hills, told us how incredible Mexico was at that time of year. Mike and I decided on a whim to fly down for a one-week vacation. As a travel destination, the town was still relatively new. We landed at this small airport in the afternoon and began trying to figure out how we'd get a hotel. Over in the corner of the airport was a small bar, and there was a guy sitting on one of the stools. He had very long hair and a beard, and we couldn't help but notice how he was looking at us—not in a scary way, but more out of genuine curiosity. Finally, he got up, came over, and introduced himself as John Barrymore Jr. He was the son of the famous actor, John Barrymore, and would go on to become the father of actress Drew Barrymore. John was living in Puerto Vallarta and offered to take us into town to get us settled.

John, who had been a working actor in the States and in Europe, was a fascinating guy. I guess he took a liking to us because he went out of his way to show us a great time. We met all his pals and managed to get into some good mischief for the next week. He even arranged for us all to take a supply boat down to Yelapa, a small coastal fishing village. Lying on the deck of that boat, which consisted of one flat area and a wheel house, was almost surreal. Huge manta rays would come to the surface of the water as if they were skimming the waves—all part of their mating dance. After the boat dropped anchor, we ran into Donovan, who was staying at the lone hotel in the little town. The poor guy had been laid up in bed with a bad sunburn; nobody bothered to warn the Scotsman about the Mexican sun.

Eventually we hopped back aboard for the return trip to Puerto Vallarta late in the day. The next morning, Mike and I rented some horses and rode along the beach. While crossing a stream where some local ladies were doing their washing, Mike managed to lose his wallet. Thank God for Barrymore, who knew enough people in town to get us out safely when the week was up. John was a gracious host and, knowing that we had to be home on a certain day to prepare for another tour, he made sure we were on the plane back to LA with Mike's exit papers.

In October of 1966, The Byrds were booked into The Village Gate, a well-known jazz club in New York City. I think we were the first rock band to get booked there, and it was an honor to be playing the same stage that Dizzy Gillespie, Carmen McRae, Art Blakey, Muddy Waters, and other amazing performers were sharing as part of the club's summer series. We played for two weeks, which was fantastic. All kinds of interesting guests kept popping in every night, including John Sebastian from The Lovin' Spoonful and photographer Linda Eastman, who came down on several occasions to take pictures. This was before she fell in love with (and later married) Paul McCartney. Mike and I became quite close with Linda who was a terrific photographer and a wonderful person. The residency at The Village Gate reminded me of our time at Ciro's, only now we were actually a really good, solid band.

Back in Los Angeles that fall, David Crosby and I were called to play on some demo recordings for a young jazz singer from South Africa named Letta Mbulu. She was being produced by the South African trumpet player Hugh Masekela, whom we'd gotten to know through Peter Fonda. Hugh was a refugee from the brutal apartheid policies of his home country, which he'd fled a few years prior. He was also an amazing player. There were some incredible jazz musicians on this recording date, leaving me and Crosby as the two white guys who couldn't read a note. But it didn't matter; we ran down the tunes and put them on tape. It was wonderful. Letta sang like an angel and, still being a very shy person, I was so uplifted when she complimented my bass playing in front of everyone, saying, "Man, Chris, you are cooking!"

I don't know what it was about the session, but it was like an epiphany for me. Feeling inspired, I went home to my house in Laurel Canyon that very night and started writing songs of my own, starting with "Time Between." The previous year I'd bought a Gibson J-45 acoustic guitar at Wallich's Music City—the last of the great record and music stores—located at Sunset and Vine in downtown Hollywood. That guitar was in my hands constantly after the Masakela demo session, as I wrote four or five songs that same week. I remember that "Have You Seen Her Face" was the final one of that first batch. Something almost unexplainable just opened up inside me after that night in the studio. My awakening as a songwriter came all at once, and it felt so right.

In the summer of 1966, we had released our third album, *Fifth Dimension,* which included "Eight Miles High," a great Crosby and McGuinn song called "I See You," and "5D (Fifth Dimension)," which was always one of my favorites of McGuinn's songs. "5D" was released as a single, as was "Mr. Spaceman" from that same album. After the problems with the radio stations over "Eight Miles High," we really didn't have another potential hit single on the album, so we started preparing for album number four, *Younger Than Yesterday.* This time around, we decided it was better to follow the lead of groups like The Beatles who weren't focused solely on hit singles, but on creating great albums that stood as a cohesive creative work. That was where our hearts were anyway, so we threw ourselves into the process with a renewed passion for making music we loved without the pressure of chasing the next radio hit.

Shortly after writing those first new songs following the Hugh Masekela session, I came up with the opening riff and first verse of "So You Want to be a Rock 'n' Roll Star," which was very much inspired by Hugh and his band. I called Jim McGuinn, who lived up the canyon from me, and asked him to come over and listen to my rough ideas. He loved the concept and completely understood where I wanted to go with the tune. Jim came up with the bridge, which was based on a Miriam Makeba song he had heard her perform. Hugh and Miriam were actually married to each other in the mid-1960s, so it seemed that everything was somehow connected. That just added to the magic of the song. It was the first thing we cut for the new album and, ready to continue stretching our musical boundaries, we incorporated Latin and jazz influences, anchoring them with my bass and Jim's twelve-string. Hugh even came to the studio and added a trumpet part. The song was a serious nod to the music we were soaking up around us, but the lyrics were our lighthearted take on the music business. Some people interpreted it as a jab at The Monkees. In reality, we had immense respect for all of them as singers and musicians. We weren't skewering the members of the Monkees, but we were taking a shot at the cynical nature of the entertainment business that will try to manufacture a group like The Monkees as a marketing strategy. For us, it was all about the music, and we were commenting on the pitfalls of the industry rather than on any of our fellow musicians.

Everything about recording "So You Want to be a Rock 'n' Roll Star" just fell into place. During McGuinn's twelve-string electric guitar solo, we even added a recording of screaming girls. On our first English tour (the "not so good" tour), Derek Taylor had borrowed Jim's new Phillips cassette player and, at one of our shows, taped the girls in the audience carrying on with their cheering and screaming. We somehow figured out a way to transfer the taped screams from the cassette onto the multi-track machine—very cool and very effective. Though it wasn't necessarily what we were shooting for, the song became a fairly successful hit and revived the band after we'd been shortchanged on "Eight Miles High." To this day, "Rock 'n' Roll Star" and "Eight Miles High" are two of my favorite Byrds records, and I think they've both really held up over the decades.

Not only was I participating more with my songwriting and singing, but David and Jim both came up with some great tunes for *Younger Than Yesterday*. The record was produced by Gary Usher, a staff producer at Columbia who had some success as a songwriter when he co-wrote The Beach Boys' "In My Room" with Brian Wilson. Gary was a good guy and a lot of fun to work with. He brought a focus to the sessions that reignited our original excitement, and he encouraged us to incorporate some outside musicians to add a bit of fresh flavor to our sound. In addition to Hugh's trumpet on "So You Want to Be a Rock 'n' Roll Star," I had Hugh's keyboard player Cecil Bernard play piano on "Have You Seen Her Face." We also brought in the fantastic Bakersfield-style lead electric guitar work of Clarence White on my songs "Time Between" and "The Girl with No Name."

Clarence was a great musician whose band, The Kentucky Colonels, was one of the best bluegrass groups in Southern California when I was playing with The Scottsville Squirrel Barkers and The Golden State Boys. He had started the group with his brother Roland, whose brief hiatus from the group necessitated Scott Hambly covering for him. And, of course, Scott was the one who taught me the important basics I needed to know to become a good mandolin player. Clarence and I met when we were both sixteen years old, and we used to run into each other all the time in our early bluegrass days. We lost touch for a while until Gene Clark invited me and Michael Clarke to serve as the rhythm section on his first solo album. During that process, I reconnected with my old bandmates Vern and Rex Gosdin, who sang backing vocals with Gene, as well as with Clarence, who played lead guitar on several songs. By that time, he'd switched to electric, and I knew I wanted to have him on the sessions. Country-rock isn't a term I've always embraced, but I've come to accept it over the years as groups like The Nitty Gritty Dirt Band and The Eagles furthered the concept and continued to make it a pure California country sound. To me, good music is good music. If I had a hand in blending the various genres I love in a way that led to country-rock, roots rock, Americana, or whatever you want to call it, then I'm glad I could contribute in a way that made an impact.

Ten of the eleven songs on the *Younger Than Yesterday* album were originals, with Bob Dylan's "My Back Pages" rounding out the lineup. David Crosby and Gary Usher butted heads on recording another Dylan song, which David thought was becoming formulaic. He believed it was pushing us a step back as we sought to leap forward. I can see why it would make sense to include one of Bob's songs given our history, but we were certainly coming into our own as a group of writers at that point. Either way, I was really proud of our work on that project. In my humble opinion, *Younger Than Yesterday* is still one of the best Byrds albums.

Not long after finishing the sessions for the album, we had a rare day off in January of 1967, and I was at home in Laurel Canyon. Today Laurel Canyon is known as a once-thriving music community that was home to Graham Nash, Joni Mitchell, Jim Morrison, Neil Young, Jackson Browne, and many others. I certainly wasn't trying to start any trends, but I think I was the first musician to locate there when I moved into my place in 1965. Jim and David soon established themselves in the area too. Though I was among the first to arrive, I was also probably the first to leave thanks to the events of that January day. Though it was winter, it was one of those beautiful, crazy Southern California days. Crazy in that the Santa Ana winds were kicking up—hot, dry, and screaming across the top of Laurel Canyon. Ominous. The Spanish used to call them devil winds—and for good reason. I had just bought a Bultaco dirt bike and was about to head out for a ride when David Crosby showed up unannounced. We went back in the house, listened to some music, had some refreshments, and hung out for a while.

After David left, I went back out to the garage and opened up the door to leave for that ride. As I was walking back toward the bike, I noticed gas was leaking from the carburetor. Not thinking much about it, I hopped on and kick-started the bike just as one of those massive wind gusts came bursting through the open garage door. You know that sound when you light an old-fashioned gas stove? I heard that sound—except about ten times louder—as the fumes blew into the gas water heater in the corner and instantly ignited on the pilot light. Suddenly, I was in the middle of a ball of flame. Realizing I was on fire, I instinctively dropped to the ground and rolled around. With smoke filling the garage, I could see the walls around me beginning to crumble from the intense heat. I jumped to my feet. I was no longer on fire, though my eyebrows and some hair had been singed off. Ditching the bike, I jumped in my car and backed up the dirt driveway. By the time I reached the road, the garage was fully engulfed, and black smoke was billowing out from the edges of the house's roof.

That house up on the canyon had a beautiful view, but it was hard to get to. It took the fire department about an hour to get up the road and go to work on it, but it was too late. The house burned to the ground. I got out with my car and the clothes on my back, but that was it. I lost everything in the fire. McGuinn, who lived across the canyon, had recently gotten a new sixteen-millimeter video camera. When he saw the flames and smoke across the way, he thought it might be my house and started filming. Derek Taylor took the film and got it on the local CBS affiliate's evening news. There it was: "Member of The Byrds' house burns down!" Two days later, I went back to see if anything could be recovered, but there was nothing more than the foundation. The dentist who owned the house lived upstairs and had been out of town when the fire happened. He happened to arrive home when I was there surveying the damage. That was one of the worst moments of my life when the landlord came home to realize that he, too, had lost everything. Despite the rough start, 1967 would prove to be an eventful and particularly memorable year for me.

By June, "Have You Seen Her Face," the first single that I'd written solo for the band, was on the charts, and we were on our way to perform at the Monterey International Pop Festival. That, in my opinion, was the absolute best rock festival ever held anywhere in the world. Monterey, California, was where they had the annual Monterey Jazz Festival, as well as a folk festival that they launched in 1963—which I had played with The Golden State Boys. Our old friend Alan Pariser, along with club owner Benny Shapiro, who first brought the Byrds to the attention of Miles Davis, had come up with the original idea of presenting a three-day "rock festival." The lineup of talent at Monterey was incredible—from Jimi Hendrix's first US appearance as a solo artist to Janis Joplin, Otis Redding, The Who, Lou Rawls, Hugh Masekela, and others. We were in between recording sessions at the time, so we Byrds all drove our Porsche 911s up to Monterey on the Pacific Coast Highway. As the festival got underway, the weather was absolutely perfect. It was a beautiful time for everyone who'd gathered to hear great music. What the audience didn't know, however, is that storm clouds were beginning to gather around the band.

By the time we got to Monterey, there had been an unfortunate breach in our brotherhood. We had recorded a song of David's called "Lady Friend" that included vocal parts by me and Jim. The original recording was pretty good, but David thought he could make it better on his own. When the rest of us weren't in the studio, he went in and replaced our vocal tracks with overdubs of his own voice—and he added some dreadful horn parts, too. The end result wasn't as good as the original version, and the whole episode created unnecessary drama. It was becoming increasingly clear to me and McGuinn that David was feeling restless and was seeking new musical outlets beyond The Byrds. I don't have a problem with that desire, if one is honest with all concerned. Unfortunately, David handled it differently.

When we got on stage at Monterey, David—without any of the rest of us knowing he was going to do it—got on the mic between songs to rant about the Kennedy assassination, LSD, and other nonmusical topics. It threw the rest of us off, and we played what felt to me like a terrible set. I was embarrassed by it, but somehow we pulled it together. It may not have turned out as bad as it felt that day, but I know it certainly wasn't our greatest moment. McGuinn and I were caught off-guard once again the following day when David took the stage with Buffalo Springfield to sub in for Neil Young, who was on a temporary hiatus from the band. We were fine with David singing with the Springfield, but we were surprised that he hadn't made us aware of his plans beforehand. I also thought it was a little ironic, as I'd been a huge champion of Buffalo Springfield early on. They were a fantastic band. I'd even briefly considered managing them early on and had convinced the owners of the Whisky a Go Go to book them in the summer of 1966. I had to practically beg Crosby to come down to the Whisky to see the Springfield play. Much to my surprise, he insisted he wasn't that impressed with their show at the time, but now, here he was onstage with them at Monterey less than a year later.

Not only were cracks appearing in the relationships among the band members, but we had also grown dissatisfied with the business side of The Byrds. On the following Monday after the Monterey weekend, we parted ways with Jim Dickson and Eddie Tickner's management company. As is often the case with artists, we decided our management team wasn't delivering what we thought they should. Now that we were writing more songs than ever, one of the areas of frustration is that they had signed each of us to their publishing company without any of us having consulted outside legal counsel. We all felt like we needed a fresh start, so firing them seemed to make sense.

Jim Dickson wasn't the only Jim who disappeared in this era. Somewhere along the way that summer, Jim McGuinn changed his name to Roger after joining a mystical Indonesian religious philosophy called Subud. We just accepted it along with all the other strange things that made up the ongoing Byrds saga. I don't think the change had any real impact on us as a band. What did have impact, however, was dumping Dickson. In hindsight, Dickson was the catalyst for the Byrds brand; he had the vision.

We thought we needed something different at the time, but it didn't lead to better things. Instead, we were swept away by a new addition to the cast—a round little man named Larry Spector that Crosby had met at Peter Fonda's house. Larry, who always reminded me of the Pillsbury Doughboy, had worked as an accountant and was somehow loosely related to the Max Factor cosmetics family. He was the business manager for Hugh Masekela, as well as two members of The Monkees, and would be involved with Fonda and Dennis Hopper as they put together the film *Easy Rider*. Quite an impressive roster. Larry managed to charm us all into believing he was a great financial manager who could save our careers. Unfortunately for all of us, he proved to be a thoroughly dishonest individual who led us down a path of extreme hell.

Before it all fell apart, however, we had some wonderful experiences together. I was happiest when we were on a stage, in the studio, or swapping song ideas. For me, it was always about the music, not the politics or the behind-the-scenes drama. I just loved getting the chance to make music. Perhaps the last idyllic moment for the original era of The Byrds came in early August when we were booked for a couple of big shows in Honolulu. Afterward, we had a couple days off, so we rented a house on the far side of Oahu and holed up together. Without any outside distractions or influences we hit on a shared burst of creative energy that led to the creation of the songs "Draft Morning" and "Dolphin's Smile." We were collaborating together like a band should. The tensions of Monterey were behind us. We had a new manager. Columbia had just released our *Greatest Hits* album, and we just knew great things were ahead for us.

The good vibes after the Hawaii trip came to a screeching halt the following week when we were back in the studio with producer Gary Usher to begin work on our fifth album, *The Notorious Byrd Brothers*. While trying to hammer out the arrangement for "Dolphin's Smile," David ripped into Mike about his drumming. They exchanged heated insults that resulted in Michael finally admitting he wasn't into the song. Before long, we were all sniping at each other and, when pressed on why he was there if he didn't like the music, Michael confessed—in his anger—that he was only sticking around for the paycheck. After a couple of days, Mike quit showing up at the studio altogether, and we had to bring in Jim Gordon to cover his spot.

I think David probably wanted to call the shots, and we all probably allowed our egos to get in the way during those early *Notorious Byrd Brothers* sessions. We'd seen hints of it at Monterey, but we knew that David was hanging out with other well-known musicians, some of whom were assuring him that he wasn't getting the attention he deserved in The Byrds and were encouraging him to take more control. It soon became clear that David just wasn't happy with the direction the band was taking, and he wasn't comfortable working with Gary Usher. He was rapidly losing interest in everything related to the band, would show up late for sessions and, when he *was* there, would usually fall asleep. Though we'd shared a great moment in Hawaii, it turned out to be an anomaly. It was obvious that David's heart just wasn't in the band anymore. Tensions escalated further when Roger and I turned down his original song "Triad," which was about a three-way relationship—nice melody; not-so-nice lyric. We just weren't on the same page.

Though we had some good original material, things got ugly when Usher brought us a Gerry Goffin and Carole King song called "Goin' Back." Crosby had raised the issue during the sessions for the previous album, but he was still adamant that we should only be recording our own songs rather than cover material. Roger and I could see his point, but we also knew that our last single, "Lady Friend" (the song of David's that had caused tensions when he replaced our vocals on the track), was the first Byrds single since "Mr. Tambourine Man" that had failed to chart at all. Though chasing big hits wasn't our goal, we still felt like the charts were at least a barometer of how our music was being received. Even in the aftermath of "Lady Friend," David hadn't softened on his stance. He and Roger got into it when David pushed back on recording "Goin' Back." Crosby left the studio, and things were icy between everyone. When we went up to play the Fillmore in San Francisco a couple of days later, David stayed at a different hotel.

David Crosby was a vital part of The Byrds' sound, but it was time to make a decision. It was not something that Roger and I *wanted* to happen, but we knew we had to part ways with him. After so many musically productive years together, things were now falling into the abyss. Roger and I drove our Porsches up to David's house in Beverly Glen and gently told him that we just couldn't work with him anymore. It was a hard conversation. Though it almost seemed like he was going out of his way to create chaos around The Byrds, David was taken by surprise when we delivered the news. He certainly didn't expect anything like that to happen. That wasn't a fun experience. I genuinely cared about David, and I was relieved and happy to see him back on his feet soon after, creating beautiful songs with Stephen Stills and Graham Nash.

We started *The Notorious Byrd Brothers* as a four-man band, but were down to only me and Roger by the end of the process. Michael was still playing live with us but only ended up recording about half the songs on the album. In addition to Jim Gordon, we brought in Hal Blaine on drums to complete a couple of the songs. Fortunately, the trio of Usher, McGuinn, and Hillman worked extremely well together in the studio, and after David's departure, the rest of the recording process came off without any serious glitches. Continuing the country thread that had begun with "Satisfied Mind" on *Turn! Turn! Turn!* and continued with Clarence White's wonderful playing on *Younger Than Yesterday,* we brought in Red Rhodes, the bandleader from North Hollywood's legendary honky tonk, The Palomino Club, to play pedal steel guitar on four songs: "Goin' Back," "Get to You" and "Change is Now," which I co-wrote with Roger, and my song "Natural Harmony." It was virtually unheard of for a rock band to incorporate the instrument, which was only associated with country music at the time.

Though it had been the source of considerable conflict, the final version of "Goin' Back" came out nicely. Columbia selected it to be The Byrds' next single with a planned release in October of 1967. We were booked to appear on some national TV shows to promote it but were down to a three-piece band. We agreed we needed a stand-in for the shows and reached out to Gene Clark to see if he'd be interested in coming back. Gene had briefly rejoined us for a residency at the Whisky a Go Go a year prior when David was having some trouble with his voice due to a sore throat. He even went up and did a couple of shows with us at the Fillmore in San Francisco after the run at the Whisky. Michael and I had been working with Gene on his solo album (the sessions where I reconnected with Clarence White), and there was a nostalgic feeling about it at the time. Gene sat in with us for old time's sake, but none of us viewed that as a permanent reunion. This time around, we thought maybe Gene might be ready to return to the fold.

We got some great national television opportunities when we played *The Smothers Brothers Comedy Hour* and *The Joey Bishop Show,* both with Gene alongside us. Joey Bishop was fantastic, inviting us into his dressing room and offering us drinks. He and Michael Clarke hit it off immediately, and Joey's introduction of us on the show was beyond generous. "These guys have sold millions and millions of records," he told his audience. Totally untrue, but it sure sounded good to our ears. Tom and Dick Smothers were also wonderful guys who took on the network by offering up topical—and almost taboo—subjects along with the music. Being on their show with Moms Mabley and Eddie Albert was amazing. One of my fondest memories is watching Eddie Albert rehearse his dance steps before we taped. Now, *that's* show business. Fabulous!

With an out-of-town gig booked in the midst of those TV appearances, Roger, Mike, and I flew to the show. Gene opted to take a train. After only one show, his old anxieties came roaring back. It was obvious that Gene's return wasn't going to work out, and he was gone almost as soon as he'd arrived. Back to being a three piece, we shot the cover for *The Notorious Byrd Brothers* in Topanga Canyon with Guy Webster, who had photographed the *Turn! Turn! Turn!* cover back in 1965. I had rediscovered my love for horses during that time after purchasing an Appaloosa/Palomino stud that I boarded at the Topanga Stables. Michael used to join me for horseback rides around the hills of Topanga, as did our friends Brandon De Wilde, a wonderful actor and friend of Peter Fonda, and Bill Wildes, a true horseman with whom I would go on to co-write many songs. Mike and I somehow talked Roger and Guy into packing up our gear on a couple of horses and shooting the cover in a run-down Topanga cabin. One of the horses is peeking out of the cabin window next to Michael, and people still ask me today if the horse represented Crosby. Maybe so, but not intentionally. That was the horse Mike was riding, and it just happened to stick his face in the window next to us. It wasn't a set-up deal—more like a happy accident.

Not long after that photo shoot, Mike announced that he, too, would be leaving us. To this day, I'm not entirely sure why he made that choice.

I know he was disillusioned and burned out, but I hated to see him go. He ended up moving to Hawaii, perhaps in an attempt to recapture a bit of the tranquility we experienced there before the *Notorious* recording sessions began. The end of the year found us with some new challenges ahead.

We turned the album in to the record label, and they set a release date for January 1968. Despite all the turmoil, *The Notorious Byrd Brothers* ended up becoming one of our most successful albums, garnering great reviews and wide acceptance with the fans. As the new year dawned, however, we had some serious work ahead. Roger and I had a band to rebuild.

# CHAPTER NINE
# DEVIL IN DISGUISE

I had heard a little about Gram Parsons and his International Submarine
Band, the name of which was inspired by a fictional group in a Little
Rascals film. The word was that Gram was a good singer-songwriter
who also played keyboard and guitar. He was signed to Lee Hazelwood
Industries but was represented by Byrds manager Larry Spector, so we
knew some of the same people. By chance, I happened to bump into
Gram in a bank in Beverly Hills one day in early 1968, and we struck up
a conversation. I hadn't heard his music at the time but was aware that his
band was exploring a country sound. Gram was an extremely charming
and personable guy. With our shared love of country influences, it was easy
to connect with him, and we hit it off right away.

During my conversation with Gram he told me his group had recently
broken up, and he was looking for something new to get involved with.
There was a Byrds rehearsal scheduled for that night, so I invited him to
come play with us. We'd recently hired my cousin Kevin Kelley, a drummer
who had been in a LA group with Taj Mahal and Ry Cooder called The
Rising Sons, to replace Michael Clarke. Given that we'd had success weav-
ing some jazz elements into our sound with songs like "Eight Miles High,"
Roger and I had already discussed adding a keyboardist to the lineup as we
rebuilt the band. I told Gram we were looking for another player—possibly
a keyboard player—and he said he'd love to come down and give it a shot.

I'm pretty sure Gram was already familiar with our material. When he showed up that night, he sounded good. He knew his way around our songs and he could sing, too. Keyboard player? Not really, but he more than made up for it with some songs he had written and brought in to play for us. Plus, he could play decent rhythm guitar, which gave us some flexibility. Roger and I both liked him and thought he would be a good addition to the band. Neither Gram nor Kevin ever became official members of the group, but we hired them both to round out our lineup and start preparing for some upcoming shows as a revised quartet.

In the meantime, Roger and I began planning our sixth record. The original idea was to create a double album that traced the evolution of twentieth-century music starting with acoustic, country, and folk material on the first disc and morphing into electronic space music on the second disc. Gram was a factor in focusing on the country material, but it wasn't a stretch for us. We had all come out of folk music and, of course, I'd started out in bluegrass with the Squirrel Barkers and The Golden State Boys. We'd already recorded "Satisfied Mind" and Stephen Foster's "Oh! Susannah." Plus, we'd recently used Clarence White and Red Rhodes, bringing country elements into our rock sessions. The Byrds was an eclectic group from the beginning, but country was certainly the part of our DNA that Gram wanted to champion, and his songs lent themselves to those arrangements.

We decided that recording in Nashville was the perfect way to kickstart our new project and, fortunately, Columbia Records had a great studio there that we were able to use. Stories have been told that we had to cut our hair short before heading to Music City USA, but nothing could be further from the truth. McGuinn and I both had short hair on the *Notorious Byrd Brothers* album cover with Michael and the horse. Such strange stories were always nipping at our heels.

We had a fabulous time recording in Nashville and got to work with some great musicians there: John Hartford on banjo and fiddle, Roy Husky on string bass, and Lloyd Green on pedal steel guitar. Songs like "I Am a Pilgrim," "Pretty Polly," and "Pretty Boy Floyd" gave us a chance to get back to square one—our love of traditional folk and bluegrass roots. And playing mandolin again was a welcome addition. We cut Gram's original

"Hickory Wind," as well as two now-classic Dylan songs, "You Ain't Goin' Nowhere" and "Nothing Was Delivered." Bob wrote both songs while he was recuperating from a serious motorcycle accident. The demos fell into our hands somewhat like "Mr. Tambourine Man" had a few years before, and we knew they were just right for The Byrds. Lloyd Green's steel work on both tracks added something extra special.

It was fun being in Nashville around the music I had grown up with and loved so much, but I'm not sure if they quite knew what to make of The Byrds. After we finished recording one night, Roger and Gram went to visit influential country DJ Ralph Emery at his radio station in hopes of having him play an acetate of "You Ain't Goin' Nowhere" for his listeners. The recording was only a few days old. I didn't go with them that night, but I heard all about how Ralph treated them on the air. When he finally did give in and play the song, he was dismissive. Our take on country music probably still had a bit too much rock influence for strict country fans of the era. I don't know if maybe Ralph and some of the other folks in Nashville thought we were making fun of their music, but nothing could have been further from the truth. We had nothing but reverence for it and were absolutely sincere in our efforts.

Columbia Records secured us a guest appearance on the *Grand Ole Opry*'s radio show, broadcast live on WSM from Nashville's legendary Ryman Auditorium. We were to be guests on the Tompall and the Glaser Brothers portion of the show for what would be The Byrds' debut in front of a live country audience—and probably the debut of any rock band ever on the *Opry* stage. This was only a couple of days after the cool reception Roger and Gram received on Ralph Emery's show, so we were a little nervous about how we'd go over with the crowd. We were scheduled to perform "You Ain't Goin' Nowhere," which was slated to become the next single, and then close our short set with "Sing Me Back Home," which was Merle Haggard's big hit at the time and something the *Opry* knew would be appreciated by the audience.

In those days you were discouraged from playing a full drum set on the *Opry,* so Kevin just played a snare drum with brushes. I played my electric bass, while both Roger and Gram played acoustic guitars. We were so honored to have Lloyd Green join us to play pedal steel. When we were introduced, there were a few laughs and some scattered "boos" in the audience. A few people were calling out "tweet, tweet" in response to our name. Nevertheless, we started the Dylan song. They might not have been enthusiastic, but they were polite enough. Tompall then got on the mic and said "That was fantastic, fellas. Now, I believe you boys are going to sing Merle Haggard's brand-new hit song 'Sing Me Back Home' for us?" Roger and I were shocked when Gram stepped up to the mic and said, "No, we're going to sing 'Hickory Wind' for my grandmother who's listening tonight." Roger and I exchanged glances but followed Gram into the unplanned performance.

Our rendition of "Hickory Wind" sounded good, but that wasn't the point. After the broadcast, Tompall was screaming mad for having been put in that awkward position. Most of the *Opry* cast members weren't too happy with us, either. Nobody said much to us backstage as we gathered up our belongings for a hasty exit. We were packing up the car when *Opry* star (and the ex-Mrs. Ralph Emery) Skeeter Davis came out the back door, "Hey, you Byrds," she called. "You sounded fantastic. Everyone here? I love 'em, but they just don't get it. I'm really sorry about how you were treated. Please don't worry about that. You sounded great." Skeeter Davis was our only friend that night.

Many years later I ran into Skeeter again in Nashville when I was back at the *Opry* with The Desert Rose Band. We started talking about that *Opry* performance from so many years prior, and I thanked her for her kindness. "Oh, that was so horrible that night for you guys," she told me. "I am so sorry for how that all happened." She was surprised when I told her I actually thought Gram was pretty rude. We were in someone else's house, and we had agreed to the *Opry*'s song requests. Then Gram just hijacked it. What he thought was so hip and cool was actually insulting to the *Opry* folks. We should have stuck with the plan. Looking back, I now view that night as a missed warning. Gram was bright, extremely funny, ambitious, and very talented. But he was also unpredictable. I should have known that night what I was in for, working with an impulsive guy like Parsons. It would take me a while to learn that lesson.

Back in Los Angeles, we continued recording sessions for the new album, with JayDee Maness on steel guitar and Earl P. Ball on piano to record the country covers "Life in Prison" and "You're Still On My Mind." We were soon joined by my old friend Clarence White, who played on the Louvin Brothers song "The Christian Life" and on "Blue Canadian Rockies," an old tune I remembered from watching Gene Autry sing it in the movie of the same name.

In the spring of 1968 we were booked on a European tour and decided to take Douglas Dillard with us to play electric banjo. If anybody could play an electric banjo, it was Douglas, a phenomenal musician and a very close friend. His group The Dillards—which also featured his brother Rodney, Mitch Jayne, and Dean Webb—changed the face of bluegrass with their fine stage act and their appearances as the fictional Darling family on *The Andy Griffith Show*. In fact, it was seeing his name on the back of a Dillards album several years earlier that first led me and The Scottsville Squirrel Barkers to Jim Dickson; so, my history with Doug was significant. His group had even toured with The Byrds in 1966 when they decided to go electric, which proved to be a short-lived experiment. It was during that tour, when we had a few days off, that I went with Doug and Rodney to visit their home in Salem, Missouri. I stayed with their family and had a great time shooting pistols that Rodney and I had recently bought over the counter, and double dating with Doug and two local Salem ladies. I was looking forward to having my old friend join us once again. He fit right in musically and played off of Roger's twelve-string, giving our sound a unique blend.

The tour was built around a rock festival to be held in Rome, The First International Pop Festival, which had the blessing of Mick Jagger and a member of the British Parliament named Lord Harlech. It was a complete bust. Nobody wanted to buy tickets to the six-day event. It was originally to be held at the Palazzo dello Sport, a 30,000-seat arena in Rome—an interesting idea on paper, but so badly planned that it ended up in complete chaos. We did manage to play a date in Rome at the Piper Club that became the refuge of the broken pop festival.

We took an unplanned detour to England after our Roman holiday, playing at the Middle Earth Club to solid reviews. *The Notorious Byrd Brothers* was on the English charts and doing really well for me and Roger. We ended our short British run with a show at Blaises, the club we had played on our disastrous first tour. Mick Jagger, Keith Richards, and Marianne Faithfull were in the audience that night. After the show, Mick and Keith invited us to take a drive out to Stonehenge to watch the sun come up, and we invited Gram to come along, too. Mick hired some cars to pick us up at 2:00 a.m. for the drive to Salisbury where the Stonehenge monument was located. Wandering around out there in the dark with the Stones was like a Middle Earth fantasy trip—except that Gram was so enamored with Mick and Keith that he was behaving like a schoolgirl with a crush on the teacher. Roger and I couldn't help but roll our eyes as we watched Gram scurrying around in an effort to keep up with them as we hiked around the monument. It was embarrassing. The actual sunrise was a little disappointing. Instead of getting a great view, we got damp feet from walking through the wet grass. Mr. Jagger, ever the consummate host, sent his driver off to buy everyone dry socks.

Two days later we were headed to New York to play the Fillmore East. When we finally returned home to Los Angeles we were offered a spot on a fundraiser for Robert Kennedy that was scheduled for May 24 at the Los Angeles Memorial Sports Arena. Billed as "SRO For RFK," a large cross section of entertainers came out to support Senator Kennedy's presidential campaign: Andy Williams, Gene Kelly, Mahalia Jackson, and Henry Mancini, to name a few. We, along with Sonny and Cher, were the pop acts booked to appeal to the younger set. I had an opportunity to meet the senator after our show, but I passed, feigning fatigue. It was less than two weeks later that he was assassinated at the Ambassador Hotel after being declared the winner of the California Primary. Missing the opportunity to say hello is one of many regrets in my life, as I always felt Robert was the Kennedy tough enough to handle the nation's highest office.

We continued to tour the States until July when we returned to England without Doug Dillard to play a charity event for The British Boys Club at the Royal Albert Hall in London. From there, we were scheduled for a two-week tour of South Africa and Zimbabwe, which was known as Rhodesia at the time. We had been warned by our friend Hugh Masekela to avoid South Africa and their racist policy of apartheid. Miriam Makeba, on the other hand, had told Roger many years before that if he ever had the opportunity to visit South Africa that he should go and see what was really happening down there. After some debate, Roger and I decided that we should go over and try to open up the country to our music. We resisted the concept of playing for segregated audiences and were assured by the promoters that the crowds at our shows would be mixed. Hugh told us that would never happen. He said the Afrikaner white majority rule would never allow blacks and whites to sit with each other, but we thought we would break through that barrier. We believed we could make a difference.

Gram traveled to London with us, but the morning we were scheduled to leave for Johannesburg, he refused to go. He said that, having grown up in the segregated South, he didn't believe in supporting the racist policies in South Africa. He claimed that he never had any intention of going with us because it would violate his ethics. That sounds like a reasonable and principled stand, but I wasn't buying it for a second. Gram knew for weeks that we were planning to go to South Africa, and though we'd all raised concerns, he never indicated that he would boycott the trip. We all had been issued work visas. We had no reason to believe that Gram was anything but fully on board and committed to doing the tour with us when we all got on the plane headed for the UK. What happened is that we got to London and the Stones told him that British acts all refused to go to South Africa. His new friends strongly advised him to skip it, and Gram was desperate to impress them. Was there room for a musician to have legitimate concern regarding the South Africa question? Of course, but in Gram's case, the truth was that he really just wanted to stay in England and hang out with his new buddy Keith Richards. The real Gram was emerging. This was pure selfishness and dishonesty on his part. I was furious, and Gram was fired immediately. This should have been my second warning about a guy I really loved but who only thought of himself.

Angry and feeling betrayed, we boarded the flight to Johannesburg. It was decided that our road manager, who only knew a few basic chords, would fill in on rhythm guitar. Roger taught him the songs during the flight—a rocky start to a tour that ended up being nothing short of a disaster. It was far worse than The Byrds' first tour of England. McGuinn caught a serious case of the flu and had to leave the stage one night. The road manager certainly couldn't cover Roger's parts, so Kevin and I were left to carry on. It was pretty bleak. Just as Hugh had warned us, the audiences were segregated, and we weren't happy about it.

There were no television stations in the country, even though they possessed the technology. It was just another way for the minority population in power to control the masses by controlling the media. For a country as rich as South Africa in 1968 to have no television, to ban all Beatles records because of John Lennon's remarks to the press, and to encourage the black population to smoke pot as a control mechanism was not only surreal, but totally outrageous. Their policies resembled Nazi Germany in the late '30s, and the only "information" outlet for the citizens was the newspaper. After we were interviewed in the press and stated our objection to racial separation, we were threatened on a daily basis, usually by angry calls to our hotel rooms that were a variation on, "Get out of our country if you don't like how we treat our blacks."

The whole experience was a living hell, usually with two grueling performances per day. Plus, we felt constantly threatened. Roger, Kevin, and I were at our hotel's bar in Johannesburg one evening when we were immediately accosted by four guys. They were ready to do battle, and as I looked over my shoulder, Roger and my dear cousin Kevin were beating a hasty retreat. I should have led them out the door since I was suddenly standing there alone, facing four crazy, drunk South Afrikaners. Summoning up all the courage I could conjure—and well aware of an impending punch out—I eventually managed to calm the wild and ignorant beasts. I somehow won them over, and we all sat down for drinks. Crisis averted. To this day, South Africa is the scariest country I have ever visited, and, in hindsight, we should have heeded Masekela's warnings. On top of all the other problems, the promoters were thieves, and I don't think we ever recovered the money they owed us from that tour.

Rhodesia was the only bright spot. Only recently having broken away from the British Commonwealth, the country was a new experiment in complete integration, and we had the opportunity to play for mixed audiences. There was a sense of hope and freedom in the air. This moment, too, would later pass as the country was taken over by the authoritarian Robert Mugabe and renamed Zimbabwe.

After having endured sickness, bad gigs, intimidation, death threats, and the possibility of arrest during our two weeks in Africa, we couldn't wait to fly out of Johannesburg and touch down again in London. We all flew home to the States on separate flights out of the UK, but each of us was subjected to an intense search and questioning at customs. This was probably the result of the controversy stirred up by our scathing press interviews in the South African media. Thankfully, the country has radically changed since the end of apartheid and the election of Nelson Mandela who singlehandedly managed to bring the country into the twentieth century. Though South Africa has continued to experience racial strife, at least now there is freedom of the press, and the apartheid laws are gone. Those were important major steps.

Our country album, *Sweetheart of the Rodeo,* was released in August of 1968. Though Parsons was gone by the time the album was released, his lead vocals were featured on three of the songs, including his own "Hickory Wind." He originally sang six of the songs, but his voice was replaced by Roger's on half of them. There's been all sorts of speculation, analysis, and overanalysis about this over the years, but there were several factors at play. As it turned out, Gram was still contractually obligated to Lee Hazelwood, whose production company had signed Gram's International Submarine Band prior to his coming to work for The Byrds. On top of that, Parsons was never signed as an artist to Columbia Records. He was a salaried musician, and Roger and I were the only two official Byrds with contracts with the label. I don't even know what conversations might have taken place, but Roger's voice was a major component of The Byrds' sound. It's possible the label wanted to hear more from the guy whose voice was strongly associated with the band rather than from a hired gun who had already been fired by the time the album was being finalized. In later years, the versions with Gram's vocals were released, but I think Roger's vocals were better in the end. The album—as it was originally released—included just the right balance of singers.

Though it has since become something of a "cult classic," when *Sweetheart* was released, it was met with critical acclaim and terrible sales. It's not one of my favorite Byrds albums, but it did open the gates for all future "country rock" bands. The Byrds were credited with "creating a new style of music," whatever that meant. We thought the influences had been there all along, so Roger and I weren't entirely comfortable with that characterization at first. Over time, however, we learned to accept our "country rock" label.

With Gram gone, I suggested we hire Clarence White as a new addition to the band. He was an incredible guitarist and singer who'd already recorded with us several times, and I knew he would enhance the sound of the group even further. Within a few weeks of hiring Clarence, we knew we needed to make a change in the rhythm section. My cousin Kevin Kelley was a decent drummer, but he didn't really fit the group. He'd originally been hired as a stopgap measure when Michael Clarke departed, but I think Roger and I knew he was more of a last-minute necessity than a long-term solution. Kevin just wasn't the right fit, and it wasn't really working out for him or for us, so I broke the news to him that we were letting him go. In his place, we chose Clarence's friend Gene Parsons, no relation to Gram; same last name, but a more reliable person. Gene was a good drummer and a good singer—plus he played both guitar and banjo, too. With the new lineup, we had four good singers and a lot more ammunition in the instrumental department.

Maybe a week or two into the new lineup, The Byrds were booked at the Rose Bowl in Pasadena, California, as part of a one-day festival—billed as The American Music Show—that included everyone from Joan Baez to The Everly Brothers. Shortly before the gig I'd discovered that our manager, Larry Spector, had renegotiated our contract with Columbia Records. He gave up a significant amount of our free recording time in exchange for a large advance payment against our future record royalties. That put a hefty commission in his pocket, but it put me and Roger in the position where we'd be in the red with the label for years. Spector completely blew it in terms of protecting us as his clients, but that was only the tip of the iceberg. As I dug further, I found out enough information that could've gotten Spector locked up for fraud for a very long time.

After our set at the Rose Bowl, I saw Larry backstage and confronted him. Tensions escalated quickly and I had a major meltdown, throwing my bass to the ground in a fit of anger. I let Spector know that I was leaving the group and wanted him out of my life forever. Right then and there, I quit the best band I had ever been involved with. Of course, in hindsight (aren't we all so much wiser when looking back?), I could have handled this in a more sophisticated manner. The band was finally right where it should be, and having Clarence and Gene onboard was the perfect recipe for bigger and better things. I really enjoyed playing with them. Maybe I should have stayed on for the music, but I was too angry at Larry at that point. For me, it was over.

I believe everything happens for a reason, according to God's will. There's a time to every purpose, as we sang, and God knew it was time for that era of my life to come to a close. I've never discounted how fortunate I was to have been a part of the whole experience of The Byrds—both good and bad. We were encouraged early on to choose material that would stand the test of time, and I think we listened. We left a lasting legacy by introducing jazz, psychedelic, and country elements to rock music. In our short time together, we made a major artistic statement and paved a path for many musicians to follow in the years to come. I will always count it as a blessing to have been a member of The Byrds along with Roger, David, Gene, and Mike. The Byrds—one of the greatest bands ever.

As for Larry Spector, he later left the music business and, with his management commission and other monies he'd taken from his clients, he opened up the famous Ventana Hotel in Big Sur. The only good that came from my association with him is that he served as the inspiration for the song "Sin City," which I would soon write with Gram Parsons. You would think I would've left Gram behind by this point, but—as I said—he could be very charming. Shortly after my insanity-fueled exit from The Byrds we made contact, and I forgave him for leaving us high and dry in South Africa. I was about to fall under Gram's spell once again.

# CHAPTER TEN
## SIN CITY

═══════════

Just before leaving The Byrds I had sold my house in Topanga Canyon and bought fifty-five acres of beautiful pristine land in northern New Mexico, near the town of Amalia. The Sangre de Cristo River ran through most of the property and the land was part of the Sangre de Cristo mountain range. I had hopes of someday building a little ranch house there but, for now, music was my priority. I rented a three-bedroom ranch house on De Soto Avenue in Reseda, down in the San Fernando Valley. After we made peace, Gram moved in as my roommate in the fall of 1968. In some ways it was like the odd couple. I serious and focused, with a disciplined work ethic, while Gram was charismatic and completely disorganized. I wanted to make great music; Gram wanted to be a star. Despite our differences, it was the start of a period that I will always look back on fondly. Gram and I shared a similar warped sense of humor and a bond over our mutual love for country music. Not many people in our world thought country was particularly cool at the time, but we both understood its simple beauty.

We also both had a shared sadness. Gram's father, like mine, had taken his own life when Gram was just about to start his teenage years. His extended family was something to behold. Though Gram came from money, the rampant alcoholism, infidelity, and backstabbing was like something out of an over-the-top Southern Gothic novel. During our time together, Gram would receive at least $50,000 a year from the family estate, which I think ultimately did him more harm than good. I didn't have a trust fund like Gram had, but we had a connection. It's not a topic we spoke much about, but there's something about facing the loss of a parent at a young age that leaves a mark on you. Neither one of us could have articulated it at the time, but there was a dull mix of anger and sadness that perhaps we recognized in one another on a subconscious level. Whatever it was, we had a real connection, and for a time, we were like brothers.

I usually woke up early in those days and, one morning, I got up and started writing a song: "This old town's filled with sin, it'll swallow you in / If you've got some money to burn...." I sketched out a couple of verses and a chorus and decided I'd better get Gram out of bed to see if he thought there was something to the idea. He woke up, grabbed a cup of coffee, and added a second verse that concluded with the strange lines, "'Cause we've got our recruits and our green mohair suits / So please show your ID at the door." I wasn't sure where the old boy was going with that line, but after I came up with the last verse about Bobby Kennedy ("A friend came around, tried to clean up this town"), it all came together.

Built on a foundation of country music and Southern Baptist gospel, each verse was a little vignette about the culture of 1968. From Vietnam to Bobby Kennedy's assassination to California's seismic shifts, each section was wrapped around the chorus, "This old earthquake's gonna leave me in the poor house / It seems like this whole town's insane / On the thirty-first floor, a gold-plated door / Won't keep out the Lord's burning rain." Larry Spector actually lived behind a gold-plated door in a condo on the thirty-first floor of a building on the Sunset Strip, so he provided the inspiration for "Sin City." At least he gave me something after robbing me blind.

Gram and I finished the song in about thirty-five minutes. He was really on his game during that time and we inspired each other in what soon became our daily songwriting sessions. In a two-week period, we wrote "Sin City," "Devil in Disguise," "Juanita," and "Wheels"—some of the best collaborations either of us were ever involved with. We could practically finish one another's thoughts while writing or singing. Gram and I were very different people, but we made a good team. The timing was right, as we were both looking for our next musical outlet.

When Roger and I hired Gram and made the *Sweetheart of the Rodeo* album, it was never intended as a permanent change of direction for The Byrds. Roger and I always viewed it as a one-off Byrds album in country music, but it was a genre I wanted to continue to explore. Traditional bluegrass music was my first love, and from that first day at Bill Smith's house in 1961, that music had only become more ingrained in me as a player, singer, and songwriter. Since Gram and I shared a common vision to bring real country music to a rock audience with a hip sensibility, we agreed it would make sense for us to join forces and carry on from where *Sweetheart* left off. With that common vision, we had forged an instant partnership. We just needed a band and a record deal.

Gram knew a bass player named Chris Ethridge who he liked, which was fine with me. After playing bass in The Byrds for several years, I was eager to return to playing guitar in the new lineup, which would give me the chance to expand on both acoustic and electric. Ethridge was from Meridian, Mississippi, and was a very soulful, slow-talking southern gentleman who moved to the West Coast to work in Johnny Rivers's band. He eventually started doing session work alongside Leon Russell, Delaney Bramlett, and other musically gifted transplants. Chris was a great R&B musician, and what he played worked very well with what Gram and I were planning.

After Chris came on board, we identified our next suspect. "Sneaky" Pete Kleinow previously sat in with The Byrds a few times and was one of the strangest steel guitar players I'd ever heard—plus, one of the more interesting people I ever crossed paths with. Sneaky's other line of work was stop-motion animation, which he excelled at. He worked on shows like *The Outer Limits, 7 Faces of Dr. Lao,* and *Gumby,* while also playing clubs with Smokey Rogers and the Western Caravan. It was Smokey who gave him the name Sneaky Pete. Considering he was several years older than me, Sneaky could very well have been working with Smokey at his Bostonia Ballroom the day I met Tex Ritter when playing there with the Squirrel Barkers back when I was a teenager. Pete played single-neck steel, as opposed to the double-neck that was the choice of most steel guitarists.

He used a strange tuning and had a unique tone that made him a brilliant player. Sneaky could be absolutely orchestral in his approach. Other times he could be coming at you from a whacked-out Spike Jones solar system. Most steel players are very precise in their playing because of the complexity of the instrument, but Sneaky threw out all the rules and came at it from a different angle. He was loose with the steel, sometimes not even bothering to tune it until halfway into a set. And that's what made him perfect for us.

With Chris and Sneaky in the fold, we were on our way to becoming the consummate "outlaw band." Gram and I discussed a few ideas about what to call our new project. The Alabama Sheiks came in among the top contenders. I liked the name a lot, but it screamed "blues band," so I lobbied strongly for one of the other options. That's when we officially became The Flying Burrito Brothers. For me, especially because it was reminiscent of *The Notorious Byrd Brothers* album title, I decided it would fit us perfectly.

The Flying Burrito Brothers. You couldn't have assembled a finer bunch of criminals! The players, the band name, and the songs we were writing were the perfect ingredients for something either truly grand or totally insane. Over the next year we'd drift back and forth between the two, but at that point, with the puzzle pieces of the band mostly in place, it was time to find that record deal. My former neighbor in Topanga Canyon, Tom Wilkes, was the Art Director at A&M Records—the label created by Herb Alpert and Jerry Moss. Tom was aware that I had left The Byrds and thought A&M would be a great place for my new venture. Although Warner Bros. was interested, we ended up signing with A&M. We were the only country act on the label, and I don't think Jerry Moss or Herb Alpert knew what to expect. They based their decision to sign us on the success I had as a founding member of The Byrds. It's possible they didn't even hear any of our music before agreeing to sign us.

My new attorney, Rosalie Morton, began the negotiations. She was a wonderful lawyer and the perfect fit for the Burritos. With her leop-ard-print briefcase, she took on A&M's legal team with full force. We were doing quite well until the subject of our song publishing came up. I'd already given away my Byrds publishing to Tickner and Dickson for pennies and thought I'd learned my lesson. During my last year with the band, Roger, David and I had enough sense to form our own publishing company, McHillby Music. Gram and I should have just left it to Rosalie to negotiate our deal with A&M, but we went to the meeting for some unknown reason. Not being businessmen, we grew bored and impatient. Wanting to get out the door and get home, we agreed to let A&M's publishing company, Irving Music, acquire half ownership of our songs. So stupid and short-sighted on my part. Rosalie was furious that we undermined her tactic of getting A&M to negotiate a recording contract with no publishing component. Her last words to us that day were, "You idiots will regret this the rest of your lives." So true.

In late 1968, Gram, Chris, Sneaky, and I began recording our debut album, *The Gilded Palace of Sin,* at the A&M studios, which were housed in the former Charlie Chaplin film studio complex. Larry Marks and Henry Lewy produced and engineered the sessions. Henry's true love was jazz, but he was open to working with the Burritos and our unusual musical blend. Larry had a better understanding of who we were and really liked the songs we were bringing into the project. Along with the material Gram and I had written, Chris Ethridge came up with two beautiful songs that Gram helped him finish in the studio: "Hot Burrito #1" and "Hot Burrito #2." Terrible titles, but fantastic tunes—possibly the best two lead vocals ever recorded by Gram, who poured every ounce of soul into those performances. Truly magical. Years later, Elvis Costello recorded "Hot Burrito #1" and wisely changed the title to "I'm Your Toy." Overall, the album was really good on a performance level, but sonically, it wasn't quite there.

The one thing we seemed to have problems with at first was keeping a drummer. We went through three or four different guys during the making of that first record. But, other than that, we kept our circle tight-knit. We were focused on making a great album, and there wasn't much of a party atmosphere in the studio at all. The only "outside" performer to appear was David Crosby, who came in to add his high harmony to the Chips Moman/Dan Penn classic "Do Right Woman." Despite the fact that Roger and I had fired him from The Byrds a year earlier, I always considered David a friend and a true talent.

With our A&M deal in place and our album completed, it was time to fine tune our stage presentation. Growing up watching the country music shows broadcast live out of Los Angeles in the late '50s and early '60s, I was always drawn to the clothes the performers wore. Their rhinestones and exaggerated embroidery made for an unforgettably multidimensional musical and visual experience. There were two main western tailors in LA back then: Nathan Turk and Nudie Cohn. I think Turk may have been around before Nudie, but each possessed his own individual style. Eventually, the striking "Nudie suits" became even better known than Turk's creations and—with the advance money from our new recording and publishing deals freshly in hand—Gram and I decided to recruit Nudie to outfit the group. To me, *real* country music included rhinestone suits, so I was really excited the day that Sneaky, Chris, Gram, and I drove over to Nudie's shop on Lankershim Boulevard in North Hollywood to order our own.

Every band member's true personality shone through with his own signature design. Manuel Cuevas, who was Nudie's son-in-law at the time, helped with the designs and did all the tailoring. Manuel remains a dear friend, as does his former assistant, Jaime Castandea, who continues to design and create wonderful stage clothes for me to this day. Sneaky, who loved dinosaurs, ordered an image of a pterodactyl on the front of his black velvet top. For whatever reason, he wanted a pullover with no buttons or pockets, very baggy sleeves, and a crew neck collar—plus big, wide, baggy pants. A strange man, but I loved the guy. Chris Ethridge opted for a long southern-style coat, all white with red and yellow roses on the coat and pants. His classy look reminded me of a modern-day version of something out of *Gone with the Wind*. Gram had the vision that fit him perfectly: a white suit with a short jacket, on which was embroidered marijuana leaves and pills. Two naked ladies, sort of like you would see on the mud flaps of a truck, were embroidered on the lapels. On the back of Gram's coat was a huge red Latino-style cross that tied in with the flames on his pants. Me, I was all over the place with my design. I couldn't quite settle on one look, so I somehow included all manner of strange embroidered pictures—from a huge sun with a face like an Aztec god on the back, to peacocks on each side of my jacket, to the Greek god Poseidon on my sleeves, and red flames running down the legs of my pants.

Barry Feinstein, another member of The Byrds' extended family, photographed the cover for *The Gilded Palace of Sin*. Barry had shot the cover of the first Byrds album in 1965 and had attempted to shoot our ill-fated music video on the beach in Malibu. After staying up all night, we drove out to the desert, arriving at dawn. We were feeling ragged, but it actually made for a great shoot. With two beautiful models in tow and a worn-out shack in the background, the title and the look of the album suggested all kinds of devious play. It was a great cover and will always be one of my favorites.

A&M was supportive of the album and planned a preview concert at their studios. All their employees, along with other music business people from around town, were invited to our "stepping out party," which they dubbed "the Burrito Barn Dance." Of course, if we were going to introduce ourselves to the world, we needed to settle on a permanent drummer. Who better than my old brother from The Byrds, Michael Clarke, who had recently returned from his self-imposed exile in Hawaii? He'd been playing with Doug Dillard and Gene Clark in The Dillard & Clark Expedition, a group that also included Bernie Leadon at that time. With the group on hiatus after a particularly disastrous performance at the Troubadour, Michael was happy to join the Burritos. The event was quite a set-up, with the label having set the stage for an unbelievable party. We shined brightly in our rhinestones, but, unfortunately, we played poorly that night. Gram was wasted, and we were way too loud and completely disorganized. I remember coming off stage and knowing that we'd dropped the ball big time.

*The Gilded Palace of Sin* was released in February of 1969, and A&M planned our first promotional tour across the country. We hired Frank Blanco and Robert Firks to handle the equipment. Frank, who grew up in the barrio in East LA, and Robert, recently paroled from San Quentin prison, were ex-paratroopers who were a bit older and more seasoned than the rest of us. Phil Kaufman signed on as our road manager. Phil had previously worked for The Rolling Stones as a personal assistant—or their "executive nanny" as he referred to himself—while they were in LA. Keith Richards introduced Phil to Gram, which is how Phil ended up in our orbit. I found these new characters interesting, to say the least. They proved to be loyal and always dedicated to the band members' protection.

Gram Parsons was so smooth he could charm anyone—man, woman, or child—out of the gold in their teeth. I think he developed this gift as a

survival mechanism, growing up in a Southern family of eccentric characters whose love of money and deceitful ways were right out of a Tennessee
Williams story. Gram went to work convincing A&M to send us by train
on this, our first tour of the Midwest and East Coast. I was to blame in the
political maneuvering too. I loved trains, and I was on the Santa Fe Super
Chief to Albuquerque on a regular basis whenever I had a little time to get
away. It's truly amazing the label eventually relented and actually agreed
to send us that way. Phil Kaufman booked the tickets from Union Station
in Los Angeles to Chicago—with stops in Albuquerque, Dodge City, and
all manner of interesting places.

When the day came, we had our big send-off from Union Station, with
friends waving as if they were saying goodbye to the troops heading off
to fight the Great War. A&M sent their head of publicity, Michael Vosse,
along with his credit card, to chaperone us, which we certainly needed.
We were assigned our own Pullman sleeper car on the train and, with
Michael and Gram along, trouble was always brewing. We passed the
time on the two-day train ride to Chicago with lots of poker games and
all manner of hedonistic pursuits. Touring by train was totally crazy and
way too expensive, but we figured the label was paying for everything,
so why worry about it? It wasn't until later that we wised up and realized
they were paying for everything with *our* money.

We finally rolled into Chicago on an early morning and prepared to
play our first show that night. Most people didn't know who we were,
other than our past association with The Byrds, but, after struggling
through "The Burrito Barn Dance" debacle, we began finding our footing.
There were some off nights, but, musically, it turned out to be a strong
tour. Gram was at his best during that first year with the Burritos, and
sometimes I would just sit back and shake my head in wonder. He was so
funny and bright, and nothing seemed beyond his reach. Rhinestone suits!
A train tour! Turbans!

Turbans? Yes, turbans—the kind worn by Sikhs or suspect magicians.
Gram was out shopping one day in Philadelphia and happened upon a
store that sold turbans. He quickly bought a handful of choice models for
the band and brought them back to the hotel. That night, those of us who
dared wore our brand-new turbans on stage, along with our Nudie suits.

I even had a blue one to match my blue suit. I felt like the 1950s R&B star Chuck Willis. It wasn't until later in my life that the great record producer Jerry Wexler explained to me why black performers sometimes wore turbans in the old days. It was a way for African Americans to try to pass as East Indian during the era of legal segregation and blatant racial intolerance in the deep South.

One of the more memorable stops on the train tour was at a club called the Boston Tea Party where we were booked on the same bill as The Byrds. It was wild being there with Roger, Michael, Gram, Clarence White, and Gene Parsons. On the final night of shows, our bands played together. That night has since become legendary, but at the time it was just a fun and mildly chaotic attempt to make some music together. For me, it was just nice to revisit with old friends. Our lives and music were already intertwined—as they would remain for many decades into the future.

A couple of months before leaving on the train tour, Gram and I had moved from the house in Reseda to yet another ranch-style home in Nicholas Canyon, just above Hollywood. We had left that house just prior to our departure from Union Station, so when the tour was over, we staggered back to LA to the new house that Phil found for us at the end of Beverly Glen Boulevard. Mike, Gram, and I moved into Burrito Manor, which was decorated with all sorts of strange furniture that Phil and his band of minions managed to purloin along the way. We started working steady gigs at the Palomino Club in North Hollywood on Monday nights and at the Topanga Corral in Topanga Canyon on Tuesday nights, and you never knew who might follow us home after the gigs. Given my two roommates, there was always a steady stream of strange people and suspect women wandering through our house almost every night. Living with Michael and Gram was like living with a couple of animals. I actually went so far as to padlock my bedroom door while living with those guys.

Somehow, during the chaos of the train tour, Gram and I managed to find time to write another semi-gospel song called "The Train Song." I already mentioned Gram's knack for pulling off whatever hijinks he could think of, but he did it again when he cooked up the idea of hiring R&B pioneers Larry Williams and Johnny "Guitar" Watson to produce that record as the Burritos' next single. Larry was best known for his songs "Dizzy, Miss Lizzy" and "Bony Moronie" (with the memorable line, "skinny as a stick of macaroni"), while Johnny was known for his signature song "Gangster of Love." It was an idea only Parsons could come up with.

When the day arrived, we were all standing in the parking lot of A&M's studios when a gleaming red Cadillac convertible pulled up with Larry Williams behind the wheel and Johnny "Guitar" Watson riding shotgun. They looked like a couple of characters straight from Central Casting. Larry had his initials emblazoned across his jumpsuit, which of course was bright red to match his Caddy. Johnny had on the coolest straw pork pie hat with a wide black band. Now, these guys were *cool*. Before the engine had even stopped, Larry was out of that car, clapping his hands. "Watson," he shouted, "let's make us a hit record!" In addition to our dynamic production duo, we brought in Leon Russell and Clarence White to play with the rest of the band.

Once we got settled into the studio and started working out the parts, Gram pulled out a big bag of cocaine. Johnny and Larry scoped out Parsons and started working their game: "Watson," Larry exclaimed, "I believe this is a hit." Johnny fired back, "You *know* it is!" Gram was soaking up the compliments when Michael whispered to me, "Does Parsons even know they're just playing him for his drugs?" Chris Ethridge, being an R&B bass player born and raised in Mississippi, gave me a wink from across the room. He knew the score, too. It was a strange session to say the least, but in the end we wound up with a genuine Flying Burrito Brothers record that sounded a little like Spike Jones and his band. What it definitely was *not* was a hit, despite what Mr. Williams had so loudly earlier proclaimed in the A&M parking lot.

The first half of 1969 was like one never-ending party, but then the vibe suddenly changed. We were still living at Burrito Manor in August when the Manson murders happened. The free-flowing culture of trust disappeared in the blink of an eye. It was like the entire city went under lock and key. People were frightened to the point of not leaving their homes at night, and it suddenly seemed crazy to have unknown people coming and going from your house. It was later discovered that one of the Manson family's intended targets was Terry Melcher, who produced the first two Byrds albums. Terry and Dennis Wilson of the Beach Boys had gotten professionally entangled with Manson, who was an aspiring singer and songwriter. When they realized he wasn't very good and attempted to sever ties, Manson became belligerent. It was shortly after that when Terry moved from his house, which was subsequently rented to Roman Polanski and his wife Sharon Tate—the home where the Manson murders happened. Rumors circulated that Manson targeted the place to seek revenge on Terry, and Terry himself went into hiding for a while.

Before the murders were solved, police were following every lead they could. Michael and I had a good friend from our Byrds days named Charles Tacot, an older guy who ran with Dickson and a lot of the Hollywood crowd. Charles, who'd been a small arms instructor in the Marines in his younger days, was a tough, no-nonsense kind of guy you could count on to watch out for you. After the murders, I opened up the *Los Angeles Times* one day and saw Charles's name as someone they were interested in talking to. One of the victims was famed hair stylist Jay Sebring, and there was some kind of conflict between Charles and Jay. On top of worrying about the random people who'd been coming and going, we were now also convinced that the cops might burst down the door of Burrito Manor, looking for Tacot, and drag us all away. It sounds paranoid now, but it's hard to describe the mood across the city in those dark days.

I decided it was time to move immediately—if not sooner. I found a house north of Malibu that Gram and I could rent for six months, so we moved out and closed up the Manor for good. I was the one who'd signed the lease on Burrito Manor, which came back to bite me two years later when I was stuck with the bill for unpaid damages done by my roommates. It was a few thousand dollars, so I just paid it and vowed that I would never live with either of those lovable idiots again. No question the original lineup of The Flying Burrito Brothers was the weirdest, craziest, and funniest bunch of characters I was ever involved with, but the fun of it all was starting to run its course in the late summer of 1969.

By the time Gram and I relocated, things were changing quickly. The other side of Malibu was too far from the action for Gram, so he was in and out, rarely ever staying there. We wrote "High Fashion Queen" and a few other songs together, but we definitely weren't productively collaborating like we were before the first album. I had no idea where Gram was coming from anymore. I poured what energy I still had into protecting the music and the band while Gram, always the charmer, was more of a hustler. He was brash and assertive and sought to advance his career by networking and ingratiating himself into the right social circles. But he was starting to trade off his career aspirations for a more hedonistic lifestyle. We both had the drive to succeed but with a very different methodology when it came to execution. It just wasn't that important to me to see and be seen, but as Gram was drawn into the trappings of Hollywood excess, I could feel him slipping away. He was drifting into dark territory, and his fascination with the party scene chipped away at the tight musical brotherhood we'd established just a few months before. It increasingly seemed that Gram cared more about fame than about the music.

Nobody held more sway over Gram than Keith Richards. If The Rolling Stones were around, Gram was like their eager puppy dog. He was determined to be in their presence, and it didn't matter what other commitments might fall by the wayside. One night we were booked at a show in El Monte, a Los Angeles County suburb. On the day of the performance, I couldn't find Parsons anywhere. Searching for Gram was becoming a daily chore, but I knew the Stones were in town cutting tracks for their next album, so I had a hunch where I'd find him. I drove to the studio, Sunset Sound, and explained why I was there. Gram didn't want to leave until, finally, Mick Jagger walked over and said, "Gram, Chris is here to pick you up; you have a show tonight and we're busy working." What Mick was really saying was, "You have a *responsibility* to your band and your fans, and we don't really *need* you here while we're recording." What a moment. Mick Jagger giving Gram Parsons a lesson in social and professional responsibility! Though Keith and Gram were tight, I had a feeling Mick never had much warmth in his heart for Gram. But Gram wanted to *be* Mick Jagger, so Mick managed to get through to him with a message I'd not been successful at communicating. I was grateful for Jagger's words, but I sensed the end was in sight.

Despite the triumph of getting Gram to the show, it still turned out to be a strange night. We played fine, but headed home afterward while our roadies Frank and Robert packed up the equipment. A bunch of gang-bangers jumped them and tried to steal our gear, but they managed to survive. Robert later told me that Frankie saved his life that day. Frank was all of five-foot-five, but he was an ex-gang member himself and a guy you wouldn't want to mess with. I'm pretty sure the guys who caused the problem had to be helped back to their respective homes at the end of the confrontation. Frank and Robert were incredibly loyal friends who stuck with me even after the Burritos.

Though there were some good shows in 1969, in all honesty, the original incarnation of the Burritos probably started going downhill after the first tour. The concept was better conceived than executed and, unfortunately, lackluster performances were a common occurrence in that band as it became clear that Parsons was more interested in getting wasted than getting his job done. I would say maybe only every fifth or sixth show was passable, and it was killing me to go out and give audiences a sloppy performance. I felt I had reached a high mark as a musician singing and playing on The Byrds' "Eight Miles High" and "So You Want to be a Rock 'n' Roll Star," but I was no longer hitting the standard I'd set for myself.

I loved working with Gram in those first months, but he simply grew more and more undisciplined. Sadly, he just couldn't consistently deliver on our promise. He had natural stage presence, but I firmly believe that the greatest hinderance to Gram's development as an artist was his steady stream of trust fund payments. He never had to suffer in his quest for a career in music, while everyone else had to learn how to scratch out a living while building a strong following. Gram had the drive, but he didn't have the hunger. Despite generally strong material, we were too often lazy and weak in our execution. And Gram's financial situation was a huge contributor to his downfall.

When it came time to start planning for another album, we were unprepared. We didn't have a strong batch of new songs, and we'd lost Chris Ethridge who, citing family problems, returned to Mississippi. Phil Kaufman wasn't the right guy to manage the band, and I often found myself having to be the adult in the room to keep everyone on track. By the fall of 1969, Phil was out, too, and I brought in the old team of Dickson and Tickner to help guide the Burritos. Sure, I'd had my differences with them during my time in The Byrds, but at least they had some experience in the music business.

With Chris Ethridge gone, we needed to bring in a new band member who could handle the chaos. I decided to return to playing bass, as I'd done as a Byrd, and recruited my old friend Bernie Leadon to play guitar. Bernie had left Dillard & Clark at the same time Michael departed, and he'd been playing in a group called The Corvettes, backing up Linda Ronstadt. Bernie was a fantastic singer and musician, and I was thrilled when he decided to switch gears and join us. With Gram losing focus, I knew Bernie would be a lifesaver in the vocal and instrumental departments.

Despite all the changes, the odds were stacked against us in terms of material. We were really desperate to come up with something for that second album. Generally, the recording process was draining, as Gram routinely showed up late, loaded, disengaged, or some combination thereof. Even with the challenges, however, there were still some memorable moments in the studio. Frank Blanco's mother brought in (and acted as translator for) a Norteño accordion player named Leopoldo Carbajal to add a bit of spice to Bernie and Gram's original song "Man in the Fog." I enjoyed recording a couple of other things for those sessions, including "Older Guys" and "Down in the Churchyard," but, overall, we weren't anywhere near the groove or unique vibe we'd come up with for *The Gilded Palace of Sin*. The songs just weren't there.

Needing outside material to round out the sessions, Gram convinced Mick and Keith to let the Burritos record "Wild Horses" even though they'd not yet released their own version. I think they'd sent a tape of it to try to get Sneaky to overdub a steel part, but when Gram heard it, he wanted us to cut it. The song didn't work for me at all. It was depressing, maudlin, melodramatic, and did not fit what we were doing on the second album. At that point, I just didn't care. I was starting to lose all interest in the band, so I just went along with it.

As it was becoming harder to maintain much enthusiasm for the Burritos, the Stones asked us to perform at their upcoming free concert to be held in December of 1969 at the Altamont Speedway in Northern California. I wasn't sold on the idea, mainly because there wasn't a lot of information about the event and because we'd be traveling there on our own dime. I finally gave in, and off we went. We flew to San Francisco and rented a car to head to the show.

It was a dark day. Clouds obscured the sky, and there was a thick, haunting presence in the air. We were involved in a car accident on the way to the gig and, when we finally arrived, it was complete chaos. It looked like a war zone. We quickly learned that the Oakland Hell's Angels were in charge of security. The Angels were in an agitated state of chemical enhancement that made them overbearing, violent, and confrontational. They were flat-out scary and had already been punching and kicking anyone who happened to cross their path. When Marty Balin of Jefferson Airplane jumped off the stage in the middle of his band's set to try to take care of some problem involving one of the Angels, he was hit in the head and knocked out.

Frankie and Robert backed our equipment van up near the stage, and we prepared to do our set. As I made my way up the steps, I saw that Crosby, Stills & Nash looked to be making a quick exit after playing a few songs. As I was heading up, Crosby was coming down. He paused and looked me in the eye. "Be careful," he warned. "This is a little strange." A *little* strange? I walked up and was greeted by two burly Hell's Angels. One of them barked, "Where do you think you're going?" I had my Fender bass in my hand. Where did he *think* I was going? Not something I would say to these guys in their present condition. Feeling like a monk explaining to two Vikings that it wouldn't be a good idea to sack and plunder the monastery, I finally managed to convince the two gentlemen stopping me at the stage that I was going up to perform.

The Flying Burrito Brothers played a good show. We managed to calm everyone down a bit, and there were no problems during our set. As we exited the stage, however, we found a very large naked man being severely beaten by a couple of the Hell's Angels. He was out of his mind on drugs and had no clue what was happening or why. As soon as the Angels found something more interesting to go after, we pulled this guy into our van and told him to stay put until we could find someone to help him. The minute our backs were turned, he escaped from the van and proceeded to get the Angels' attention again. They were immediately back on the attack. This was turning into an unbelievable nightmare. It was like a living Hieronymus Bosch painting unfolding before my eyes.

I gathered my belongings and—along with Sneaky, Dickson, and our friend Jet Thomas—beat a hasty retreat toward the car. Gram took off with the Stones, and I didn't know where Bernie and Mike had ended up. It wasn't until 2010 that Bernie told me what happened to them. The two of them got a ride back to the Sausalito Inn with our friends Toni Basil and Annie Marshall. The hotel was seventy miles from the speedway, which tells you something about how well planned the whole thing was. Mike didn't even have a room, but he was able to talk the desk clerk out of the key to Gram's room, where they stayed that night. By the time they finally made it to the hotel, Sneaky, Jet Thomas, Dickson, and I were on the way to the airport. We heard the horrible news on the radio that a young man had been stabbed to death by someone in the Hell's Angels right in front of the stage.

Altamont was a far cry from the Monterey Pop Festival, which was just two and a half years prior. That's when everyone got along, with very little security, for a nice, peaceful weekend. With the darkness descending around Altamont, it was almost predestined to end in tragedy. The promise of peace and love that had marked the 1960s was now a shattered dream. The decade wasn't fading out with a whimper, but with a very evil and abrupt end.

# CHAPTER ELEVEN
# START ALL OVER AGAIN

**B**urrito *Deluxe* was released in April of 1970. There's really not much I can say about that record except that it was flat-out bad. They say you can't judge a book by its cover, but that might not be true for albums. At least it isn't true for *that* album. In addition to a lackluster set of songs, it featured really terrible artwork. There's nobody to blame but Parsons for that. Gram came up with the idea of the science lab jump suits, as well as the plastic gloves. Why did I allow this to happen? Out of the many records I had already done, this was the worst album cover I had ever been involved with. But I let it happen. Once again, I was giving Gram the reins when I should have stepped up and asserted myself more forcefully. The cover alone would have hampered our attempts at getting on any radio playlist, not to mention the music inside. And that's exactly what happened—no airplay and no sales.

Today plenty of folks in the Americana and roots music crowd cite the original incarnation of The Flying Burrito Brothers that Gram and I started as a pioneering musical experiment and an important influence. In 1970, however, we were a commercially unsuccessful group with a hit-or-miss track record as a live band. I always knew the potential, but by that point it was becoming way too stressful hoping Parsons would show up for gigs. And then hoping, if he did show up, he wouldn't be so high on something that he couldn't perform. There were many nights when we would count off an up-tempo country shuffle only to have Gram start singing a slow ballad in a different key. Not an easy task to pull off. It became like a Keystone Cops routine with everyone crashing and banging into each other during a four-bar interlude to try to rescue the song. It was becoming embarrassing.

And then it all came down to *that* night.

Gram was twenty minutes late when he staggered into the Brass Ring, the San Fernando Valley club where we were working. He was stoned out of his mind, and when the show began, Gram completely destroyed it. Once again, we all started playing one song and Gram came in on the vocal with something else entirely. Multiple times. Total train wreck. After the first set, I stomped off the stage and retreated to the dressing room, where I was furiously pacing back and forth. Suddenly Gram came into the room, glassy-eyed and slurring his words. "What's the matter, Chris?" I turned to face him and saw that his guitar was still strapped on. My mind was racing. *That guitar. I hated it. We all hated it. The guitar was little more than a prop, and he could barely play it.* My blood was practically boiling. *It was a terrible instrument, and really terrible considering he never played with any finesse. That's what was missing with this guy. Finesse. He was like a bull in a china shop. He just didn't care!*

I was in a rage. I took a few steps toward Gram and stuck my finger in his face. "You're fired!" I screamed. "You have no respect for anyone, and I'm done with it. You're through!" Gram smirked. "You *can't* fire me," he drawled. I launched into an angry tirade about selfishness, professionalism, self-respect, and who knows what else. As my voice kept rising, I lost all control and smashed my fist through the front of that stupid guitar. "Be thankful that wasn't your head," I snarled as I stormed out of the dressing room and headed for my car.

A day or two later, I was walking across the A&M lot, feeling bad about the guitar, but not about firing Gram. As I discovered immediately after that fateful confrontation, Sneaky, Mike, and Bernie all agreed with my decision. We were tired of feeling used, and it was time to move on. As I was walking, I saw Gram coming toward me. "Chris," he said, "What's going on here? What did I do?" I told him that it was time to part ways and that my mind was made up. "You can't fire me, man," he whined. "I *made* this band. You can't do it without me." I just shook my head. "No, Gram," I replied softly, "we *both* made this band, and I can absolutely do it without you. I did plenty of things before you came along, and I'll do plenty of things after. I'm sorry, but this time it's truly over. You're fired."

Nobody could stay mad at Gram for very long, but I was resolved that he wouldn't come back to the band. And he didn't. It might have been one of the few times in his life that Gram didn't charm his way out of the consequences of his bad behavior. He had his pain, but Gram was also a spoiled rich kid who almost always got his way. He had to learn an important lesson, and I was at peace with the decision. I really loved Gram, but he was the least professional guy I ever worked with. Still, I knew he would bounce back, and I hoped that maybe this would be a wake-up call that would trigger him to refocus his natural talents. Gram still needed to grow and mature, but I wasn't going to let him do it on my dime anymore.

After we parted ways, Gram returned to England. He reached out to Keith Richards, who invited Gram and his fiancé Gretchen Burrell to stay for a while. They moved in to Keith's Redlands estate outside of London, and the two of us lost touch for a good while. In the meantime, the Burritos, as a four-man lineup, vowed to stay together at least a little longer to see if we could rebuild ourselves into a real band again. The challenge fostered a camaraderie between the remaining members that hadn't existed before.

Our first show without Gram was at the tail end of a package tour in June of 1970. The traveling Festival Express Tour, featuring The Grateful Dead, Janis Joplin, Ian & Sylvia, and other acts, was making its way across Canada on a chartered Canadian National Railways train. We got on board for the last two shows. With the change in personnel, we had to rework the set list and tweak our arrangements. Bernie and I swapped off singing lead and harmony vocals, and it felt good. In fact, years later, when a CD and DVD of those shows was being prepared for release, Bernie and I were able to view the footage and give our input on what should or shouldn't be included. We both agreed that our take on Gram's song "Lazy Day" should be included because it was a fine performance. Actually, it was more than a fine performance. It was the best the band had played all year. It was plain to see what could have been if Gram hadn't allowed his talent to wash away in that period. It made me sad to see what could have been—and what *should* have been—much earlier on.

Despite the fresh opportunity and the improved tightness of the group, we were still in somewhat of a rut, both musically and financially. We needed to bring in another singer and songwriter to keep the fires stoked, and that's when Rick Roberts arrived at our doorstep. Tickner ran into him when Rick was hitchhiking one day on Sunset Boulevard. He brought Rick to our rehearsal that night, and I liked him immediately. He was a solid singer and nailed the harmony parts. On top of that, he'd written some good songs. But, most importantly, Rick was full of ambition and highly professional. We weren't looking for another Gram; we were looking for a reliable collaborator to help us move into the next phase of the life of the band.

Soon after Rick came into the group, we were offered a tour of Holland and England, which we immediately accepted. It felt a bit strange when we landed in Amsterdam and were met by a large group of fans at the airport. After clearing customs, we were ushered into a press conference—something I hadn't experienced since The Byrds. Turned out we were big stars in Holland. The Dutch fans loved our music, and Sneaky Pete was the most popular guy in the group by far. It was great to see him get such positive feedback from audiences.

Robert Firks found us bed-and-breakfast style lodgings on the Prinsengracht Canal called the Weichmann Hotel. It was run by an American named Ted Boddy and his wife Nikki, whom he'd met in the early '50s while stationed in Europe. Nikki's family had converted the beautiful historic building into a hotel before it was taken over by the Nazi high command to house some of their officers during the occupation in World War II. It was a beautiful spot on a charming street—a great find on Robert's part. We became close friends with the Boddys, and I visited with them often over the years. As word got out about their openness to musicians, a lot of bands camped out at the Amsterdam Weichmann Hotel.

While the rest of us enjoyed the hotel, Mike was soaking up every last bit of the Amsterdam experience. It's always been a very liberal city where one could buy hashish legally over the counter. It was Michael Clarke's dream come true. He was in his element and enjoyed every second we were in Holland. Everyone in the band was given a week's per diem, and Michael went through his in approximately three hours on the first night we landed there. He then proceeded to borrow money from the rest of us for the entire stay in Amsterdam. I think he even hit up Mrs. Boddy for a few guilders.

We had a fabulous concert at the Concertgebouw Opera House in Amsterdam and worked some other venues around the Netherlands before flying to London. Expecting the same reaction we got in Holland, we hopped off the plane at Heathrow airport to—crickets. Nobody was waiting for us except the tour promoter. At least we played some great shows around England to appreciative audiences. It was just as successful as the Netherlands—though in a far more reserved manner.

Bringing Rick into the fold injected some new life into the band, as well as some new sensibilities. He came from more of a pop background, and our respective strengths worked well together as we began writing songs for the third Burritos album. Dickson was going to produce the record and, unfortunately, just as The Byrds had done a few years prior, Rick signed a publishing deal with Tickson Music before I could warn him. Regardless of what was going on from a business perspective, however, we cut a really good album. We had good songs, we carefully rehearsed the tracks and the vocals, and Bernie and Sneaky got to expand on their solo ideas, with Bernie playing more banjo and acoustic guitar. The final product, simply titled *The Flying Burrito Brothers,* was completely different from the first two albums. Some have argued that it didn't sound like a Burrito Brothers record, but I disagree. It was an expansion on who we had been as singers and songwriters, and an exploration of a wider range of influence, while staying within the parameters of country music. As a bonus, the album was much more successful than our first two efforts. It received excellent reviews, and sales were far better than they'd been for the previous records. Finally, the Burritos were living up to our promise and building an audience around the country. For the first time, we were doing great business.

Though we were hitting our stride, Sneaky decided to leave the Burritos after we finished recording the third album. His first love was stop-motion animation, and he wanted to stay home where he could work in his chosen industry and be available for recording sessions. He wound up working on some great TV shows and films and playing on some fantastic records too. I was sorry to see him go, but I understood.

There weren't many steel players like Sneaky Pete, but Tickner once again showed up with just the right guy. Al Perkins had just moved to town from Texas and was not only brilliant on steel guitar, but also a fantastic lead guitarist. He had a lot of experience working in bands and, like Rick Roberts, was a total pro. It was yet another step in the right direction. We were booking a steady stream of gigs, primarily at colleges on the East Coast, and perfecting our new identity as a tight, kick-ass band that was able to play straight country, bluegrass, and rock and roll. We had new blood, new energy, and the audiences were loving it. Truly, the best lineup of The Flying Burrito Brothers that ever existed was me, Michael, Bernie, Rick, and Al.

That lineup, unfortunately, was short lived. With Rick joining the group, I could tell that Bernie was feeling a bit frustrated. Having put in a solid year with the band, he was looking for a new challenge. He didn't want to leave us high and dry, but he let us know that he had his feelers out for another opportunity. Soon after, he was invited to start a band with one of Al Perkins' old bandmates, Don Henley. Leaving with my blessing, Bernie joined Don, Glenn Frey, and Randy Meisner to transition from being a Burrito Brother to an Eagle. It was through that group that the dream Gram and I envisioned of introducing country music to a young rock audience found its greatest commercial success. Moving to that band was a wise decision for Bernie that proved to be a monumental success story.

Even after Bernie's departure I was still feeling good about our lineup. We continued to play some really great shows. In fact, as we thought about what we wanted to do for our fourth album, I decided it would make sense to record some live performances. Dickson was on board to produce, and we planned to tape two upcoming university performances back East. I wanted to enhance the show by adding Byron Berline and Roger Bush from the bluegrass group Country Gazette—as well as my old friend Kenny Wertz from the Squirrel Barkers—to join us for a bluegrass set in the middle of the show. I played mandolin, Roger was on bass,

Kenny handled the banjo, Rick played rhythm guitar, and Byron was on the fiddle for both the bluegrass segment and the electric set. And of course Michael on drums.

Released as *Last of the Red Hot Burritos,* the live LP became my second favorite Burritos record after *The Gilded Palace of Sin.* Although the liner notes had nothing to do with the actual music and should have never been a part of the final artwork, the album captured a moment in time when the audiences went wild and we were selling out wherever we played. It was a complete turn-around for the band, and we achieved it through raw perseverance and dedication. We had finally broken through, and we were working as a team—a truly golden era for me in terms of live performances.

It's funny that a West Coast band like The Flying Burrito Brothers would work most steadily on the East Coast, but that's where our strongest audience was in the early 1970s. One of the premier clubs in the country at the time was the Cellar Door in the Georgetown neighborhood of Washington, DC. We were booked there one night when Rick Roberts and Kenny Wertz casually wandered into a nearby bar called Clyde's during the break between our sound check and the show. After a little while they returned, raving about a talented young woman they'd just heard performing solo with an acoustic guitar. They insisted I come down and hear her before our show started, and I agreed.

I walked into Clyde's and was immediately taken by the voice of this great singer. She had a natural honesty and charm that shined through with every note that came out of her mouth. That was the first time I heard Emmylou Harris. She was wonderful but completely unknown to anyone outside the scene in and around DC. I was so impressed that I invited her up to the Cellar Door to sit in with the Burritos when she finished her set. She agreed and got up on stage with us that night to sing "It Wasn't God Who Made Honky Tonk Angels." I think we asked Emmylou to join the Burritos on the spot, but she wisely turned us down. Georgetown had a thriving music scene, and she was happy staying in her comfort zone and playing her various gigs around town.

Meanwhile, Gram Parsons was beginning to wear out his welcome at Villa Nellcôte, the French mansion that Keith Richards rented while The

Rolling Stones recorded sessions for their *Exile on Main Street* album. He and Gretchen had been living and traveling with the Stones for almost a year when Keith's wife Anita politely asked them to leave. They packed up and flew back to the US where Gram would try to kickstart his career. He came to our show in Baltimore, and we made peace with one another—yet again. After joining me for a couple of songs on stage, we stayed up most of the night catching up with one another. Gram had stopped taking drugs, and I was reminded that when he was sober and somewhat coherent, he could be a wonderful friend and confidant.

At some point during our conversation, Gram mentioned that he wanted to make a solo album and was looking for a girl singer to work with. Emmylou popped into my mind since she was nearby in Washington DC. I encouraged him to call her up, but he wasn't convinced. I revisited the topic several times that evening, telling Gram how great she was. He finally gave in and picked up the phone. They arranged to meet in DC the next day, so Gram booked a train ticket. The rest, as they say, is history. The two hit it off, and Gram flew Emmy out to LA for rehearsals and recording. Coming from a folk background, she wasn't quite the country music devotee that Gram was, but Emmylou Harris was getting ready to embark on a great adventure that would change her life forever.

Gram wasn't the only old friend I ran into out on the road. We had a night off in Cleveland during a string of shows and heard that Stephen Stills was playing in town. After achieving huge success with my old bandmate in Crosby, Stills & Nash (and, later, Young), he decided to take some time away from CSN and strike out on his own. After scoring with radio hits like "Love the One You're With" and "Change Partners" he was touring with his own band.

Stephen and I went way back to the mid-1960s when he formed Buffalo Springfield with Neil Young, Richie Furay, Dewey Martin, and Bruce Palmer. I got to know Dewey when he was playing drums for The Dillards when they briefly experimented with going electric during a three-week tour of the States opening for The Byrds. After the tour ended, I ran into Dewey again, and he invited me down to hear this new band he was playing with. I met the Springfield guys and heard them rehearse. They had the goods: great songs and great vocals. They were being managed by Barry Friedman and Dickie Davis, two old friends of mine. When Barry and Dickie approached Whisky a Go Go co-owner Elmer Valentine about hiring them, he passed. He just wasn't interested. I stepped in and talked to Elmer about giving them a couple of nights to play the club in the summer of 1966. Elmer and his partner Mario Maglieri did hire them for a weekend on my word, and they were a hit. Elmer held them over for another week. They then became the de facto house band there for nearly two months—which ultimately led to their landing a record deal.

Now here I was in Cleveland, Ohio, watching Stills on stage. I hadn't seen him since CSN had become world famous, so it was great to spend a nice evening catching up after the show. It was only a month or two later when I ran into him again while playing a Burritos show at a club called Tulagi's in Boulder, Colorado. Stephen was living in the area at the time. That night I was playing a 1950s Gibson F-5 mandolin that I'd bought in Virginia during a Byrds tour in 1968. Although I'd played mandolin in the Squirrel Barkers and The Golden State Boys, I didn't even own a mandolin during my first few years with The Byrds. After finding that Gibson, I began making up for lost time with a daily practice regimen. It wasn't a great instrument, and after I had it for a couple of months, Ed Douglas stripped off the finish and left it natural, hoping to get some more tone out of it. The first thing out of Stills's mouth when we saw each other after my show was, "The band sounds great, but I think you need a better mandolin." I laughed it off and we headed out to his cabin in Gold Hill, just outside Boulder, where we spent the evening continuing to catch up.

After that tour, I was hanging out at home one day at the house I shared with Bernie Leadon. We were still roommates even though we weren't bandmates, and we lived in a place on the canals in Venice Beach. Built in the 1920s, the Venice Canals were intended to recreate the romantic vibe of its Italian sister city. By the time we lived there, however, the neighborhood had lost its luster and was jokingly called "the slum by the sea." There were certainly no singing gondoliers passing by on the waters outside my window. An occasional used piece of furniture might float past, and once I happened to glance outside to see a duck riding on top of a mattress. The free show was interrupted by a phone call. It was someone from Stephen Stills's camp calling to ask if I was available to come down to Criteria Studios in Miami and play some sessions for a new solo album he was starting to work on. Stephen had some material that was leaning toward a bluegrass/country feel and he needed mandolin, fiddle, and steel guitar. They wanted Al Perkins and Byron Berline to come down with me. I was completely up for it and, since the Flying Burrito Brothers already had shows booked on the East Coast during the weekends, the three of us would be able to travel down to Miami during the week for the sessions. It would be great to work with Stills, and besides, I hadn't been to Miami since The Byrds appeared at the Columbia Records Convention there in 1965.

Arriving the day before the session, we were picked up at the airport and driven to a large mansion on the bay that Stills and the band were leasing. I met the other musicians: Dallas Taylor, Fuzzy Samuel, Paul Harris, and Joe Lala. I had actually met Joe before when his band Pacific Gas & Electric opened for The Flying Burrito Brothers in San Diego. They were all very nice guys, but I was still a bit shy, so I was feeling a little apprehensive about what to expect at the following day's session.

There was no reason to feel nervous. The studio was fabulous, and the engineers were brothers Ron and Howard Albert, two wonderful guys and incredible talents who would figure prominently in my life for years to come. We'd only been there a few hours when we took a short break. "I have something you should see," Stephen told me. One of his road guys handed him a small oblong case. He popped it open and pulled out what looked like an old Gibson F model mandolin. "Try this out and tell me what you think." I carefully picked it up, realizing it was a 1924 Lloyd Loar F-5 "Master Model." It was the very finest mandolin Gibson ever built— the rare mandolin equivalent to a Stradivarius violin. I played a little bit.

"This is outstanding," I said. "Where did you get it?"

Stephen replied, "You like it?"

I said again, "This is an *outstanding* instrument."

Stephen nodded. "Good," he said. "It's yours!"

I was in shock. I couldn't believe he was offering me such a beautiful instrument. It was such an overwhelmingly kind gesture that I felt like I shouldn't take it.

"Stephen," I protested, "I can't accept this gift. It's far too generous and it's too good of an instrument for me."

Stills just shook his head and laughed before straightening up and looking me right in the eye. "I'll never forget what you did for the Springfield," he said with the deepest sincerity. "You got us our first real job at the Whisky, and that's how all this began. I want you to have this mandolin to know how much I appreciate it."

I fumbled around for an appropriate response and finally managed a simple "Thank you." I wanted to throw my arms around him and give him a big bear hug, but I don't think he would've been comfortable with that kind of display of affection.

After that, I was floating high above the ground playing my new mandolin. I was loving every minute of the sessions and spent about three days recording tracks and adding some harmony vocal overdubs to a few songs. When the weekend came around, Al, Byron, and I rendezvoused with the rest of The Flying Burrito Brothers for some shows before returning to Miami for some additional recording sessions that wrapped up over the long Thanksgiving weekend.

It was on the last day of recording when Stephen approached me with an unexpected offer. Stills wanted to start a new band with me, Al, Dallas, Joe, Fuzzy, and Paul. Of course, it sounded like a great idea, but what about CSN? How did they fit into the equation? Stephen assured me that he wanted to go in a different direction and do some exploring with a solid band that could handle any material from straight country and bluegrass, to rock and roll, to blues, and even a little Afro-Cuban flavor thrown into the mix. If I was going to do it, however, it would mean giving up The Flying Burrito Brothers.

The Burritos had gotten to the point where we were a great live act and had developed a real camaraderie onstage. No matter how great we sounded, however, what was the end game? We weren't selling any records. I had put nearly three years into this, and as good as we were sounding on stage, it was time for me to move on. The hardest part would be breaking away from my pals, but they would all land on their feet. I knew in my heart it was the right thing to do. Game over. When Stephen made the offer to me "I said, let me think about it, and I'll get back to you." It was just under three minutes when I turned around and looked him in the eye and said, "I'm in, when do we start rehearsing?"

# CHAPTER TWELVE
# IT DOESN'T MATTER

In December of 1971, Dallas Taylor, Joe Lala, and I spent Christmas Eve at the Carlyle Hotel in New York City with the Stills family: Stephen, his mother, and his two sisters, Hannah, and Taicita. Stephen was recovering from a knee operation, so we camped out there for a few days of shopping, going down to the Village to hear music, and hanging out. It was an unusual way to spend the holiday, but being in New York during Christmas is always a beautiful time.

On Christmas day, we all headed to JFK and boarded a flight to London. The rest of the band and crew soon joined us to begin rehearsals for a world tour promoting the upcoming album. Stephen leased Ringo Starr's home in Surrey, near Elstead, which was a small town outside of London. The idea was to have everyone living together under the same roof for the next two months while we rehearsed. It was a beautiful Tudor-style English country manor complete with a house staff, a full-time gardener, and stables with two horses. We each had our own bedroom, and I lived at the end of the hallway on the second floor. My room was referred to as the "monk's cell," and it could easily have passed for a monastic cave. I was told that most of the heavy oak timbers in the ceiling were taken off the Spanish Armada, most likely after the battle of Trafalgar in 1805. It was a comfortable temporary home with loads of English charm. The weather, however, was a different story. England in January and February isn't paradise for an ex-surfer from California. The sun might have briefly popped out every now and then to taunt me, but I really just remember those damp overcast skies greeting me every day when I awoke.

The other band members and I were under the impression that we would rehearse each day in the manor's adjoining garage studio. We did, but not according to any set schedule. Our rehearsals were sporadic and would start whenever Stephen was ready. Sometimes that meant the festivities didn't get underway until midnight, or one or two in the morning. Having always followed a strictly-scheduled and structured rehearsal time in the other bands I had played in, this was a huge adjustment for me.

Despite the idyllic setting, Elstead could start to feel like a prison at times with the foul weather and crazy rehearsal schedule. It got to where there was an oppressive air when we were all confined to the house. One day, a few of us took a hike out into the pastures, wearing what looked like army jackets. Out of nowhere, two military jeeps full of soldiers, with guns drawn, pulled up and surrounded us. They were English army troops from nearby Guilford. This was in the days when the IRA was setting off bombs in and around London, and they thought we might be suspicious characters. When they realized there wasn't an Irish accent among us, we were saved. So much for getting out for a little fresh air! When we knew we weren't needed for rehearsal, we'd venture a little further and take the train from Guilford station into London just to have a little taste of freedom. Joe Lala, one of the funniest people I've ever known, used to say, "We're going on a vacation from each other together!"

Sensing our restlessness, Stephen decided we should take a few days off and fly over to France for a little break. Stephen, Dallas, Paul, Joe, and I landed in Paris and stayed the night at Bill Wyman's house. The Stones weren't touring or recording at the time, and Bill had already popped into Stephen's album sessions in Miami to play bass with us on "The Love Gangster." Bill was a very nice man and a great musician. He opened his home to us and treated us to a wonderful dinner at a nearby restaurant that evening. Wyman supposedly once said that he would have left The Rolling Stones to join Stephen's band if he'd been asked, which tells you something about the quality of that group of musicians. If he had, I would have enjoyed playing with him. Bill was always a lovely man and someone in the Stones whom I truly admired.

The next morning, we booked tickets on a train to Rome. It was a comfortable ride, and we all had our own private compartments. As we disembarked the train to make a change in Zurich the next morning, we discovered that Stephen must have stayed up a few too many nights. He was beginning to hallucinate. A porter was loading our luggage onto a large cart, and Stephen was sure the kid was stealing our stuff. He confronted the poor guy, pulled out a folding knife from his pocket, and threatened his life. The porter grew wide-eyed and took off running. Paul and I calmed Stephen down, got him to hand over the knife, and convinced him to go wait in the train station bar. We threw the knife in the bushes across the street from the station, found the porter, and managed to sooth his fears with some kind words and a generous tip.

When we boarded the next train to continue on to Rome, we all hid from Stephen in Joe's compartment. Joe, never one for confrontation, hid out in the railroad station bar as soon as Stills started to get agitated about the porter. While there, he met a new friend who sold him some wonderful treats that did much to calm our anxiety in the wake of "the Zurich incident." We kicked back, howling in laughter as we headed for Italy. We all had a great time sightseeing together in Rome before flying back to London a few days later. It was just the break we'd needed.

Refocused and reenergized, we put together a two-hour show that presented the entire album. Stephen settled on the name Manassas for both the band and the record. It was a reference to the Virginia town that was the site of the first major land battle of the Civil War. Well-trained and ready for battle ourselves, we moved out of Elstead and hit the road to go play our first show together. The venue for our debut performance was the Concertgebouw in Amsterdam, the same beautiful theater I had played with The Flying Burrito Brothers a couple of years earlier. We followed that up with some very good shows in England and around the European continent. That band was sounding so good.

After our European shows we were booked to headline Australia's Rock Isle Mulwala Pop Festival over Easter weekend. We boarded a BEA jet for Melbourne with stops in Beirut, Tel Aviv, Hong Kong, Perth, and a plane change in Sydney. The second group on the festival's bill was Canned Heat, who came in from the US. We all arrived at the Sydney airport at about the same time from opposite ends of the earth—Manassas from the west and Canned Heat from the east. We all went through Immigration and Customs and boarded our final flight for Melbourne. In an instant, five customs agents appeared and summoned us off the plane. We were accused of smuggling drugs into the country by hiding them in our amplifiers. After a complete search of everything, they realized they had the wrong band. The drugs belonged to Canned Heat.

We were finally allowed to fly on to Melbourne. I'm not sure what happened to Canned Heat, but they did show up for the festival the next day without the contraband they brought along. It was a very hot day and poor Bob Hite, their lead singer, passed out on stage in front of the crowd of 30,000 people. Being a rather large fellow whose nickname was "the Bear," a fork-lift had to be brought in to move him off to the side of the stage.

Following the Australian festival, both bands flew to Hawaii. It was my first time back to the United States in months, and I managed to avoid being grilled by the authorities. Stephen wasn't so fortunate. He decided to wear a nice suit on the plane, while the rest of us wore our normal everyday wear. Upon landing in Honolulu and lining up to go through US customs, the head agent pointed to our group. "Okay, you people," he said, "welcome home. You can come on through except for you in the suit. You need to go wait over there." I guess Stephen stuck out like a sore thumb with his beautiful English suit, while the rest of us were in our typical gear. He ultimately managed to convince the agents there was nothing nefarious going on.

Our return to the States coincided with the release of the *Manassas* record. Thanks to the marathon recording sessions, there was plenty of material for a conceptually engaging double LP. It was divided into four distinct sections: "The Raven" was a rock section with some Latin influences; "The Wilderness" was country and bluegrass; "Consider" was folk-oriented; and "Rock & Roll is Here to Stay" was, well, what it sounds like. It was a wonderful album, the critics loved it, and the band was fantastic—both in the studio and on stage. In terms of songwriting, Stills and I worked together quite well, having written "It Doesn't Matter" and "Bound to Lose." The album hit the *Billboard* Top 5, and I just soaked up the experience of playing great shows in large venues all across

America—including an unforgettable show at Carnegie Hall. That first year with the band was fantastic, and I loved working with those guys. At the conclusion of the tour, I moved to Boulder, Colorado, where Stephen and the band were based.

With the triumph of *Manassas,* Stephen Stills was at the top of his game in 1972. He'd just come off back-to-back smashes with the *Crosby, Stills & Nash* album and the follow-up, *Déjà Vu,* with Crosby, Stills, Nash & Young. His two previous solo albums were both big sellers, and he'd had a handful of hit singles on his own with "Love the One You're With," "Sit Yourself Down," "Change Partners," and "Marianne." I must admit I was in awe of the man and, at times, felt a little intimidated working with him because he was such a good musician, singer, and songwriter. But he kept me on my toes and encouraged me to think out of the box. I was still wrestling with my own insecurities in those days, and sometimes I allowed them to get the better of me. I had brought the Burritos back from the dead and led the band during its best period, but now I was back to the old familiar "second in command" position. At some point, I realized that was actually fine with me, as it confirmed that I was most comfortable playing mandolin, acoustic guitar, bass, or singing. All the other stuff that came along with leading a band and taking care of business was fine, but my heart was in making good music.

In the music business, there's always the danger of the second album jinx. It happened to a lot of artists; after achieving success with a debut release, the pressure was on from the record company for more "product." This often created problems if the artist didn't yet have strong follow-up material. To try to meet the demand, the artist would scramble to finish a song in the studio, which could become a very expensive proposition as the clock ticked away on those hourly studio rates. And that's exactly what happened to Manassas. We continued to tour throughout 1972 before returning to Miami's Criteria Studios to begin work on our second album with Howard and Ron Albert at the helm. We weren't ready, and we didn't have a clear plan of where we were headed with our music. The songs lacked the depth and substance of the first album's material. The process dragged on for a long time, and we never regained the momentum we had when making the previous record. Not to mention this was 1972 when rock and roll excess was in full swing. It's no secret that the 1970s was an indulgent decade—especially in the music world. Self-destructiveness ruled the day as hard drugs began to take a toll, and lots of gifted people fell into the abyss. In short, our personal lifestyle choices were not helping matters. In fact, they were causing major problems in the studio.

We finished up the record in Colorado and Los Angeles, finally releasing the *Down the Road* LP in the spring of 1973. The project was uneven, and the reviews were mixed. We continued touring, but the band started to splinter due to various personal problems, as well as increasing pressure on Stephen to rejoin Crosby, Nash, and Young. Our final stretch of dates ran from September to mid-October, including a show at the Winterland Ballroom where David Crosby and Neil Young joined us onstage.

Our final show was on October 14, 1973, in Marquette, Michigan. There was no big blow-up or anything dramatic that led to the end of Manassas. We just quietly faded away and realized it was time to call it a day. I loved Manassas and loved working with such talented musicians. It was a unique group, and I learned a lot from Stills, both as a guitarist and songwriter. He was a mentor to me, and being in that band toughened me up for what lay ahead. After all these years, I still hold Stephen in high regard as both an artist and a good friend.

In 1972, while I was still a member of Manassas, Asylum Records came up with the idea of the five original members of the Byrds reforming for a one-off album. The project wasn't conceived as a long-term reunion so much as a collective of Roger McGuinn, David Crosby, Chris Hillman, Gene Clark, and Michael Clarke getting together to perform new material. With CSNY on hiatus, the label thought we might work as a supergroup and, just maybe, we'd even recapture the magic of 1965 while reflecting the current times. It was decided that David Crosby would produce the album. I was still living in Colorado, so I traveled to LA to reunite with everyone to work up the songs for the record. It was good to make music with my old friends again after several years apart, and I think we all felt reinvigorated by the prospect of working together without all the baggage of our collective past.

As for the resulting album, which was simply titled *Byrds?* It was a noble concept, but a failed undertaking. The songs were lackluster, and we didn't have strong leadership to guide us. David's production left a lot to be desired, and he brought in an engineer who was incapable of getting a decent sound on us. The main problem, though, was that we were all so committed to keeping the peace and avoiding old interpersonal conflicts that the material really suffered. Instead of pushing or challenging our fellow band-mates, we were all tiptoeing around each other, carefully avoiding the possibility of reopening old war wounds. Bringing out the best in one another took a back seat to being polite. The two songs I contributed, "Things Will Be Better" and "Borrowing Time," ranked as lower-echelon mediocrity at best. We were probably all holding back our best material for our own personal projects, and it showed.

The only guy who really delivered the goods on *Byrds* was Gene Clark, who provided some redemption with his songs "Full Circle" and "Changing Heart," as well as his renditions of Neil Young's "See the Sky" and "Cowgirl in the Sand." But that wasn't enough to save us. The record came out in March of 1973. We weren't trying to recreate the past of eight years earlier, but the album didn't even *remotely* sound like The Byrds in their heyday, which only ended up disappointing the fans. Unsurprisingly, there wouldn't be any kind of tour or band reunion to accompany the failed experiment. In the end, it wound up being the final Byrds album.

While we were recording the *Byrds* album I stayed at the Chateau Marmont on the Sunset Strip. Gram Parsons was living there at the time, sharing a room with a filmmaker named Tony Foutz. The pair lived on the floor above me, so when I had a few friends over to celebrate my birthday on December 4, 1972, Gram showed up too. It was a welcome surprise. As I always say, you couldn't stay mad at Gram for too long. The night started out nicely enough but later turned ugly. Even though Gram had stopped using drugs, he was drinking heavily and could be a mean drunk.

The more Gram drank, the meaner he became, tossing out insulting off-handed remarks to those in the room. After working all those nights in the country/western bars around LA with The Golden State boys, I had little tolerance for obnoxious drunks. Things were getting very uncomfortable as the party became an awkward scene worthy of *Who's Afraid of Virginia Woolf.* As the evening wore down, everyone seemed to get up at the same time and make for the door, leaving me with a very inebriated

Gram Parsons. It seemed he'd driven them all off. Jesus said we're supposed to forgive others "seven times seventy" times, but after having forgiven Gram more times than I could count, I'd had it. I went into DEFCON 2 level "Hillman mad," which was a terrible place to be for both me and whoever happened to be on the receiving end of my vitriol. Verbally speaking, I let Gram have it with both barrels before picking him up with one hand by the back of his pants and the other on his collar, like you see in hundreds of old movies. It actually worked! I kicked open the door, threw him out, and slammed the door shut behind him.

As I began picking up bottles from around the room, I could hear Gram moaning outside my door. "You don't understand, Chris," he pleaded as he banged on the door. "We're brothers. I love you, man." I moved over to the door and looked through the peephole to see my old friend staggering outside. He looked like a broken man. "I love you too," I called through the door. "I won't ever stop caring about you, Gram, but it's over. We're done."

I didn't see Gram again until the following July when tragedy struck the Byrds family and the tight-knit Southern California music community. My dear friend Clarence White was struck and killed by a drunk driver one night as he was loading up his car after a show in Palmdale. I—along with just about everyone I knew in the music business, including Gram— attended Clarence's funeral at St. Mary's Catholic Church to pay respects to a brilliant musician and friend who had touched us all with his unique guitar style. I had known Clarence since we were both teenagers playing bluegrass, and one of my regrets in life is not having stayed in The Byrds longer to have gotten to work with him more than I did. It seemed so senseless that such a unique talent would be taken from us so suddenly.

After the service, we all went out to the gravesite for the burial. Gram and our old road manager Phil Kaufman, who was still working with Gram, were pretty drunk. Understandable, as we were all so upset about losing Clarence. In their altered state, Gram and Phil made a pact that day. Should anything happen to either of them, they agreed that, whichever of them died first, the other would take his friend's body out to Joshua Tree National Monument in the Mojave Desert and light the remains on fire.

Given that Gram was already on a destructive path, it was sad but not surprising when he died of a drug overdose two months later on September

19, 1973. He was twenty-six. Gram was at his old haunt, the Joshua Tree Inn when it happened. Just before his body was put on a plane in Los Angeles to be shipped back to his step-father in New Orleans, Kaufman and Gram's friend Michael Martin borrowed a hearse and convinced the airline personnel at LAX to turn the body over to them. They drove Gram's remains back out to Joshua Tree and, in an alcoholic stupor, honored the pact by dousing the open coffin with gasoline and throwing a match on the body. Eventually, the charred remains were found and the police figured out that Phil and Michael were responsible. Since there was no explicit law on the books about stealing a body, they were charged with stealing the casket, paid a fine, and that was it.

Gram's story has been told many times, so there's no need to go through all the details yet again. His legacy lives on with loyal fans around the world that still hold him close in their hearts. To many, he was a legend. To me, he was a musical partner and friend. Our few short years together were complicated and often frustrating, but despite his gregarious charm, I don't think Gram had many real friends. In fact, I believe there were only three people who really knew, loved and understood Gram Parsons: me, Emmylou Harris, and Rev. Jet Thomas, who was his student advisor at Harvard during Gram's brief time there. In the end, none of us could save him.

# CHAPTER THIRTEEN
# LONG, LONG TIME

S outher-Hillman-Furay. David Geffen, who was the head of Asylum Records, came up with the idea of putting J.D. Souther, Richie Furay, and me together in the hope of creating another "supergroup" in the vein of CSN. I knew Richie from Buffalo Springfield and his band Poco, and I knew J.D. from Longbranch Pennywhistle, his duo with Glenn Frey that was a precursor to The Eagles. We were all considered singer/songwriters, which was the musical identity the 1970s was built on. On paper, joining forces looked to be a sure-fire winner.

In reality, the chemistry between the three of us was a little slow taking hold at first. We cautiously approached one another like stray dogs, determining if it was safe to proceed. Rather than collaborating, we each brought our own songs to the table, and everyone's material had his own personal signature attached. As we began arranging the vocals, however, the music started to gel. I brought Paul Harris and Al Perkins into the group from Manassas, and Phil Kaufman even came back on board for a short time as our road manager—all veterans from my past campaigns. We still needed a good drummer. One day I happened to run across Jim Gordon, who had stepped in to play on *The Notorious Byrd Brothers* when Mike Clarke went AWOL. Jim was one of the greatest drummers in the business. He had just left working with Eric Clapton in Derek and the Dominos and was looking to do something new. He was also an in-demand studio session player, but even though making the decision to join a touring band would cut into his studio work, he decided to go with us. With everyone contributing his own songs, we had plenty of material to begin recording.

Richie Furay recommended we use Richie Podler and Bill Cooper to produce and engineer the album. They were well known, having recorded and produced Three Dog Night with great success. We cut the sessions at American Recorders in Los Angeles with Richie and Bill, two of the most eccentric but talented studio guys I had ever worked with; they knew how to make hit records. With a great group like Al Perkins on steel guitar and lead guitar, Paul Harris on keyboards, and the phenomenal Jim Gordon on drums, I was happy to go back to playing bass full time.

The first album, *The Souther-Hillman-Furay Band,* was released with an extensive tour of the US. It started off fine, but we then discovered that Jim Gordon had some serious mental problems. He could be violent and unpredictable. We had no idea about the extent of his issues when he was hired, but I started to figure it out after he attacked me one night in a Holiday Inn bar. He was sitting by himself a few feet away from where I was sitting with some of the other guys in the band. I'm not quite sure what triggered the outbreak, but all of a sudden, a glass came flying toward our table, shattering right in front of me. I had a fierce temper in those days, so this was like poking a tiger through the bars of a cage. I got up, brushed the glass off of my shirt, and walked over to where Jim was sitting. I slammed him in the nose with an open palm strike—an old street technique I had learned in my Kenpo karate days. Jim was a good 250 pounds and about six-foot-four inches tall, so I knew if he got loose, he would take me out. Thank God, he backed down.

That wasn't the only incident with Gordon. His behavior was getting scary. One night, we had to stop the car on the Pennsylvania Turnpike and let him out. Richie actually fired him on stage at one point. It was ten years later, in June of 1983, that Jim came home to his mother's house and proceeded to beat her with a hammer and then stab her to death. At his trial, he claimed to have been hearing voices. He was diagnosed with schizophrenia and sentenced to sixteen years to life for second-degree murder. This very talented man now sits in the psychiatric ward of the state prison in Vacaville, California, where he'll likely remain for the rest of his life. An unbelievable horror story.

Another change that had to be made came when I let Phil Kauffman go as our road manager. That's when Ronald Perfit came into the fold. Ronald had worked for Richie's band, Poco, and ended up helping SHF. We became fast friends, and he was the absolute best road manager I ever worked with. In fact, he worked with me all through the '70s and early '80s when he wasn't working for The Eagles, Jackson Browne, or Tracy Chapman. Ronald could keep everyone on the road laughing and relatively calm with his gift of making everything happen with less stress. His handwritten itineraries and daily memos were priceless. He was one of the brightest guys I have ever known and will always hold a special place in everyone's hearts. He passed away in 1997, and I still miss getting his famous crazy postcards.

There were several great relationships that came out of the Souther-Hillman-Furay period. The first SHF album reached number eleven on the *Billboard* album chart and earned Gold certification. We sang and played well, but, ultimately, we never fully came together in the way I'd hoped. It was as if we were three separate singer/songwriters performing with a backup band rather than functioning as a fully cohesive group. We lacked the substance and depth that The Byrds had, and somehow it just never felt "right" musically.

In August of 1974, SHF played a show at the Santa Monica Civic Auditorium, where I reconnected with someone very special. I first met Connie Pappas in December of 1968 when I was hanging out with Michael Clarke at the Troubadour. Mike turned to me and said, "Look who's coming through the front door; it's the Pappas sisters, Reneé and Connie." I told him I didn't really know them, but that I'd sure like to meet Connie. I'd had my eye on her since seeing her at the Golden Bear, where she worked part time in the office for her cousin, George, who owned the club. Mike said, "I'll get them to come over." He introduced us, and we talked for a few minutes before the girls headed into the main room to hear whoever was performing there that night. Connie was so beautiful, and after our brief conversation at the Troubadour, I realized that not only was she beautiful, she was very intelligent. What a refreshing concept after some of the women I had been out with the past few years!

The next day, I called Reneé and asked her if I could take Connie out. "That's totally up to her," Reneé said. "I suggest you give her a call at Sunset Sound where she works." I did, and we went out for our first date. We continued to see one another other, and we had so much fun together whatever we were doing. One time we drove out to Joshua Tree—with my two dogs Ned and Sophie along for the ride—just to watch the sun come up. Thank God, she loved dogs too. Connie was even there with me for the infamous Burrito Barn Dance on the A&M Records lot. My previous dating habits bordered on major promiscuity, but with Connie, it was as if we were always on an innocent high school date every night. Prior to that 1974 show at the Civic, the last time I saw Connie was when she drove me to Union Station for the infamous Flying Burrito Brothers train tour. We exchanged postcards and letters for months, but we never got back together after that. Our lives were going in different directions.

It was five years later when I saw her again. Connie was backstage at that concert, and oh my God, she looked beautiful. In the meantime, she'd risen up the ranks to become the vice president of a successful international music management company and had been invited to the show by some of the executives at Elektra/Asylum Records. It seemed like we talked forever that night. What she did for a living wasn't my concern, other than being very proud of all she had accomplished in those five years. My concern was hoping she would forgive me for ending our relationship so abruptly. Unfortunately for me, Connie would spend the next several months and virtually the entire next year traveling around the world for her job. This was before cell phones, so our communication was primarily leaving messages on one another's answering machines. I couldn't stop thinking about her, but it just wasn't yet possible to really establish a long-term relationship. The timing was not in our favor.

From mid-January to the end of February 1975, SHF went through the motions of recording a lackluster second album, appropriately titled *Trouble in Paradise*. Since Richie and I both lived in Colorado, we decided to record at the Caribou Ranch, which was located up in the mountains above Boulder.

(L) A&M Records co-founder Jerry Moss sits in on a Flying Burrito Brothers publicitity shot in 1969. (L-R) Chris Ethridge, Sneaky Pete Kleinow, me, Jerry, and Gram Parsons (Photo by Jim McCrary). (R) A Flying Burrito Brothers' poker game with Mike (left) and Gram (right) on the Super Chief to Chicago during the infamous train tour, 1969. (Photo by Michael Vosse)

My Burrito Manor roommates, Topanga Canyon, 1969: Mike on the left and Gram on the right. (Photo by Jim McCrary)

Onstage with Sneaky Pete at the Fillmore Auditorium in San Francisco, 1969. (Hillman Archives)

The original lineup of The Flying Burrito Brothers, backstage at the Hollywood Palladium, 1969: (L-R) Chris, me, Gram, Sneaky, and Mike with a newly-casted broken ankle. (Getty Images)

Gram and me trying to get through our performance at Altamont Speedway in December of 1969 as violence explodes around us. (Getty Images)

The Flying Burrito Brothers, post Gram: (L-R) Bernie Leadon, Sneaky Pete Kleinow, Rick Roberts, me, and Mike Clark. This was shot at the A&M Records compound, formerly The Charlie Chaplin Studios. We are on what was known as the "backlot." (Photo by Jim McCrary, Getty Images)

Manassas rehearsal in Elstead, Surrey. (L-R) Al Perkins, me, Stephen's sister Taicita, Stephen, and Bernie Leadon, who came to visit us from London. Bernie had been mixing the Eagles first album with Glyn Johns. (Getty Images)

Manassas at Stephen Stills' house in Nederland, Colorado, 1972: (L-R) Dallas Taylor, Fuzzy Samuel, Stephen, Joe Lala holding the photo shoot refreshments, me (with epic hair), Paul Harris, and Al Perkins. Such a good band! (Hillman Archives)

(L) Happy guys, Manassas! Enjoying the encore with Joe Lala and Stephen. (Photograph by Phillip Rauls)
(R) On stage with Stephen Stills and Manassas in 1973, playing my beautiful Lloyd Loar
mandolin that Stephen gave me a year earlier. (Photo by Bob Jenkins, Hillman Archives)

Manassas at the Hollywood Bowl, July 16, 1972. (L-R) Byron Berline sitting in with us,
Dallas Taylor, Al Perkins, me, Fuzzy Samuel, and Stephen. (Photo by Henry Diltz)

The Souther-Hillman-Furay Band, taking a break during the recording of our first album for Asylum Records: (L-R) Al Perkins, Jim Gordon, J.D. Souther, me, Richie Furay, and Paul Harris. (Photo by Henry Diltz)

Chris, Richie, and J.D. Trouble in paradise. It looked so good on paper! (Photo by Henry Diltz)

McGuinn, Clark and Hillman in front of Gene's fabulous Cadillac convertible, 1978. (Photo by Henry Diltz)

Performing with Gene and Roger as McGuinn, Clark and Hillman in Minneapolis, Minnesota, Summer, 1979. (Photo by Brad Skramstad)

(L) The day that changed my life forever was the day I married my beautiful Connie.
(R) Some of our wonderful friends enjoying the reception with us: (L-R) Stephen Stills,
Jerry Wexler, me, Connie, Roger McGuinn, and Joe Lala (Photos by Henry Diltz)

I had so much fun playing in our bluegrass group Ever Call Ready: (L-R) Bernie Leadon, me, Al
Perkins, David Mansfield, and Jerry Scheff, Sacramento, California, 1985. (Photo by Kent Lacin)

Early photo of The Desert Rose Band in front of the Palomino night club in North Hollywood, California: (L-R) Jay Dee Maness, Herb Pedersen, me, John Jorgenson, Bill Bryson, and Steve Duncan. (Photo by Jay Dusard, Hillman Archives)

(L) Backstage at the Grand Ole Opry with my dear friend Skeeter Davis. We had a good laugh over my previous visit with The Byrds in 1968. (Grand Ole Opry Archives). (R) At the BMI Country Music Awards in Nashville, October 1, 1991: (L-R) Steve Hill, me, BMI President Frances Preston and Vice President Roger Sovine. It was always exciting when Steve and I were recognized for our songwriting. This time, it was for "In Another Lifetime." (Hillman Archives)

I loved singing with Emmylou Harris and Vern Gosdin on The Nashville Network's *American Music Shop*. (Hillman Archives)

(L) Me and Bill. In 1989, *Rolling Stone* magazine contacted me to be part of an article focusing on artists and their mentors. I chose Bill Monroe, who showed up to the photo shoot right on time, looking sharp. We started playing our mandolins and singing his song "The Old Crossroads." When I forgot the lyric in the second verse, Bill gave me a good smack on the leg to jog my memory. What a day, and what a great music lesson from one of my all-time heroes. (Glenn Hall Photography). (R) Hot night at the Roxy Theatre in Los Angeles, after a Desert Rose Band show: (L-R) Lyle Lovett, Stephen Stills, the fashionable Elton "Tex" John (seated), and the amazing Bernie Taupin visiting with me backstage. (Hillman Archives)

Buck Owens visiting with The Desert Rose Band after sound check at the Academy of Country Music Awards in Los Angeles. We loved having Buck in our corner! (Hillman Archives)

Dwight Yoakam put together an amazing tribute to Buck Owens for the Academy of Country Music Awards. (L-R) Travis Barker of Blink-182 on drums, me, Dwight, Brad Paisley. Not shown: Tom Brumley on steel guitar, Billy Gibbons of ZZ Top on guitar, and Buck's son Buddy Alan. What a great band. (Getty Images)

The Roy Orbison Concert to Benefit the Homeless, February of 1990 at the Universal Amphitheatre in Los Angeles. Roger, David, and I had not been on stage with Bob Dylan since Ciros in 1965. (Photo by Kevin Mazur, Getty Images)

Backstage at the Roy Orbison concert: (L-R) Roger and Camilla, Jan and David, Connie and me. (Photo by Kevin Mazur, Hillman Archives)

The Rock & Roll Hall of Fame induction ceremony at the Waldorf Astoria
in New York City, 1991. It was the last time we were all together.
(Photo by Larry Busacca, Courtesy of the Rock and Roll Hall of Fame and Museum)

(L) Herb and I have known each other since 1963 and have been singing together for over
fifty years. He is a big part of my musical life and is like a brother to me. Here we are
warming up before our live recording at Edwards Barn. (Photo by Zarek). (R) Playing together
well over twenty-five years with two of my favorite people: Multi-instrumentalist John
Jorgenson (left) and super vocalist Herb Pedersen. (Photo by Joe Atlas Photography)

*Bidin' My Time* sessions at The Clubhouse, January, 2017. Herb Pedersen and John Jorgenson prepare for the track while Tom Petty and I discuss where we're going with the arrangement. (Photo by Josh Jové)

The *Bidin' My Time* sessions at Tom's Studio, January, 2017. Herb prepares David Crosby for his vocal overdub while Tom and I ponder the mysteries of the music business. (Photo by Josh Jové)

Me and Roger McGuinn backstage at the Ryman Auditorium in Nashville, 2018 with Marty Stuart and his Fabulous Superlatives during the Sweetheart of the Rodeo 50th Anniversary Tour: (L-R) Marty, me, Chris Scruggs, Roger, Harry Stinson, and Kenny Vaughan. (Photo by Alysse Gafkjen)

(L) Me checking out Marty Stuart's incredible guitar playing on Clarence White's B Bender Telecaster, July 24, 2018, at the Theatre at Ace Hotel in Los Angeles. (Getty Images). (R) Two Byrds in flight again: Me and Roger on the Sweetheart of the Rodeo 50th Anniversary Tour, September 24, 2018, Town Hall, New York City. (Photo by Jeremy Gordon)

My beautiful family—Connie, Catherine, and Nicky—near our home in Ojai, California, in October of 1993. (Photo by Jody Q. Kasch, Hillman Archives)

We were fortunate to get well-known and respected producer Tom Dowd to produce the record. Caribou was a wonderful recording environment, perfectly suited for many of the top rock acts of the time. We began rehearsing, but we didn't have Jim Gordon on board with us. Jim was such a good drummer that we'd all been spoiled while working on the first album. The drummer we used was someone that J.D. met and hired on the spot. Unfortunately, the man couldn't lock in, and it was very difficult to capture the groove that we had with Jim.

The album came out in the spring and sounded like an attempt to hit all the required chapters you would find in a Rock Music 101 course. Our manager, Ron Stone, convinced the powers that be at Asylum that we were set for an extensive concert tour in the summer so that the label would promote the album. But there were never any dates booked, as he knew. We all knew. It was the end of SHF. We slowly walked off into the sunset after the last session, remaining friends, but never recording together again. Since we'd all been signed to Asylum Records as individuals, the door was open for each of us to record a solo album.

When I first started to write my own songs I, like many other musicians, was ignorant about the business and the value of owning music publishing rights. Tickson Music, during the Byrds era, and then Irving Music, during the Burrito era when I was signed to A&M Records, were the companies that controlled half of the ownership of my songs. Having written songs with Stephen while in Manassas, I then signed with his company, Gold Hill Music. I just wasn't very business savvy about that kind of thing. After Rosalie Morton tried to tell me not to give up my publishing on that fateful day in the A&M offices in 1968, you would have thought I would have learned something. Finally, I figured it out. I called Stills up one day and explained that I felt it was time for me to have my own publishing company. Stephen was so gracious and encouraged me to do it. That's when I started my own company, Bar None Music. Years later, Stephen generously gave me back all the publishing on the songs he had under Gold Hill Music—a truly honest guy.

Though I'd moved to Colorado to work with Manassas in 1972, I continued to live there after the band broke up and stayed on through the Souther-Hillman-Furay years. The Colorado period was not a bright time in my life. I was in a very dark place, and I knew I had to get my life back on track. I was preparing for my first solo record, which was a new experience after having always been a team player in a band. I had written some good songs and believed it was finally my time to step out. I must admit I was feeling a bit apprehensive and not quite sure of myself, but this time I met the challenge head on.

There were a few bumps in the road on the way there. The first recording session was a train wreck—not because of the players on the date, but because of the producer I'd hired to do the album. He was a gentleman from Nashville who had produced Bob Dylan and Johnny Cash, so I thought he'd be the perfect guy to work with. We just didn't communicate well, and it bordered on a bad nightmare from day one in the studio. I needed someone I could relate to who understood what I was trying to accomplish. A good producer, like a good film director, has to wear many hats: big brother figure, amateur psychologist, pal, and, most importantly, someone who knows how to use every trick to get the best performance out of the artist. I was still learning to use my voice—to sing with feeling, commitment, and phrasing—and I needed patient direction from the guy in the booth. The person I hired didn't have a clue, and I can't even imagine how he managed to have success with Dylan and Cash. When I tried to discuss my concerns he insistently reminded me of who he was and what he'd accomplished in the music business. Either that or he'd respond with some inane remark about everybody on the session being laid back and drinking organic apple juice. He actually said that to me. I thought, "Who *is* this guy? This isn't Woodstock!" We were recording in Sausalito, and maybe that was part of the problem. I was seeking focus and direction, not mellow vibes.

Feeling completely lost I turned to my old friend Stephen Stills. I called him up and told him what was going on. "Get rid of this guy," he said. "Let's get Ron and Howard Albert to fly out and produce your record." It wasn't an easy task, but I let the man from Nashville go. Afterward, I flew down to LA and met up with the Albert Brothers. Ron and Howard, knowing me as they did, took charge and made everything easy. They booked a good studio, Cherokee Recorders in Hollywood, and we all decided together on what players to use on the tracks. A lot of old friends worked on those sessions, which would become the *Slippn' Away* album: Herb Pedersen, Bernie Leadon, Tim Schmit, Al Perkins, Paul Harris, Joe Lala, Jim Gordon, Russ Kunkel, Lee Sklar, Rick Roberts, Donald "Duck" Dunn, Mark Volman and Howard Kaylan from The Turtles, and one of my true guitar heroes, Steve Cropper. It was a remarkable cast that assembled for my first solo effort, and, because Ronnie and Howard were such great producers, the whole project came together quickly and smoothly.

With the release of *Slippin' Away,* it was time to put together a band to go out and promote the new record. I used some players from the Boulder area, including my old pal Rick Roberts from the Burritos, along with Jock Bartley and Mark Andes. Jock was an extremely talented lead guitarist, and Mark Andes had already found success with the bands Spirit and Jo Jo Gunne. These guys were great players, and I even produced a demo of their own group, which was called Firefall. They ended up joining forces with our old brother Michael Clarke, landing a recording contract with Atlantic Records, and going on to achieve great success in the late 1970s with songs like "You Are the Woman" and "Just Remember I Love You."

I was thrilled for the Firefall guys, but as they were concentrating on their own career, I had to find a band. I recruited some new guys, including Skip Edwards on steel guitar and keyboards, Al Staehely on bass, Bernie Leadon's close friend John Brennan on lead guitar, and, for a while, Al Garth, Merle Brigante, and Larry Sims from the Loggins and Messina Band. All these guys were excellent players.

In the spring of 1977 The Chris Hillman Band, as we were called, was booked for a triple-bill European tour alongside Roger McGuinn's group, Thunderbyrd, and Gene Clark's K.C. Southern Band. What seemed like a great plan ended in disaster. After two sold-out performances at the Hammersmith Odeon in London, the tour began to fall apart. The promoter failed to pay all three bands, as well as the travel agents representing the tour. My attorney advised me that the promoter's company was in breach of contract and that I should consider leaving the tour. I gave the promoter thirty-six hours to make good on the deal and warned Gene and Roger that the arrangement was taking a turn for the worse. The time limit expired, and I made plans to depart. Roger and Gene decided to stay, playing two more shows without getting paid.

That reunion with Roger and Gene was short-lived. That version of The Chris Hillman Band would be short-lived as well. We toured around the country with enough success to warrant another album for Asylum Records. I began work on another solo record, using my live band in the studio, but this time with a different producer. It was clearly another case of the second album jinx. *Clear Sailin'* came out in 1977, but the songs were weak, and it didn't have the Albert Brothers' magic touch. I had lost my momentum somewhere along the way and was back to spinning my wheels. I was still playing shows but having some minor problems with the band members, so I decided it would be best if we all went our separate ways.

There was something about the decade of the 1970s that was clouded by a spirit of misery and death. Of course, we'd lost Clarence. Then we'd lost Gram, who got trapped in the quicksand of excess and was ultimately overcome by his personal demons. It's hard to explain, but there was something about that ten-year span that affected so many of us. There was a darkness and oppressiveness that seemed to be nipping at our heels. I was slowly realizing that I couldn't outrun or bury my own pain. My long-held internal anger was reaching its highest point as my father's suicide continued to haunt me. Controlling my temper would prove challenging as the '70s rolled by. At the same time, I was making personal choices that contributed to my restlessness and unhappiness. So much of that self-destructiveness, I now realize, was rooted in anger. I think the only reason I survived a decade that many others didn't was because of the wisdom and guidance my parents instilled in me during the first twelve years of my life. They gave me values, morals, and a sense of responsibility that kept me from becoming another statistic in those days. It was becoming increasingly obvious to me that I needed to change.

An important part of that realization was Connie, who had walked back into my life when I was very near the breaking point. By 1976, her travel schedule had settled down, and we were able to spend more time together as she guided me into a positive, loving place that was unlike anything I'd felt since before my father's death in 1961. By that point, I had sold my place in Boulder and purchased a small house in the Birdrock neighborhood of La Jolla, California. I decided to take a short hiatus from recording and touring, though I was still writing every morning. And I was back into surfing too. I missed the ocean while living in Colorado. Anyone who grew up near the Pacific Ocean can relate to the power of the ocean that was luring me back. My new house was blocks from Tourmaline Beach, a perfect point break to ride. I filled my time living easy by the ocean, reading, coming up with songs, and, most importantly, going up to Los Angeles to visit Connie on the weekends. We were madly in love, and her insight and advice were what kept me going.

As I was seeking clarity on what to do next, another opportunity arose with Roger McGuinn and Gene Clark. Roger was represented by Ron Rainey, who had been booking shows for Roger and Gene as an acoustic duo. In early 1978, Ron was putting together a solo deal for Roger at Capitol Records. The label offered more money when there was talk of adding Gene to the mix. Then, through Ron's business contact with Connie, he tried to recruit me into the deal as well. At first I wasn't interested, but with Capitol salivating about signing three former Byrds they put a strong offer on the table that began to sound attractive. Ultimately, we signed a three-album contract and made plans to record in the fall. That gave us time to do a month-long tour of Australia and New Zealand with some scattered shows around the States.

I convinced Roger and Gene to go to Miami, Florida, and work with Ron and Howard Albert at Criteria Studios. I'd loved working with those guys during the Manassas sessions and my first solo album, so I knew they'd be the right partners to help with the album that would become *McGuinn, Clark & Hillman*. All three of us were prepared and had some great songs. Roger brought in a drummer he'd been working with named Greg Thomas, who turned out to be one of my favorite drummers of all time. Joe Lala played percussion; Roger was on six- and twelve-string electric guitar; I played bass; and the Albert brothers recommended a lead guitarist named John Sambataro who turned out to be a welcome addition to the session band, and then the touring band with McGuinn, Clark & Hillman. With strong material, proper rehearsal, and a shared focus, we were prepared. This was not going to be a repeat of the Byrds reunion debacle of a few years prior.

Following the Manassas game plan, we leased a big house on Pine Tree Drive in Miami, with the plan of spending two weeks at Criteria and then finishing up the sessions in Los Angeles. With the Albert Brothers guiding us, we made a great album and had a top-twenty chart single with Roger's song "Don't You Write Her Off." We hit the road, and it all worked well. The band was tight, and the shows were consistent. For some unexplained reason we did not call it The Byrds, maybe because David and Michael were not involved. It was a huge step forward for Roger, Gene, and me. We had all survived some major low periods in the '70s to emerge professionally refreshed and grateful for another chance.

Roger had met and married a lovely woman, Camilla Sproul, in the spring of 1978, both of them making a commitment to Jesus Christ and pursuing a life of faith. Their love and their spiritual values were another marker on my path of beginning to refocus on what really mattered. I knew that Connie coming back into my life was divine intervention, and I was certain we were meant to share the rest of our lives together. It was a form of pure love unlike anything I had ever experienced before. We were married in October of 1979, in Los Angeles with our dear friend Rev. Jet Thomas officiating. Roger serenaded us with a beautiful acoustic version of "Turn! Turn! Turn!" Many of my closest and dearest friends, and our extended families, came to celebrate that special day with us over forty years ago.

Real life, however, is rarely a linear story of triumph, and there continued to be challenges. As McGuinn, Clark, and I started to regain our notoriety in the music business, Gene began to struggle with his own personal demons once again. He was focused and singing so beautifully during the recording of the first album. He had contributed some wonderful new songs, and the three of us were having a great time after dealing with obstacles over the last few years. Like Gram, Gene unfortunately fell under the spell of alcohol and drugs after the album was released, which only intensified his personal issues. He was such a gifted and talented singer and writer that it almost made me wonder if that old myth of madness feeding the creative spirit was actually true. I've never known anyone like Gene Clark, who was so poetic and insightful in his writing, yet hardly ever read a book. He possessed a gift, being able to grab the most beautiful passages and rhyming sequences right out of the air. But, sadly, we began to lose him to that familiar dark force that had seduced so many friends.

It was becoming so predictable, like a bad movie that keeps playing over and over: the band forms, everyone is excited, and, with the right amount of luck and talent, has a couple of hits and touring success. Then it proceeds to splinter, usually due to outside negative influences. My simplistic analogy of a musical group is that it's like five individuals, each holding a paintbrush and each working together to paint the Mona Lisa's smile. When it works it's spectacular, but when one or two drop the brush, it's the end. Roger and I tried to keep the momentum going with our MCH band pals Johnny and Greg, but it was like were headed down the same road with Gene that we'd already traveled back in 1966. We did another album called *City,* but then Gene was gone, and Roger and I were left, once again, attempting to hold a crumbling entity together.

Even though our second album was not as sparkling as our first, Capitol wanted one more, per our contractual obligation. Connie's sister Reneé was married to producer and legendary Atlantic Records executive Jerry Wexler, who had been producing R&B artists like Aretha Franklin, Ray Charles, and LaVern Baker since the 1950s. We asked Jerry if he would be interested in working with Roger and me, and he agreed to do it if we would record in Muscle Shoals, Alabama. Roger and I started writing together every night, preparing for this next adventure.

Jerry brought in Barry Becket to assist. Both were brilliant producers and record men, but neither of them had a clue what McGuinn and I were all about. Jerry kept trying to turn us into Sam and Dave. He even had me sing a version of Graham Parker's "Soul Shoes" in a Mick Jagger style, which was totally out of character for this country and bluegrass guy. It was, by far, one of the strangest records I've ever been involved with. There were a couple of decent songs from the sessions, including "Turn Your Radio On/Songbyrd's Flight," which Roger and I wrote together. We wrote another one during that period called "Here She Comes Again" that we didn't get a chance to record until thirty years later on my solo album *Bidin' My Time.*

By the time we finished in Muscle Shoals, McGuinn-Hillman was staggering on the ropes. Capitol refused to release the record at first, and who could blame them? It was not at all cohesive or anywhere near an accurate representation of who we were. They were finally pressured into putting out the album, but by that time we were practically down for the count, musically speaking. On a personal level, the real fighting was just beginning.

We were on a tour of the East Coast to promote McGuinn-Hillman with new band members, including my dear friend Al Perkins, who'd worked with me in The Flying Burrito Brothers, Manassas, and many other projects. But the new blood wasn't enough to reinvigorate us after a bad album experience. Things were tense between me and Roger. We were both feeling the frustration, and we were struggling with a lack of direction. The record company was barely going through the motions, and I was always on the brink of a terminal meltdown.

One night, we were booked into the Bottom Line in Greenwich Village. After our first show, I came off the stage only to be cornered by a drunk promotion man from Capitol Records. I repeatedly told him to wait just a moment until I had time to change in my dressing room, but he kept pushing, shoving, and interrupting. I didn't have a lot of tolerance for that kind of behavior, so, in a "Sinatra moment," I hauled off and punched him. Our road manager, who was a large man, grabbed me from behind and pulled me into the dressing room. Bright and early the next morning, as we were leaving for JFK airport, my attorney phoned to tell me that I was off Capitol Records. I'd been dropped from the label because, as the Capitol legal affairs executive explained to my attorney, "Your client's pugilistic tendencies and general attitude are no longer welcome here."

It was a long plane ride back to Los Angeles. What happened at the Bottom Line wasn't the first time. Poor Roger must have witnessed three or four of my fights with various people during the MCH era. I wasn't a tough guy by any means, and I was lucky nobody killed me during one of my meltdowns. Gene and I came close to blows a few times, and I would have probably ended up on the canvas if the strong Missouri farm boy's drug use hadn't messed him up pretty bad by that time. When we arrived at LAX, Roger turned to me and said, "Chris, I don't want to work with you anymore." Short and to the point. MCH was done, and now McGuinn-Hillman was dead and buried with it. Looking back, I don't blame Roger one bit. I wouldn't want to work with me either. It was getting to the point where I should have added "extremely volatile and unpredictable" to my resume. I would have never been able to explain it at the time, but the truth was I was angry at my dad for leaving us. Those feelings had never been dealt with, which only allowed them to grow. It would take a little more time before I was able to completely forgive him. And myself.

# CHAPTER FOURTEEN
# DESERT ROSE

===

Within the last six months of the MCH band, Connie and I had sold our homes—mine in La Jolla and hers in Los Angeles—to buy a house on the beach in Ventura. It was our first home together, and we were a happy couple. I was putting the nightmare of my outburst in New York behind me and trying to get myself sorted out. Just when things were looking up, however, I received notification of a lawsuit from the English promoter who put together that disastrous English tour I'd quit in early 1977 after he failed to pay us. Though I'd given him thirty-six hours to rectify the situation at the time, he failed to do so, and that's when I walked away. Though Roger and Gene were part of the equation, for some reason I was the guy who was held responsible for the collapse of the tour. In addition to the lawsuit from the crooked promoter, there were some other unresolved legal issues that all seemed to land on me at once. I was scared until Connie said to me one night, "If we have to sell this house and move into a studio apartment for a while, that's fine. We'll still be together." That was all I needed to hear. I knew then that God had brought this beautiful woman into my life.

The two of us flew to London together for the trial at the Queen's Bench Division of the High Court. The proceedings lasted three days, but I was fully exonerated of all the charges against me. Great! I was proven innocent at a cost of $75,000 in travel and legal fees. But my wife was by my side through it all. Another reminder of what's really important and how blessed I was.

Shortly before the trip to London, I found out that Sugar Hill Records, a small independent label in North Carolina, was planning to re-release the album I recorded with the Gosdin Brothers and Don Parmley back in 1963. Though we never landed a record deal at the time, Jim Dickson released it on a label called Together Records in the 1970s after I'd had some success. It even included some dreadful liner notes supposedly written by me that I didn't write. For some reason he put it out under the name The Hillmen rather than The Golden State Boys, which was our actual name, but then it disappeared. Despite those irritations, the music was good, so it was exciting news to find out it would get a better release. I assumed the album had vanished forever. Dickson, who owned the masters, was in negotiations with Barry Poss, the head of the label. I met Barry through a phone call, we discussed the album's release, and he asked if I would write the liner notes—for real this time. I agreed and then asked him if he had any interest in me recording a solo album. He was more than interested, and we began planning a record for Sugar Hill.

Sugar Hill was what you would call a boutique label by today's standards. It was primarily geared toward folk and bluegrass, which was perfect for me. I had already decided to rediscover what really got me involved in music and that it was time for me to play acoustic guitar and mandolin again. I asked Al Perkins if he was interested in playing together as a duo, with me on vocals, mandolin, and guitar, and Al on dobro, vocals and guitar. We began touring throughout the US and Canada, and we sounded good. Al was a pleasure to work with on the road and in the studio. He was and is a very patient and loving man, and he had such a calming effect on me. Finally, I had found my passion again by going back to my roots in folk and bluegrass. Musically, it was the happiest, most comfortable, and most motivated I'd felt in years.

When it was time to make the record, I brought in all my old pals again. In addition to Al, the festivities were joined by Herb Pedersen, Kenny Wertz, Byron Berline, Emory Gordy, and Bernie Leadon. We called the album *Morning Sky* after a Dan Fogelberg song and recorded some great tunes by John Prine, Bob Dylan, and Kris Kristofferson, as well as J.D. Souther's great song "Mexico" that we'd recorded on the second SHF album, and Jerry Garcia's "Ripple," a Grateful Dead favorite. My old friend Henry Diltz shot a great image of me holding my Lloyd Loar mandolin with my arm around my sweet Springer Spaniel, Heather, that was used on the back cover. The album was a true labor of love, recorded with a budget in the neighborhood of only $6,000. It was 1982, but revisiting my early influences helped me take a major step forward as I reconnected with the music that first ignited my passion in 1960.

For me, to perform acoustically without a full electric band was singing and playing at its purest essence. Playing with Al helped me reclaim the acoustic dynamics I'd lost during my "band years." After the album was released, Al and I added Bernie Leadon and the great bassist Jerry Scheff to complete the first acoustic quartet version of The Chris Hillman Band. We were good. *Very* good. Bernie, Al, and I had a blast trading off solos while Jerry, still one of the finest musicians I've had the pleasure of playing with, made it all swing. Bernie had parted company with The Eagles and, like me, was having a lot of fun playing the music we both grew up with.

*Morning Sky* did well enough around the States, Canada, and Europe to bring in some incredible festival and theater bookings. I was pleased, and Sugar Hill was pleased. The beautiful part of my experience with the label was my close relationship with Barry Poss. Here was a man of honesty and integrity in the record business. What a refreshing concept! Sugar Hill recording contracts were a total of two pages with no options or restrictive clauses. They could only offer a small budget, but they paid a fair royalty return.

When Sugar Hill wanted to do a second album, I asked Al Perkins to produce it. Even though I had fully immersed myself back into acoustic music, I really wanted to explore doing a traditional country record with an electric backing band, but with material I would be able to duplicate with the acoustic band during the live shows. We got the greatest musicians to record the tracks for the album that would become *Desert Rose,* including the alumni of Elvis Presley's Las Vegas band: Jerry Scheff on bass, Ron Tutt on drums, Glen D. Hardin on piano, and James Burton on lead guitar. We also recruited guitarist Bob Warford, Jay Dee Maness on steel guitar, and Ray Park and Byron Berline, who came in to play some fiddle parts. Al played the dobro, and Herb added his acoustic guitar and vocals. I wanted to keep the vocals in two parts, lead and tenor, like the old brother duets, such as the Wilburns, the Everlys, and the Louvins. Herb was the perfect duet partner and totally understood what I wanted to do. We recorded some of my favorite country classics like "Why You Been Gone So Long," The Wilburn Brothers' "Somebody's Back in Town," and The Louvin Brothers' "I Can't Keep You in Love with Me." All those afternoons after school at Bill Smith's house and my time playing on *The Cal Worthington Show* had paid off. I think we really captured the energy of West Coast country music on *Desert Rose*. The players and Al's production were far more then I probably deserved.

The *Desert Rose* album created a number of new opportunities, but it was nothing compared to the blessing Connie and I would receive on that wonderful morning in the fall of 1983 when our daughter Catherine was born. This beautiful little girl who entered my life became the center of my world. Holding her in my arms was an indescribable feeling of pure love. With a renewed musical passion and a sweet young family, I felt like the luckiest man alive. This was what life was supposed to be—the pure blessing of God's grace. The blinders were off, the light was shining brightly, and nothing seemed impossible anymore. It was a spiritual reawakening.

Not only did I have Al Perkins to thank for helping me recapture my musical passion, but he was also a true friend and a spiritual guide. The 1970s could have easily been my swan song with the bad choices I was making. I knew I was headed down a dead-end road, but I could almost hear a small voice in my heart crying out for mercy. Al was a devout evangelical Christian who remained ever-faithful no matter what mischief was going on around him in The Flying Burrito Brothers and Manassas. He and I had discussed the Christian faith on several occasions, but it all became very real in 1973 during a rough plane ride with Manassas. Al and I were sitting next to one another, and I was feeling helpless and scared as the plane bounced and bobbed wildly. On that flight I reached out to God and, with Al's help, I prayed and accepted Jesus Christ into my life. It was one of those moments they sometimes call a "foxhole conversion." There's danger all around, and you promise God your heart and soul in a moment of fear. Then, when the threat is gone, you forget all about it. I may have abandoned God the next morning after that frightening plane ride, but God never abandoned me.

When SHF was recording our second album at Caribou Ranch in Colorado, Richie Furay was dealing with some personal issues in his life and began exploring the Christian faith. There was a dining room at the studio with a long, heavy wooden table where everyone would congregate for meals. One night, Richie was having a hard time trying to understand Al, who was ministering to him about Jesus. At the other end of the table, Souther was holding court with a couple of our road crew guys, where I joined them. Souther had a great sense of humor—very dry, very witty. When he looked over at me, he said, "Want to join our new club?"

I said, "What's the name of this club?"

J.D. replied, "Why, it's the Heathen Defense League, or HDL for short." I couldn't help but laugh. It was typical Souther humor—funny, but not mean-spirited against Al or Richie.

After that foxhole conversion moment on the plane, there were some poor lifestyle choices, self-destructive behaviors, and a few angry outbursts, but over the next ten years, thanks to the miracle of becoming a father and guidance from Al, I found my way back to God and slowly worked my way out of the Heathen Defense League. Accepting Jesus Christ into your life is not an easy ride because the evil one is always there to take you down a different path, but this time I was determined to stay committed.

During that time Al introduced me to a man named Steve Hill who lived near me in Ventura. Steve was a musician and a devout Christian. Within a few days of meeting each other, Steve and I wrote a song together called "Love Reunited." It was the bridge to a long-lasting bond between the two of us. I later found out that Steve was also an ordained evangelical minister who held Sunday services in Oxnard Shores. He baptized me in the Pacific Ocean in late 1984, further sealing my renewed commitment to Christ.

Not only were Al, Bernie Leadon, and Jerry Scheff my musical brothers in my acoustic quartet during the 1980s, they were also all Christians. We joined forces with another fine musician—fiddle, mandolin, and guitar player David Mansfield—to record a gospel album under the name Ever Call Ready for a Christian record label called Maranatha. We stayed within a bluegrass-influenced gospel style, recording mostly older songs right out of a Baptist hymnal—with the exception of one, "Panhandle Rag," an old Texas swing song. We had so much fun playing it in the studio, we decided to include it on the album. That record is right up there with some of my favorite earlier efforts, and I loved the spiritual and musical bond I shared with those guys.

In addition to the Ever Call Ready album, we continued to tour as an acoustic quartet. When Jerry decided to change course, I met and hired a wonderful singer and bassist named Bill Bryson. Our revised quartet continued playing dates around the US and Europe. We made a lot of great memories together with that lineup, including a European tour that took us to Bergen, Norway. The Norwegian promoter had a small boat and graciously invited us out fishing on our day off. Bernie, Bill, and I signed on for the voyage. Bergen is located right on the fjords and may have been one of the ports the vikings sailed out of on their way down the coast to raid monasteries in England, Scotland, and Ireland. It was an amazing sight, looking back on those long, sloping mountains rolling into the North Sea as we set sail at sunrise. Little did we know our goal was going to be catching the elusive killer squid, a Norwegian delicacy. We hit the jackpot and soon began hauling in squid on grappling hooks faster than you could recite the first line of *Moby Dick*. Bryson proved to be the master squid hunter, with me and Bernie taking a close second.

Following our European adventure, upon arriving back in the States, Bernie was ready to move off in another direction. We parted ways on great terms. Here was a guy I had known since he was in high school when he took over for Kenny Wertz on banjo in the Squirrel Barkers. Bernie was like my little brother, and we remain good friends to this day. I knew I was going to miss Bernie in the acoustic group, but I also knew I wanted to continue with that kind of lineup. I would need an equally adept musician, and I certainly found him. Bill Bryson had already been telling me about this young guy around town named John Jorgenson. Bill couldn't say enough about John's talent, and he brought John by one day to meet me. After playing a few songs, I knew I had found the perfect guy. John was beyond incredible on guitar and mandolin and—I was later to learn—also a phenomenal electric guitarist. Actually, he was a master of just about anything with strings, including the piano. John had graduated from the University of Redlands as a woodwind performance major. I had never worked with a genuine "schooled musician" before, other than on an occasional recording session. I soon discovered there was nothing different about working with someone at John's level, as he approached bluegrass, country, and rock like everyone else I had ever worked with who played by "ear." John was playing with a bluegrass band in Frontierland at Disneyland, which took up most of his time, but when I offered him a job in the quartet, he jumped at the chance. We arranged to work our schedule around his.

My acoustic quartets always remained one step above any of my prior pursuits, in terms of the quality of musicianship and the integrity of the people I worked with. By the mid-1980s, my long apprenticeship had come to an end as I began to finally feel comfortable in a leadership role. Sometimes, however, being a leader means having to make some hard decisions. One morning I got a call from Howard Rose, who was Dan Fogelberg's agent. Dan had recently recorded a bluegrass album that Herb Pedersen and I had worked on called High Country Snows. Dan was planning a long tour to promote the record and he wanted me to put together a quartet to back him up. An acoustic quartet? That had become my specialty.

The only caveat was that Dan wanted Herb to be part of the group. Made sense to me since Herb is such a fine singer and musician. Fogelberg was a huge Manassas fan and loved Al's work in that group, but he needed Herb's voice and banjo and didn't want to have a five-piece group. I made sure John could get time off to go with us and secured Bill and Herb for the tour, but I had to tell my dear friend Al that he wouldn't be a part of this group. Breaking the news to him was one of the more difficult undertakings I've ever faced. I knew Al was very upset. Who wouldn't be in his situation? Ultimately, however, we were all able to move on.

The tour with Fogelberg ran from June to July of 1985 and was very successful, especially for me, Bill, Herb, and John. A special bond was forged between the four of us on that tour that ended up taking me far beyond anything I could have imagined at that point in my life. When we first arrived back in Los Angeles, I naturally drifted into what I'd been doing before the Fogelberg tour—more acoustic shows, and even some trips back to Nashville for television appearances on *Nashville Now* and *This Week in Country Music*. John, however, was convinced we should start a country band with Herb and Bill, but also bring in Jay Dee Maness on steel guitar and Steve Duncan, a multitalented singer and drummer. I knew Jay Dee from working with him on The Byrds' *Sweetheart* album. Plus, Gram and I would go sit in with him at all-night jam sessions at the Aces Club in the City of Industry back in the early Burrito days. I didn't know Steve yet and wasn't in a drummer mood, so I fought the idea. The last thing I wanted to do at that moment was to put together another electric band. But John was persistent, almost to the point of becoming annoying. He was young, ambitious, and, ultimately, persuasive. John began to win me over.

The six of us finally got together and ran through some tunes. I had a few new songs, and we revisited stuff from the Byrds and Flying Burrito Brothers catalogs, as well as some Buck Owens and Merle Haggard songs. I already knew the other guys were good, but Steve was also a fine musician. I hadn't played with a good drummer since Greg Thomas in MCH and, before that, with Jim Gordon in SHF. By the end of the rehearsal, it was clear we had enough material to book a gig, and we set up a trial show at the annual LA Street Scene Festival. It wasn't necessarily earth-shattering, but singing with Herb created a perfect blend between our two voices. Bill and John added some great three- and four-part harmonies too.

I was still a bit skeptical about the electric band idea—too many bad memories from the various 1970s groups I was involved with. But John Jorgenson, ever vigilant, was on a mission, and he found some other places to play around town. In early 1986, we played the Palomino Club a few times, which was the old Flying Burrito Brothers stomping grounds. By the second time we played the room, people began coming in to see us. Word of mouth is a powerful tool, and the word about the new band was good. My attorney, who had negotiated most of my recording contracts in the 1970s, mentioned us to another of his clients, Jim Halsey. Jim was a well-respected country music manager, agent, and promoter who handled Roy Clark and The Oak Ridge Boys—two extremely successful country music acts at the time.

On our second or third night at the Palomino, Jim came down with William Golden from The Oak Ridge Boys. They were impressed, and even though we were still developing our sound, they both saw our potential. Jim offered us a two-week run, opening for The Oak Ridge Boys at the MGM Grand in Las Vegas in May. Coincidentally, the Oaks had recently recorded one of my songs, "Step On Out," that I had written with Peter Knobler, former editor of *Crawdaddy* magazine, and they made it the title track of their album. Things were happening in a way I had never anticipated.

When we accepted the generous offer to play the MGM, we didn't even have a name yet. We were still calling it The Chris Hillman Band, and I remember gazing up at the MGM billboard with "The Oak Ridge Boys" in large letters that glimmered in the lights. Underneath, in small letters, it read "Chris Hillman." Their fans probably thought that was the comic who opened the show. It was during that run in Vegas that the band started to hone a unique sound. For me, those dates were the deciding factor. Let's do this!

Back in Los Angeles, we caught the attention of Dick Whitehouse, a notable music and entertainment lawyer. Dick was a huge music fan and was always out on the town, checking out new acts. At the time, he was the head of legal affairs for Curb Records, which was located in Burbank. Dick started coming in to see us on a regular basis and, on one visit, brought along Paul Worley, a Nashville producer. Paul was recording The Nitty Gritty Dirt Band, who were having a great run of success on the *Billboard* charts after crossing over to country music. Dick saw what Jim Halsey and William Golden had seen—a band with great potential. I was absolutely ready to give it a go, but I was still watching everything with a wary eye. I'd been down the band road many times, so I was determined to walk slowly and carefully.

Dick offered us a recording contract, and Paul Worley agreed to produce our first record. We would be signed to Curb Records, which, at the time, had distribution deals with other labels, such as MCA Curb or RCA Curb. It looked like we would be on MCA Curb. I certainly didn't go out looking for another record deal, and technically, I was still signed to Sugar Hill. When I told Barry Poss about the offer, however, he was happy for me and wished me luck. It was like the old saying, "When you're least seeking the gold, it will fall at your feet." I doubted if there would ever be any gold falling at my feet, but we made the deal and prepared to record in Los Angeles with Paul and his assistant, Ed Seay. And we came up with a new name, The Desert Rose Band, after a song I had written with my friend Bill Wildes.

I had known Bill Wildes since 1968, when I lived in Topanga Canyon and had gotten back into owning and riding horses. I first met him at the Topanga Stables, where he boarded his horse Sonny. Bill, a cutting horse trainer and an incredible all-around horseman, became a very close friend of mine. We shared many adventures together, and on one of my trips to New Mexico to visit my property, I took him with me. We were up in the Red River Valley, near Questa. My friend George Wiseheart, who sold me my land in Amalia, got me, Bill, and a couple of locals into a poker game. It started to turn into a scene from an old Western movie. As the night wore on, one of the guys at the poker table, who had a little too much to drink, accused Bill of cheating. Bill Wildes was not a man to trifle with, and upon hearing those words, he jumped up, threw his chair back, and said, "Are you calling me a liar?" The other man quickly backed down. George managed to calm everyone down, and we finished the game before Bill and I called it a night. In those days, I had no clue that Bill wrote, but I later discovered he was a wonderful lyricist with a good musical sense about him. We would go on to write many successful songs together.

We started the Desert Rose Band record in October of 1986 with sessions at Amigo Studios and Sunset Sound in Hollywood. With Paul and Ed producing and engineering, we made a good record that included three songs I'd written with Bill Wildes, two with Steve Hill, and some interesting covers. When it came time to do the cover artwork I thought of using Jay Dusard to photograph us. Jay was a fantastic photographer. I met him through Ian Tyson, who had Jay photograph many of his album covers. He captured the true essence of The Desert Rose Band, from the cover portrait, to the back shot of us in front of the Palomino Club in North Hollywood.

Our first album for MCA Curb, *The Desert Rose Band,* was released in June of 1987. Jim Halsey became our manager and his son, Sherman Halsey—along with Bob Burwell—handled all our logistics. For the first single, the label released "Ashes of Love," which had been written and recorded by Johnnie Wright and Jack Anglin back in the early 1950s. As usual, I didn't pay much attention to what the record company selected, having gone through this before when A&M would release singles from The Flying Burrito Brothers to no great acclaim. At that point, the last chart single I was involved with was Roger McGuinn's "Don't You Write Her Off," from the first MCH album in 1979, so I didn't have big expectations for chart success. To my surprise, "Ashes of Love" actually made a good start, charting in the twenties on the *Billboard* country chart. I loved the band and was happy to get any radio play. The Desert Rose Band members were great musicians and singers. What a pleasure it was to work in a band that shared such a professional attitude.

As people started to pay attention, I suggested to the band that we might want to investigate getting rhinestone suits. Everybody jumped on the idea, especially Jay Dee Maness, a true county music veteran who'd once played in Buck Owens's legendary backup band The Buckaroos. Manuel Cuevas had set up his own shop after leaving Nudie's, and new stars like Dwight Yoakam were wearing his designs and bringing the flash of country music's golden era back into the mainstream. We all ordered our suits, but kept them within the confines of good taste. This wasn't the "outlaw Flying Burrito Brothers"; this was The Desert Rose Band—a real country band.

After getting through the door of country radio with "Ashes of Love," MCA Curb released the second single, "Love Reunited." It was the song Steve Hill and I had written the first day we met, and it began slowly but steadily climbing up the charts. Dick Whitehouse, still our greatest fan, would call every week with the numbers. Eventually, "Love Reunited" reached the Top 10 on the *Billboard* country chart. I couldn't believe it. This wasn't supposed to happen. I was so accustomed to commercial failure for years, and now a song I wrote and sang was a big hit? I had learned to become a good band leader, was playing with great musicians, was getting the attention of country fans, and was really believing in myself again. I would have been happy if it all stopped there, but it kept getting better. We ended up having two more hit singles off the first album: "One Step Forward," another song I'd written with Bill Wildes, reached number one in *Cashbox* magazine and number two in *Billboard,* also becoming a big line dancing hit. Soon after, "He's Back and I'm Blue," written by a friend of mine from Colorado named Michael Woody, climbed to the top spot in on the *Billboard* country singles chart.

The Desert Rose Band was even invited to appear on the *Grand Ole Opry*. To be able to return after The Byrds' infamous appearance on the show in 1968 was a moment of personal redemption for me. All the artists who were there that particular night were very gracious and encouraging. One of my heroes, Bill Anderson, was the host for the evening's performance and asked me what we were considering playing. I thought "Love Reunited" would be appropriate since it had recently been a Top 10 single. Bill took me aside and kindly suggested we do "Ashes of Love" instead. "Chris," he told me, "most of the folks in the audience know this song so well, and it might be a better one to open the crowd up to you." I had huge respect for Bill, and I took his advice. I was so happy I did because the people went crazy when they heard us play. I think Bill got a kick out of our stage wear too. "I love your suits," he told me. "I'm going to get mine out of the closet and start wearing them again." And he did!

With the chart success from the first album, the Halsey Agency was landing us some impressive bookings, including opening shows for Reba McEntire, The Judds, The Oak Ridge Boys, and Merle Haggard. We were also getting some good TV slots, including bookings on *The Arsenio Hall Show*, *The Tonight Show* with Jay Leno, Dolly Parton's network program, and Pat Sajak's short-lived nighttime show. We were even on Dick Clark's *American Bandstand*, a show I had done many times with The Byrds. The Desert Rose Band had the ability to play the mainstream shows and still appear on country programs like *Hee Haw* and *Nashville Now*.

With the success of *The Desert Rose Band* came recognition. The album was nominated for a Grammy award; I was honored as a songwriter by BMI, my longtime performance rights organization, for the airplay success of "Love Reunited" and "One Step Forward"; we were nominated for the Academy of Country Music's Top Vocal Group award; and we won the Band of the Year honor. In Nashville, the Country Music Association nominated us for the Horizon Award and as the Vocal Group of the Year. I didn't get into the music business to win awards; it never crossed my mind. When I began my career in 1963, the Grammys were a new show, and it would be several years before they were aired live on television. The Byrds were nominated for Best New Artist in 1965, but we lost to Tom Jones. Though it was never about awards for me, I must admit I didn't mind the recognition. It had been a long road to The Desert Rose Band, and I was riding high. I was about to get a crash course, however, in good old-fashioned music business politics.

# CHAPTER FIFTEEN
# PAGES OF LIFE

═══════════

In early 1988, The Desert Rose Band was back at Sunset Sound Recorders in Hollywood with Paul Worley and Ed Seay, who were producing our second album. Steve Hill and I were on fire, writing together every day at my house in Ventura. Seven of our songs made the final cut of the album, including the title track, "Running," which was about my father's suicide. It was something I had never previously tried to write about, but it became a powerful song that had a lot of integrity and treated my father with dignity. Steve and I had a bond that was so strong that he was the only person I could have ever written that song with.

When the album was completed, I called Tom Wilkes, my old friend from A&M records, and asked him if he could find Barry Feinstein to photograph the cover. Barry had shot The Byrds' first cover for Columbia in 1965 through a fisheye lens and then, in 1969, photographed the first Flying Burrito Brothers album, which Tom had designed. Many years later, we all returned to the high desert to shoot the *Running* cover. Feinstein, Wilkes, and the desert again. A tie-in with *The Gilded Palace of Sin?* Coincidence or conspiracy?

The first single released from *Running* was "Summer Wind," one of the songs Steve and I wrote. Country music was a little late catching up to the success of MTV, but this time around we were entering the video age. Other than The Byrds' self-sabotaged attempt at making a film for

"Set You Free This Time" with Barry Feinstein, music videos were new territory for me. The one for "Summer Wind" was filmed on the beach in Ventura with my young daughter taking a prominent role in the production. Both the video and the single earned strong airplay, propelling the song to number two on the *Billboard* country chart. The follow-up single—"I Still Believe in You," another of my songs with Steve Hill—went all the way to number one.

One of the best videos we ever made was "She Don't Love Nobody," which was filmed in Nashville. The song was written by John Hiatt and had been pitched to us a year before we recorded it. When I first heard it, I didn't *hear* it. What I mean is, I didn't hear it as a Desert Rose Band song. When we were working on the album the following year, Bill Bryson said, "Take another look at that John Hiatt song." I rearranged the background vocals in an "answer back" pattern, and it all came together. Yet another big hit. John Hiatt was happy; we were happy; everyone was happy. And the happiness just kept right on when we followed it up with Herb taking the lead vocal on a Top 10 remake of "Hello Trouble," an old Orville Couch song that Buck Owens had covered.

As The Desert Rose Band found more and more success on the country charts, I was hoping one of our records might cross over to the pop charts. We were doing quite well where we were in country music, but despite critical acclaim, acceptance among our peers, and fantastic airplay, we weren't selling as many albums as I thought we should have. I hoped maybe a crossover single might help boost up our sales. At first, I was confused about why the huge airplay and generous award nominations weren't translating into record sales. I soon figured out it was a problem of supply, not demand.

We had the usual complaints that most recording artists have regarding their record label affiliation: no product in the stores, no one working the radio stations, and the label generally becoming the scapegoat for every perceived wrong. We certainly had some real issues, however, particularly with getting product into the hands of the fans. We would have a number one single on the radio and be playing large venues opening for Reba McEntire or Merle Haggard in major cities, but there would be no records available anywhere in the area where we were appearing. This wasn't just a hunch; it was a proven fact. Herb and I would go into the local record stores when we were on the road and walk out totally dejected. I couldn't figure out if it was Curb's deal with MCA or MCA's main acts getting the distribution over their co-label deal with Curb. This was beyond frustrating because we ended up not selling that many records, even though we should have with all the radio play we were getting.

When it came to sales, I was getting a whole new education in how everything worked. In country music, the real trick was getting into the racks at the Walmart stores. The concept is that the shopper moves through the store, buys a new rake, some shoes for the kids, and throws a Desert Rose CD into the basket along with their other stuff. We could only hope. Who knows what kind of politics are involved in such things?

The politics certainly didn't end there. By the time The Desert Rose Band was nominated for Vocal Group of the Year for the second time at the CMA awards, we'd built up a strong track record of a half dozen Top 5 singles. I actually thought we had a good chance of winning. So, there we were in Nashville the evening of the broadcast where, having already performed on the show, we were quietly waiting in our seats for the final outcome. Mary Chapin Carpenter read the voting results for the category, and I swear she paused and shook her head as she finished reading, "The Kentucky Headhunters." It came out like a question rather than a statement. The Headhunters were a fine group, but they had only had one hit, no track record of any merit, and were so obviously a one-hit wonder. Angry, envious, and ready to howl at the moon? Absolutely! "No justice," I quietly screamed inside. Later I found out the real reason we didn't win that night. The Kentucky Headhunters were on a major label, and I discovered that record companies traded votes for certain artists. Why? Because one good nationally-televised trophy win equals another hundred thousand units sold. Totally cutthroat. I didn't know how it worked back then, which is why I was naïve enough to think we might win. With time and a little wisdom, I rose above it. It didn't really matter. As an old country music legend once said, awards shows were created to make *everyone* feel bad!

Of course, playing music was where the real fun was. We had a great couple of years, but I was still looking for ways to unlock our sagging record sales. It was a true mystery when we had such huge radio airplay acceptance. The first step is always a textbook play—change management. And that's what we did. Was that the best option? Did anything drastically improve? We were still getting Top 10 hits, as well as Grammy, CMA, and ACM award nominations, and were already at work on our third album, but still not making very much headway with sales. Fortunately, we were savvy enough not to move to Nashville, keeping our West Coast identity intact. We did win the Band of the Year (Touring) award three years in a row from the Academy of Country Music, which was based in Southern California.

Whatever frustrations there might have been, it was during The Desert Rose Band heyday that I was reminded, once again, what actually matters in this world. Not long after my birthday, in 1988, our son Nicholas was born. There is nothing comparable in this world to holding a newborn baby in your arms for the first time. He looked just like the early pictures of me, and he would bring even more happiness and love to our growing family. I vowed that my family would, now and forever, take priority over any career aspirations or frustrations.

I loved my family so much that it was always difficult to leave home. The Desert Rose Band tours were long, usually a month to two months, but they were good. We'd come a long way since our very first outing, traveling across Canada opening for The Oak Ridge Boys in 1985. Somebody at the Halsey office had found a bus for us to lease that was owned by a nice Canadian guy named Scott Cadillac. Scott was great and always ready to please, but his bus was beyond funky in both appearance and temperament. We broke down every two weeks on average, whereupon Scott would put on his overalls, grab a wrench and a role of duct tape, and patch up the old-timer once again so we could be on our way. Having a little success brought us up a couple of notches in the tour bus leasing arena.

The Desert Rose Band must have gone through five or six road managers during our time together, and every one of them was a character if not a criminal. One noteworthy road manager was Alan Hopper, a sweet and kind man who was an employee of our new management firm. Unfortunately, Alan had the terrible habit of stretching the truth about the distance between shows. What was really 550 miles to the next show would become 300 miles in his mind, and some of those night-into-day bus rides could be grueling. Still, he was a great guy and was always upbeat. One morning we woke up on the bus to discover that Alan was gone. He'd just vanished! We later found out that when the driver made a late-night stop to refuel, Alan had gotten off to buy something in the truck stop. We were all asleep, and the driver, upon finishing refueling, simply assumed everyone was onboard and drove off. Alan walked outside the store and watched the bus disappear in the distance. There he was, somewhere in rural Louisiana, with three dollars, no wallet, and wearing only shorts and a t-shirt. Somehow, through the kindness of strangers, he managed to hitch a ride to the next town and called our manager, Chuck Morris, who got him on a plane to meet us at our next show. Chuck swore up and down that I left Alan behind on purpose, all in fun, but I was completely innocent. I was sound asleep in the back bunk when poor Alan was left to the wolves.

Every traveling musician runs into these same kinds of incidents on the road at one point or another. Sometimes it's accidentally leaving a man behind, and sometimes it's just dealing with the unsavory characters who have a habit of populating the live music circuit. In the early days of The Desert Rose Band, I remember settling up with a club owner in Georgia who made sure I saw his .357 magnum, which he "casually" set on the desk while counting out the money. That was nothing new to me. Prominently flashing guns has always been a part of the world of nightclubs and music promotors. In The Flying Burrito Brothers days I played a festival in Palm Springs, California. I went to the office, along with Paul Butterfield, who was also one of the acts on the bill. Paul always carried a .38 snub nose pistol in his briefcase, a habit he formed after years of working the clubs on the Southside of Chicago, where a weapon could come in mighty handy. Sometimes the occupational hazards might even come from fellow musicians. There was a club in Tupelo, Mississippi, where the house band had to take the night off when The Desert Rose Band was booked to play. They weren't happy and tried to set us up by asking me if I had brought some of that good "California bud." I spotted that con a mile away. These are the sorts of little adventures that any musician from the old days has experienced from time to time.

In 1989, The Desert Rose Band began recording the *Pages of Life* album. By that point, we'd been together over five years, which was the longest I had ever been in a band. Steve Hill and I continued to write at my house, and we wrote six songs for the project, including "In Another Lifetime," the Top 10 singles "Story of Love" and "Start All Over Again," and "God's Plan," which was later recorded by Roy Rogers and Dale Evans along with their son Dusty. What an honor. Herb offered up his great song "Our Baby's Gone," and I think we knew when we were recording the album that it was shaping up to be our best yet. What we didn't know was that changes were coming in the world of country radio airplay that would affect many artists. We also didn't yet know that it would be the last album recorded with the original lineup of the band. Jay Dee decided to leave to spend more time doing studio work for movies and television. We had worked together since the *Sweetheart* sessions in 1968, and it was always an honor to play with one of the most highly regarded steel guitarists in the country.

With the dawn of a new decade, all looked good on the horizon. My family was doing well, and our children were growing up. I was working and relatively happy. *Pages of Life* was released in January of 1990, and I was feeling good about the future of the band. Our next video, "In Another Lifetime," was shot in the Mojave Desert near the small town of Zzyzx, California, complete with a cast of snakes and tarantulas climbing over our boots. We continued to tour and get great press, thanks to the efforts of our wonderful publicist Sarah McMullen, who also worked for the Roy Orbison estate.

Just as I was looking ahead at what was to come, I had an opportunity to revisit the past. In fact, it was the memory of Roy Orbison that was the catalyst for bringing me together with my old bandmates Roger McGuinn and David Crosby. We were invited to play for Roy's widow Barbara at a tribute concert that was staged at the Universal Amphitheatre in Los Angeles. The audience went crazy when Bob Dylan joined us onstage for a memorable version of "Mr. Tambourine Man." It felt so good to be playing music with my old friends again. These sorts of Byrds mini-reunions always worked out well and were fairly tame. If we'd tried to do it for any longer it would have opened up some old war wounds, and it wouldn't have been pleasant for any of us.

The legacy of The Byrds was receiving fresh attention at the time. The previous year, The Nitty Gritty Dirt Band asked Roger and me to sing a version of "You Ain't Going Nowhere," the Dylan song we had recorded on *Sweetheart of the Rodeo,* for their *Will the Circle Be Unbroken: Volume Two* album. We met up in Nashville in late January of 1989 and recorded the track with Randy Scruggs producing. We had no idea that this would end up being released as a single with our names as the artists. It reached number six on the *Billboard* country chart, earned a CMA nomination, and resulted in us getting nominated for a Grammy for Best Country Vocal Collaboration. The nomination was amazing, since we were almost completely ignored when the original *Sweetheart of the Rodeo* version was released in 1968. Even more amazing, I was nominated for *two* Grammys that year, since The Desert Rose Band was up for Best Country Performance by a Duo or Group with Vocal for "She Don't Love Nobody." My past and my present were coming together in a wonderful moment of both looking back and looking forward.

After The Desert Rose Band returned from a long tour of Canada, Europe, and the States in 1990, I learned that Sony, which owned Columbia Records by that point, was in the process of putting together a box set of The Byrds. Not only did they want to gather up the best tracks from our time together, but they also wanted new songs for the package. Roger brought in Bob Dylan's "Paths of Victory" and a new song, "A Love That Never Dies." I brought in Julie Gold's "From a Distance," which I assumed Crosby or McGuinn would tackle. I ended up singing the lead vocal, so I guess the bass player won that vocal competition. Stan Lynch, who played with Tom Petty's Heartbreakers, was brought in to play drums, along with John Jorgenson, who added some guitar overdubs. Ed Seay produced and engineered the sessions in early August at Nashville's Treasure Isle Studios and did an excellent job, just as he'd done on all The Desert Rose Band recordings.

Revisiting our work with The Byrds gave us an opportunity to ensure the legacy of the band by protecting its name. By the late 1980s, Michael Clarke and Gene Clark had their own version of The Byrds and were out on tour with some new players. This became a problem for Roger, David, and me because these "Byrds" were not very good. Frankly, they presented a bad version of what was once an incredibly talented and unique band. To protect the ticket buyers—and to at least get Gene and Mike to bill themselves as a "tribute to The Byrds" rather than "The Byrds"—Roger, David and I reformed again. Some dates were booked in California to establish and protect our rights to the name. We played three shows, beginning in San Diego and ending up in Ventura. We also had Steve Duncan and John Jorgenson from The Desert Rose Band sitting in. The performances were fantastic, and by the time we hit our last show in Ventura with Tom Petty joining us on guitar, we sounded as good as we did in the mid-1960s. It was important to the three of us to keep the integrity and the legacy of The Byrds intact, and not allow it to be diluted for a quick dollar.

That legacy was further cemented when, in January of 1991, The Byrds were inducted into the Rock & Roll Hall of Fame—a huge acknowledgment from our peers and the record industry. The ceremony was still fairly new at the time and was not yet televised, which made the black-tie event—in the beautiful ballroom of the Waldorf Astoria Hotel in New York City—a private and special occasion. All five original members— Roger, David, Gene, Michael, and I were in attendance. Roger, David, and I were seated at a table together, along with our beautiful wives. Michael and Gene's wives were not able to attend, and somehow those guys were seated at a different table. Camilla McGuinn, who is gracious and loving, saw to it that Gene and Mike were relocated to be with the rest of us. We were all together, and it was wonderful. That, in and of itself, was a rarity, as just about every group of inductees usually aren't speaking and haven't been for years. Normally, separate tables are the best-case scenario, but not in this case. We were back together as a band, honored for that special moment in time.

Just before the program began, the images on the video projectors were interrupted. Rather than videos of the inductees, a news broadcast came on. President George H.W. Bush announced that the Desert Storm operation had begun. This was almost a mirror of our first year of success in 1965 when the Vietnam War loomed large and was changing our whole way of life in America. In that moment at the ceremony, it felt like the times weren't changing, so much as turning in a circle. We had made a complete revolution.

Once the evening was underway, Don Henley of The Eagles gave the induction speech. He talked of growing up in Texas and being strongly influenced by The Byrds in 1965. He was eloquent and very complimentary, his words very much appreciated by us all. We went up on stage when they introduced us, and each gave a short speech. Then, the five of us with—with Jackson Browne and Don Henley sitting in—played three songs, "Mr. Tambourine Man," "Turn! Turn! Turn!" and "I'll Feel a Whole Lot Better." Roger played twelve-string and I played bass, while all five of us contributed vocals. Paul Schaffer and the house band helped back us up. It was a perfect evening, and it was wonderful to be recognized and honored for our very best time together as a group.

The only downside to the evening was seeing how Gene and Michael were struggling. Mike was drinking quite a bit, while Gene's hands were shaking. He looked frail, and I knew they were both battling personal demons. David gently offered help with his kind words, "If you ever want to get right, I'm here to help you in any way I can." David, having been incarcerated, strung out, and now completely sober, was reaching out to Gene and Mike. Sadly, it didn't turn into a happy ending. Four months later, Gene was gone. I received a call from his manager on the morning of May 24, 1991. In a frantic voice, he told me, "Gene's dead." He had passed away in the middle of the night from what was later reported to be a massive heart attack. Such a huge talent—an incredible singer and songwriter who, after leaving *The Byrds* in 1966, spent the remainder of his life writing fantastic songs, making albums, and slowly destroying himself. So tragic and tortured a life, but he left us such beautiful songs. I loved Gene. I didn't always *like* him, but I never lost my respect for him and his art.

Over the next couple of years I kept hearing bad things about Michael Clarke and the toll his drinking was taking on his body. I wanted to reach out, but I didn't know where he was living at the time. Finally, I managed to get a phone number for a house in Florida. On the morning of December 19, 1993, I dialed the numbers in hopes of reconnecting with Mike. A woman answered the phone, and I asked to speak to him. "Who's calling?" she asked. "It's Chris," I replied. She identified herself as Robin, Mike's former wife and the mother of his son Zack. "Honey," she said in a very sad tone, "Michael passed away two hours ago. He died in his mother's arms." Oh my God! No words could describe how I felt at that moment. I managed to hold back the tears long enough to finish the call, but as I slowly put down the receiver, they came in torrents. Mike, Gene, and I were younger than David and Roger, so we formed a brotherly bond in the early days of The Byrds. I was closest to Mike, as we anchored the rhythm section together and shared a mutual love for blues and R&B.

Everyone loved Michael, who always lived in the moment and always had a beautiful woman on his arm. I don't think he ever made an enemy in this world and, despite his cunning and larceny, he was a joy to know. We all forgave him because we loved him so much. Michael was never one to be afraid, and I had so many memorable adventures with him—from our time in Puerto Vallarta to hanging with Otis Redding at the Whisky a Go Go. Michael had walked right up to Otis and introduced himself. Before I knew it, we were both sitting with him as he bought us drinks. We had a nice conversation. Otis Redding was a lovely man and such a huge talent. Another time, in The Flying Burrito Brothers, I walked into the bar at the Gramercy Park Hotel in New York after a show one night to meet up with Mike. I spotted him and sat down. Michael said, "Chris, meet Chuck Berry." There was a guy sitting on the other side of him and it really *was* Chuck Berry. Once again, Mike had immediately made a friend. I reached out to shake Chuck's hand. He looked at me and said, "Charles Berry, nice to see you." That's all. And that was good enough for me!

I was close with Mike's mother, Suzie, and, after Michael passed away, we were able to send one of his beautiful paintings to her. Connie also helped his son Zack in sorting Mike's record royalty accounts. Michael was an amazing man who accomplished so much in his short life. After his time with The Byrds, The Flying Burrito Brothers, and Firefall, he played drums for Etta James and Jerry Jeff Walker. As a drummer, he could be lazy, but when he was focused, he could hold his own with the best. Mike put a lot of soul into his music, and that's what it's all about. But, for me, the best thing Michael ever did was introduce Connie into my life. If not for Mike, I would never have known the wonderful woman with whom I have raised a family and shared some of the happiest moments of my life.

# CHAPTER SIXTEEN
# LIKE A HURRICANE

In the summer of 1991, my family and I moved to Ojai, California, a small town that's inland from Ventura. Our new house was located on two acres, with a lot of open space and a wonderful pool. It was a perfect place for the kids. Catherine loved to swim and play tennis, while Nicky loved to climb trees and shoot his Daisy BB gun, just like his dad had done so many years before. We shared some pretty good memories together there, although living in a gated community sometimes felt like we were trapped among our neighbors. At times it was like being locked in with some serious mental patients.

The Desert Rose Band had two albums in 1991: *A Dozen Roses: Greatest Hits* and *True Love*. Following those albums came some changes to the band. I always thought John would be the first to jump ship. He was very talented and driven to success, and I knew he wouldn't be happy to remain a guitarist and background singer forever. When he grew restless, I encouraged him to make the move. Steve Duncan left as well. It was all fine with me. I didn't want anyone to feel unhappy or unwanted, and I thought they should follow their dreams. We hired Tim Grogan to play drums and Jeff Ross, a friend of John's, to play lead guitar. Jeff wasn't a country player, but he added a different element to the sound, and it all worked. After Jay Dee left, we needed a new steel guitarist, and, to our great fortune, Tom Brumley, the legendary musician from Buck Owens's

Buckaroos and Rick Nelson's Stone Canyon Band, was interested in joining us. Needless to say, I was thrilled. Tom—along with Jay Dee, Sneaky Pete, Al Perkins, and Lloyd Green—was one of my favorite steel players. I can safely say I've been tremendously privileged to work with the very best steel players in the world.

With our new bandmates coming in the new year, 1992, the revised Desert Rose Band was ready to hit the trail. We continued touring and prepared to record another album, but country radio programming was rapidly changing. There was a brief moment in the mid-to-late-1980s when a special crop of great singers and songwriters like Dwight Yoakam, Steve Earle, Lyle Lovett, Randy Travis, Patty Loveless, The O'Kanes, and so many others came along and illuminated the country music industry with a fresh new light. They had new perspectives, but they were deeply rooted in country music's traditions. Then Garth Brooks came along and completely changed the face of the genre forever—and not necessarily in a bad way. His presence simply launched a new business model. Garth was the consummate showman—a good singer and entertainer who held a degree in advertising from Oklahoma State University. And he put it to good use. The days of Hank Williams, Lefty Frizzell, Buck Owens, Kitty Wells, and all the great "brother duos"—all that represented solid, genuine country music in my mind—were suddenly gone from the airways. Things change, and it had a ripple effect on many artists who broke out in the second half of the 1980s.

Doing our best to hang in there in the face of a changing landscape, The Desert Rose Band switched management companies yet again. It would prove to be a very bad decision. We were rapidly going from bad to worse, and our airplay continued to dwindle. After eight Top 10 hits between 1987 and 1990, we suddenly found our singles falling shy of the Top 40. All our peers who had previous success seemed to be suffering as well. The effects soon trickled down to our live bookings too. The talent buyers for the state and county fairs booked the following year's acts based on how well they were doing on the charts at the time. Since we weren't scoring the big hits like we used to, The Desert Rose Band was quickly relegated to the "Budweiser Stage" for the summer of 1992. That meant you went from being a main stage headliner, performing one show per night, to playing a smaller stage sponsored by a beer company that required three shows per day. We were working steadily, including another tour of Europe, but I was very conscious of the change in the air.

After coming off the road, we headed to Nashville to record the album *Life Goes On*. "What About Love" was the first single, and I felt it had a good chance of earning some heavy radio play. How wrong I was! Curb Records was done with us. Their plan, as I learned on a forty-five minute phone call with Mike Curb, was to try to market it to Christian radio. That was certainly one of the strangest ideas I had ever been presented with. We'd given them Top 10 radio hits and, in turn, the stores still weren't stocking our records. Was it the label or was it the management? In hind-sight, everything points to the management company, which should have been on top of their game and motivating the label; that's how it works. In the end, Curb released *Life Goes On* in Europe and Asia. It wasn't even released in the United States. How quickly the tide can turn.

The Desert Rose Band's final show was in 1994 at the Riverside County Fair in Indio, California. That was the end of the trail. Going all the way back to The Scottsville Squirrel Barkers in 1963, I had never been in another group as long as I was in The Desert Rose Band. There were many wonderful moments and enough stories to fill three books. Though the end was frustrating, I can confidently say the good far outweighed the bad. I loved that band, but it ended at the right time. I needed to stop the excessive touring; I needed to be back with my family—to really "be there" for them as a husband and a father. My family—then, as now—was far more important to me than anything in the world.

After disbanding the group, I went home to Ojai and enjoyed the time to jump into some new projects that had nothing to do with music. In the early '70s, I had taken karate lessons at one of Chuck Norris's Tang Soo Do studios in the San Fernando Valley. I always wanted to finish my training but never had time to do it because of my touring and recording schedule. Now that I had the opportunity to pursue it, I resumed training and studying in Ed Parker's Kenpo style, which incorporated both linear and circular motion techniques. Parker was precise in his development of this Chinese-based martial art; Elvis Presley even studied with Parker and used some of the "kata" moves in his Vegas show. The Flores Brothers,

Refugio and Jesus, had a big studio in Oxnard and a branch down the road from my house in Ojai. Once I signed up for lessons to resume where I had left off, I was totally committed. My son Nicky soon joined the "Little Tigers," a special class for young kids. He loved it and was as committed as I was. Best of all, we could share in something together.

I spent about five years, working my way up the ranks until it was time to take the black belt examination. Everyone who was qualified to take the test spent an entire month preparing and, per Ed Parker's rules, had to write a fifteen-page essay on a subject related to the martial arts. It was an exercise to challenge both the mind and the body. When the day came, my black belt test took a little over three hours. It was grueling, trying to remember two hundred techniques as the instructors called them out. To add to the challenge, Ed Parker's methods taught you to improvise on the spot. At the end of the test, we each picked a partner and put on our safety equipment to spar a few rounds. I passed! I was so excited as I received my belt from my sifu (instructor). I had stuck it out through intense workouts and sparring, and, at fifty-three years old, I'd never felt better. The martial arts were just the kind of strict regimen I needed at that point in my life. The discipline kept me focused and grounded in a way I had never experienced before.

After a period of self-imposed exile, I missed playing music. In 1995 Herb Pedersen and I worked out another deal with Barry Poss at Sugar Hill Records to record a semi-concept album centered on the Bakersfield Sound of the 1950s and '60s. We put together a great band with Jay Dee Maness on steel, Lee Sklar on bass, Willie Ornelas on drums, and Larry Park playing lead guitar. Our entire budget was around $8,000, which meant we had to be totally prepared before walking into the studio. Perfect! Now, *that*'s the way to make a record, and I think it turned out to be one of our best ever. We recorded songs that were originally cut by classic artists like Buck Owens, Merle Haggard, The Wilburn Brothers, and Wynn Stewart, as well as a couple of tunes I wrote. One, "Just Tell Me Darlin,'" was written with my old pal Bill Wildes. The other, "Bakersfield Bound," was a song I wrote with Steve Hill about the Dust Bowl and the subsequent migration to California in the 1930s. That became the title of the album, and Herb and I had the wonderful Henry Diltz photograph us for the cover while driving into Bakersfield in a beautiful classic Cadillac convertible. Herb and I grew up in California with that music in our DNA, so it was only natural to make that album together. Nearly twenty years later, country star Vince Gill made a similar-themed album called *Bakersfield* with Paul Franklin accompanying him on steel guitar. Herb and I were honored to see musicians of Vince and Paul's caliber follow in our footsteps to help keep the Bakersfield Sound alive.

Shortly after Sugar Hill released *Bakersfield Bound,* Herb and I ran into our old friend Larry Rice. I had known Larry and his brother Tony since 1963 when they were living in Los Angeles. They were already incredibly skilled musicians at a very young age, having been around bluegrass music since their dad, Herb Rice, was playing mandolin with The Golden State Boys. Their uncle, Hal Poindexter, was the lead singer of the band at the time as well. That was the group I would be sure to dial in to hear on *Cal's Corral* that was broadcast live from Los Angeles on channel 13. That show and that band had been such a huge influence on me when I was growing up. Larry had the idea that he and Tony should make an album with me and Herb. That was the birth of Rice, Rice, Hillman, and Pedersen—yet another group that sounded more like a law firm than a band. Just to be able to work with Tony was itself a huge honor. Tony Rice was one of Clarence White's protégés and to this day remains an amazing musician.

Larry put a deal together with Ken Irwin, who ran Rounder Records. Sugar Hill and Rounder had a friendly arrangement where acts from both labels would sometimes move between the two imprints with different projects. Herb and I flew down to Nashville to begin recording with Jerry Douglas on dobro, Ronnie and Rickie Simpkins on bass and fiddle, as well as Mike Auldridge, Vassar Clements, and a very good piano player, Danny Crawford. *Out of the Woodwork* was released in January of 1997. We didn't tour much at all—maybe six or seven shows, and mostly festivals. Looking back, I'm not even sure if we viewed RRHP as an official band or a great side project, but we managed to make three very good records for Rounder. The last one, *Running Wild,* was released in 2001. We tackled some really interesting songs during our time together, from The Beatles' "Things We Said Today," to Stephen Stills' "Four and Twenty." I contributed a couple of songs for each record; some were originally for The

Desert Rose Band but eventually made it to these projects, including "I Will," "The Walking Blues" and "Change Coming Down." One of my favorites was one I wrote with Herb called "No One Else," which was inspired by his lovely wife Libby. Larry Rice was a wonderful songwriter and contributed some great songs to all three albums as well. Sadly, we lost Larry to cancer in 2006. He was a wonderful mandolin player, singer, and songwriter. A very talented man.

In between the first two RRHP albums, Barry Poss wanted to record another solo record with me for Sugar Hill. Richie Podolor and Bill Cooper produced and engineered *Like A Hurricane,* which we recorded at American Recorders in Los Angeles in the fall of 1997. I hadn't done a project with Richie and Bill since the first Souther-Hillman-Furay record in 1974, and it was wonderful to work with them again. Steve Hill and I had come up with some interesting new songs, and Michael Woody and I wrote another called "Second Wind." I always loved Jackie DeShannon's "When You Walk in the Room," which the English band The Searchers had recorded. It was a song I used to play with The Byrds during our shows at Ciro's, so I decided to put that on the album as well. In addition to what Richie and Bill contributed, John Jorgenson produced the songs "I'm Still Alive" and "Living on the Edge," while Herb produced "Heaven's Lullaby" and "Carry Me Home." Along with John and Herb, the musicians we used included David Crosby, Hal Blaine, Steve Duncan, Jay Dee Maness, Lee Sklar, Jerry Scheff, and Skip Edwards—all veterans from past campaigns. It was wonderful to be surrounded by close and talented friends while making a record for an honest man who ran a prestigious record label. It was a joy to be making music on my own terms with the people I wanted to work with.

By that point, Connie and I had been married almost twenty years. Life was good, my family was doing well, and we were very happy. I continued to embrace my Christian faith but was beginning to question and reexamine my own understanding and interpretation of the scriptures. Connie's parents Pete and Vasiliki, who were Greek, raised her in the Orthodox Church, and our children were baptized Greek Orthodox. Connie and the kids attended services every Sunday, and our marriage was blessed in the Orthodox Church in the late '80s with Connie's aunt Mary Ellen and her cousin Helen as our witnesses. In our own ways, Connie and I both believed in the Holy Trinity, and we shared a love of Christ as a family. But the traditions we followed were different. I would attend church with the family on Easter, Christmas, and special feast days but never really understood the intricacies of the liturgy, or what is called the mass in the Catholic Church. The smell of the incense and the sight of the icons on the walls overwhelmed my senses. It was so different from the evangelical worship services I was used to.

As I was feeling restless with my spiritual journey as an evangelical Christian, I began to experience a strong pull toward the Eastern Orthodox Christian Church. This was, of course, long after we had taken our wedding vows. Connie never pressured me into converting. She did, however, pray fervently for me in hopes that perhaps God would guide me to that decision. In 1997, that guidance became very real in my heart. I felt a strong presence leading me and God's gentle voice whispering in my soul. I told Connie I wanted to talk with her priest, Father Constantine, about the church. I explained to him that I was interested in joining the Orthodox Church, which was followed by many sessions where he began teaching me about the sacraments, the true meaning of the church, and when the early Christians established the first churches in the five patriarchates of Alexandria, Antioch, Constantinople, Jerusalem and Rome.

I ultimately made the decision to join the Greek Orthodox Church. My baptism that Steve Hill had performed was recognized, and I was chrismated into the church on October 26, 1997. The sacrament of chrismation is somewhat similar to the idea of confirmation in other traditions. I stood near the altar while the priest prayed over me and then anointed me with holy oil, which is called chrism. I then recited the Nicene Creed, my personal confession of faith. While I was sitting in the pew, waiting until the end of the liturgy when Father Constantine would call me up, Nicky was sitting next to me. He was all of eight years old, but he grabbed my hand, looked up, and said, "Dad, you're going to be just fine." What a beautiful sentiment. The wisdom and love my little boy displayed in that moment was yet another sign that God had directed me to that time and place. I felt so much love that day from all the parishioners who welcomed me into the family—especially Father Constantine's wife Mona, whose friendship and constant presence in our lives is a true blessing. That day also established a stronger bond between me and Connie's family. I was home. My path to Orthodoxy was divinely sent, a direct work of God. I was part of the apostolic church, the church that endures now and forever.

In addition to my spiritual revitalization, I was feeling very physically healthy. My karate workouts, bike riding, and surfing were keeping my body strong, and I planned to stay that way for as long as God willed. At least I *thought* I was healthy. In 1998 I made an appointment with my doctor for my yearly physical. After what seemed like a routine exam, my blood test came back showing I had elevated alanine transaminase enzymes (ALT), which is an indicator of inflammation or damage to the liver cells. I had a further test that determined I was positive for hepatitis C. I assumed all would be fixed with a simple medical treatment until my doctor sat me down and explained that hepatitis C, which had only been identified in the late 1980s, was a far more deadly virus than hepatitis A or B. There was no vaccine. The virus causes the destruction of the healthy liver cells, which can then cause scarring, cirrhosis, and liver failure or cancer. In short, it could kill me. He explained that the disease is passed through blood and can hide in your system for years before showing up. I didn't understand. How could I have contracted it? I flashed back to the time I got a tattoo on my forearm during the end of the Flying Burrito Brothers days in 1970. I remembered looking at the tattoo needle at the time and wondering if it was sterilized. It probably wasn't. Maybe that's how I got the virus, but at that point it didn't really matter how I contracted it. The point was I had it. And I didn't even feel sick. I was completely blindsided by this bad news.

Like it or not, I was going to have to deal with hepatitis C. Once again, Connie stood by my side and took charge of the situation. She made an appointment with Dr. Kip Lyche, a highly-rated gastroenterologist who treated hepatitis C. Dr. Lyche explained that, while there was no surefire cure, some patients were benefiting from the combination of interferon injections and ribavirin pills. He explained that the treatment had only recently been approved by the FDA and encouraged me to get a second opinion. I knew exactly where I could turn for guidance. David Crosby had been diagnosed with hepatitis C and complete liver failure in 1994.

Connie and I visited him at UCLA hospital when he was awaiting a transplant donor. Sick and near death, David wasn't able to make a living in a hospital bed. I was fortunate enough to help him financially. Now I needed David's help. It was four years after his transplant surgery that I called him, and he was there for me. David had his personal physician—Dr. Gary Gitnick, who headed up the gastroenterology department at UCLA—call me and arrange for a second opinion from his team. Connie and I drove down and met with Dr. Paul Martin, who agreed that Dr. Lyche was right about his approach to treatment.

I still didn't feel sick, but we decided to go ahead and start the treatment. Interferon was like chemotherapy in a slightly different form—not at all pleasant. Dr. Lyche told me in no uncertain terms that when I began the treatment I would feel horrible and would be sick every day for as long as I was on the medication. I would inject myself with the interferon three times a week and then add the ribavirin pills to the routine. The last thing he said to me at the end of that office visit was, "You're going to hate me in two weeks." After his nurse gave me my first injection and showed me how to administer them myself, we headed home. I told Connie that evening, "This isn't so bad. I don't feel anything from that shot." Then, around 10:30 that night, I was overcome by chills, and my body went into heavy convulsions. Connie gathered up every blanket in the house and piled them on top of me. Eventually, she laid on top of me too! I was flying off the bed like Linda Blair in *The Exorcist*. It was that bad.

That was only the beginning. The interferon kicks the immune system into high gear on a hunt-and-kill mission in your body, seeking out and destroying the virus. It was the absolute most horrible thing I have ever felt. I grew weak, both physically and emotionally. One of the possible side effects listed on the waiver I signed was suicidal ideations. Those never became serious thoughts, but there were many times I would just break down and cry. And my poor wife was bearing the brunt of it all while taking care of Catherine and Nicky and running her office in Beverly Hills. I was reminded, once again, that this amazing woman has an inner strength most of us can only wish for. I hung in there and maintained a strict regimen with the treatments. I refused to surrender, and I was encouraged by David Crosby. He was a champ who continued to check in on me throughout my treatment period.

In the midst of that trying time in 1998, my mother experienced a severe stroke that resulted in the loss of a lot of her capabilities. This wonderful, very bright woman who had battled diabetes for forty years, finally gave out as her body stopped functioning. She held on but had lost so much physically, unable to speak and barely able to move. We gathered around her, and I prayed for God's grace. At one point, while in the hospital, I held her in my arms and gently told her to surrender, to go with God. I know she heard me because I could see the understanding in her eyes. A few days later, she fell asleep and never woke up again. I loved my mother so much—her strength, her courage, her intellect and wit. She encouraged and believed in me. She was my greatest fan and the faithful friend whom I could call to discuss life, family, and so many other topics on which she could advise me.

My mom was the one who suffered the most after my father's suicide, but she was understanding and tough enough to rally us to go on with our lives. The last year of her life, she gave me a card, writing how proud she was that I'd grown up and become the man she always knew I could be. My poor mother patiently waited through my dark years, silently praying for me to get through those days. She adored Connie and our children, and that meant the world to me. I owe so much to my mother and my father for all they taught me and my brother and sisters. We all survived and achieved success as a result of their guidance.

During the summer of 1998, as I battled a disease and grieved the loss of my mother, I felt like Job in the Old Testament. My faith being challenged, but I was determined not to surrender. Though my body was weak, I was resolved to pursue a healthy lifestyle. I started by calling up Maria Basiotto, a fourth-degree black belt in Kenpo Karate who taught classes in Ojai. I explained my condition, and Maria, who was also a nurse, understood my situation. She agreed to take me on a as student. Standing over six feet tall, Maria was a no-nonsense instructor. During our first lesson together, she looked me up and down and asked, "So, you have a black belt?" Before I could respond, she said, "Now I'm going to teach you *real* Kenpo Karate." I was confused and began to reply, "But I thought

. . ." She stopped me midsentence. "I'm going to teach you the *true* art of Kenpo." As I studied with her over the next year, I learned that Maria was tough but also patient and gentle. She pushed me harder each day until I earned a second-degree black belt. Maria Basiotto was instrumental in my fight against hepatitis C.

The other person who guided me through my daily battle was Dan Mackey. Dan owned a gym in Ventura—an actual old-fashioned gym with free weights. I had been going there since 1982 and already had a good relationship with Dan. He had even helped train me for my first black belt test. After I started the therapy, I asked Dan if I could still come in and if he would help me train. I was so frail that I couldn't do it without help. He readily agreed and started training me, as well as teaching me visualization techniques to use every time I injected myself with the toxic interferon.

Of course I wasn't able to travel that summer, which eliminated any chance of playing music on the road. The moments of joy I was able to capture came as a result of my time with Connie and the children's activities. I might have been weak, but Catherine and Nicky's tennis camps and surfing camps created some beautiful family time together. After four months of treatments, however, I was slowly dying. I was so toxic from the medication that my skin had a greenish tint, and my hair had become thin and straw-like. The doctors were attempting to draw blood from me every week until it was finally impossible for the nurse to find a vein. It took great difficulty to function each day, and I struggled with the effects the medicine had on my mind. I lost thirty pounds. The only good part of the hell I was going through was that I could eat anything I wanted without gaining weight. But, I'll tell you, the trade-off sure wasn't worth it.

Seeing that I was struggling, Dr. Lyche suggested that I join a support group that met at the hospital each week. I got to know an interesting group of people from all walks of life, including a dental hygienist, a real estate broker, and an older woman who was a Holocaust survivor. She still had her "camp tattoo" from Auschwitz, and I held her in great reverence for all she had endured in her life. To realize that now, at this late stage of life, she had the additional burden of battling hepatitis C helped put my own suffering in perspective. Support groups are wonderful. Sharing with and listening to others who can relate to what you're going through while facing a terminal health issue can lessen the stress and help give you hope.

By the sixth month, my body was falling apart from the treatment; I was toxic. I felt like I was ready to die. I developed additional disorders as a result of the initial problem, so it was as if the bulk of my time was spent seeing doctors. In the fall of 1998, after half a year on the medication, Dr. Lyche took me off all the treatments. It was killing me. I was relieved to stop putting all that stuff in my body, but I continued to feel weak. I assumed I was just really tired as a result of the toll the previous year had taken on me. But when I started having trouble breathing and continued to get weaker each day, Dr. Lyche scheduled a series of blood transfusions. Talk about a creepy procedure. Laying on your back for hours while receiving someone else's blood is *not* fun.

Living in Ojai had become difficult for all of us, especially Connie, who was raising two children and still overseeing her office while caring for me. We needed to simplify our lives, so we sold our house. We had a great last Christmas there before moving into a Spanish-style home on the hillsides of Ventura in January of 1999. Just days after settling into our new house, one of Dr. Lyche's partners called and told Connie that my creatine level was critically low. My kidneys were beginning to shut down, and they urged her to take me to the emergency room right away. After another round of tests, I was admitted back into the hospital with a new set of questions, one of which was, "Have you ever been in a third-world country"? Of course. South Africa, 1968. That's where, according to the doctors, I may have been exposed to a strain of tuberculosis. The dormant infection surfaced during the hepatitis C treatment because my immune system was so compromised.

It didn't take long before my kidneys started to fail, and I was transferred to the intensive care unit. Father Constantine came to the hospital room and gave me communion while Connie, Catherine, and Nicky stayed by my bedside. I could tell they were very upset, but I didn't think I was going to die just yet. If I *was* going to die, I was at peace. That night, when everyone was gone, I prayed to God. I asked Him to take care of my family if it was my time to go, and I told Him that I was ready either way. I was perfectly at peace with whatever His will might be. I just wanted everything to be okay with the family in the event I didn't make it through this alive. Then I drifted off to sleep.

The next morning Dr. Lyche walked into my hospital room and said the words you rarely hear a doctor say, "We prayed for you last night, and I think God answered our prayers. Your kidneys are back to normal; this is truly a miracle." My nightmarish year of hell was coming to an end. I had come to the brink of death, but now I was on the mend. I truly owed my life to God, Connie, Catherine, Nicky, Dr. Lyche, all of my other physicians, Maria, Dan, and everyone who prayed for me. God wasn't finished with me yet. There was still more I was meant to do on this earth before my time was done.

# CHAPTER SEVENTEEN
# THE OTHER SIDE

A s my strength started returning, I resumed my music career with daily practice and plans for some shows. But first, in June of 1999, we took a trip to Greece. I had promised the family that when I got better, we would all take a vacation. We traveled through the islands and had a wonderful stopover on the Peloponnese Peninsula at Vervena, the village from which Connie's maternal grandparents emigrated in the early 1900s. It was such a wonderful trip, and we would continue to visit there over the next ten summers. Finally, after some very dark times, the future was looking bright.

The following month saw the release of a Gram Parsons tribute album that Emmylou Harris organized and produced. It included a new performance of The Flying Burrito Brothers' song "High Fashion Queen," which I recorded as a duet with Steve Earle. In September, I flew to New York to film a concert that would accompany the record. It was my first performance since getting over the disease, and I was certainly jumping in with both feet. Not only was it being filmed for television broadcast, but it included an impressive cast: Emmylou, Sheryl Crow, Gillian Welch, Steve Earle, and John Hiatt, who also served as the host.

The show ended up coming out great, but the best part of the trip was that my ten-year-old son Nicky came along as my road manager for the weekend. It was fun to visit New York together, and we enjoyed spending time with my nephew, Hillman Curtis, and his wife, Christina, who lived there. Christina and Hillman, who was a groundbreaking and very successful digital designer and filmmaker, even entertained Nicky by graciously taking him on a tour all over the city while I was at the rehearsals for the show. I was devastated when Hillman died in 2012 after a long and hard battle with cancer. Christina and their children, Jasper and Tess, were at his bedside—as were his sister Rebecca and his mother, my sister Susan—when he quietly closed his eyes and went to sleep with the Lord.

I had the opportunity to gather with great musicians and pay tribute to another old friend the following year for a live concert at the Santa Monica Civic Auditorium that was billed as "A Gathering of the Clan." Fred Walecki—who owned a shop called Westwood Music and was a dear friend to many of us in the Los Angeles music community—had contracted cancer of the esophagus. Bernie Leadon and producer Glyn Johns organized a two-night benefit that included Jackson Browne, Ry Cooder, Emmylou Harris, Don Henley, Jeff Bridges, Linda Ronstadt, Warren Zevon, Bonnie Raitt, Graham Nash, David Crosby, Herb Pedersen, and Randy Meisner. Roger McGuinn wasn't scheduled to be on the show, but he and David and I happened to be doing a photo shoot for *Vanity Fair* magazine on the first day of the two-day event. We talked Roger into coming down to the auditorium to be part of the show that night. We hadn't played with one another at all since nearly a decade before, at the Rock & Roll Hall of Fame induction ceremony in 1991. Fortunately, Roger had brought his Rickenbacker twelve-string along, and when he plugged it in at sound check and hit the opening notes of "Mr. Tambourine Man," everyone stopped what they were doing backstage and lined up to watch us rehearse as if they were in a trance. Suddenly, the mythical Byrds had reappeared.

As other performers were doing their sound check, Herb Pedersen and I visited with Linda and Emmylou in one of the dressing rooms. The four of us, with just one acoustic guitar, sang an old gospel song together. What an amazing vocal blend that was! I was already on a musical high when Herb and I came out on stage at the show that night to do a short guitar and mandolin duet. The crowd was shocked when David and Roger appeared at the end. The three of us—with a borrowed bass for me, and Glyn Johns' son Ethan sitting in on drums—played "Mr. Tambourine

Man" and "Turn! Turn! Turn!" We had a wonderful performance that night—just two songs—but they were spot-on, as if no time had passed. The audience gave us multiple standing ovations and called for more, but that was it. It was only meant to be a brief moment. There were only three of us original Byrds left, but it was a reminder of the impact we made with our music. Roger and Camilla had to pack up to head back to their home in Florida the next morning. That was over twenty years ago now, but it was the last time The Byrds ever performed. And it was a beautiful night.

By that point, Herb and I were playing regularly together as a duo. He's one of my oldest friends from music and is such an incredible guitarist and singer—probably the best I've ever encountered since working with Vern Gosdin and David Crosby in my early days. Having known each other since 1963, Herb and I just fit together like brothers. In the early 2000s, we were offered a record deal with a small label called Back Porch/Narada that was a subsidiary of Virgin Records. We recorded an album called *Way Out West* that was released in 2002. It's one of my favorite "Chris and Herb" records and includes many of the usual suspects: Bill Bryson, Willie Ornelas, Jay Dee Maness, Larry Park, multi-instrumentalist Dennis Caplinger, and Sharon Soldi, who added some beautiful accordion. Steve Hill and I wrote some wonderful new songs for the project, which was mixed in with covers of the Ray Price classics "Invitation to the Blues" and "You Done Me Wrong," The Louvin Brothers' "You're Learning," the Felice and Boudleaux Bryant song "Problems," and the Doc Pomus-penned classic "Save the Last Dance for Me." My niece Kim did all the artwork, which was nothing short of brilliant. She used old pictures of me and Herb as young kids growing up in California. It was a great package, but, as things sometimes go, the label completely folded not long after the release due to poor business management within the company. Sadly, the master recordings for that album may have been lost forever, which is a shame. It was a great record, and I believe that someday—somehow—it will see the light of day again with a proper re-release.

I used to refer to the mid-2000s as my "awards time." In 2004 I was honored by the Americana Music Association with their Lifetime Achievement Award for Performance. My good friend Marty Stuart presented it to me at the ceremony in Nashville, which also gave me a chance to play a short set with Herb, Bernie Leadon, and Al Perkins—all friends from the many groups we'd played in together over the years. Then, in 2005, while on a tour of England with Herb, I was honored with the *Mojo* magazine Roots Award. There were so many interesting people receiving awards who attended the show, including Bill Wyman, who treated us all so well in Manassas, Jimmy Page, Robert Cray, Dr. John, Steve Earle, and Jeff Beck. Stars galore! That kind of event is normally something I would shun, but being honored that night was such a thrill. And getting to catch up with some old friends, like Bill, made for a perfect evening.

In June of 2005, Sovereign Records released my solo album *The Other Side,* which Herb produced. This time we approached it all acoustic, though I used the same players we'd been working with: Bill Bryson on bass, Larry Park on lead acoustic guitar, Skip Edwards on accordion, Gabe Witcher on fiddle, and Sally Van Meter on dobro. That was yet another fun project, with just the right people working together on songs as diverse as "Eight Miles High," "It Doesn't Matter," and "The Water Is Wide." It was a chance to give some Byrds and Manassas songs a different feel in a different setting, and it worked so well. Herb was a good producer who knew exactly how to wrangle a wild man like me.

On March 17, 2006, Herb and I played at the Crystal Palace, Buck Owens's beautiful club in Bakersfield, California. Buck came down and listened to us warm up at rehearsal. I'll never forget when he put his arms around me and Herb and told us how much we reminded him of the duets he used to sing with his right-hand man Don Rich. Such a compliment. Having been a fan of Buck and Don's amazing vocal blend for so many decades, it was an honor to have the blessing and approval of one of my heroes. At the end of our show that night, Buck's assistant handed me a check for our fee, but it was more than we were owed. I found Buck, who was still in the club, and alerted him to the mistake. "Buck," I said, "you overpaid us by $1000!" He gave me a wink. "You boys keep it," he replied. "You earned it." As he walked away, he turned back and, without missing a beat, added, "and save your money!" Not only was Buck country music royalty, but he was also a shrewd businessman. What a great guy. We lost Buck the following week when he passed away in his sleep right after playing his last show at the Crystal Palace. He wasn't feeling too good that night and had planned to go home early, but he decided to take the stage when he found out some fans had driven all the way down from the Northwest just to hear him perform. Herb and I were honored to be asked by the family to sing "Turn! Turn! Turn" at Buck's funeral at the Valley Baptist Church in Bakersfield. He was a truly amazing artist and an amazing man.

The Academy of Country Music awards show was held in Las Vegas on May 23, and Dwight Yoakam was asked by the show's producers to put together a band to honor Buck's memory with a medley of his hits. Dwight invited me to play bass and sing harmony. Tom Brumley—a veteran of both The Desert Rose Band and the classic lineup of The Buckaroos—played steel guitar, while Brad Paisley and Billy Gibbons played electric guitars, and Travis Barker of Blink 182 held down the drums. We played bits of "Act Naturally," "Together Again," "Buckaroo," and "Cryin' Time" before Buck's son Buddy joined us for a rousing version of "Streets of Bakersfield" that was dedicated to the memory of his father, as well as his mother, Bonnie Owens, a singer who was married to Buck before she later married Merle Haggard. Bonnie, too, was an important part of the Bakersfield Sound that reshaped country music forever. It was a lot of fun to participate in that tribute, and I always say it was the very best band I was in for less than fifteen minutes. Dwight has remained a close friend for many years—a very intelligent, well-read, and multitalented man who always makes a point of playing up my contribution to country music. I've been honored to have him record some of my songs, and he has kept the Bakersfield Sound alive through his music and his XM satellite radio show.

Sadly, losing musical friends like Buck Owens was becoming increasingly common. So many of my old friends were dying after struggles with health issues. Sneaky Pete Kleinow had been diagnosed with Alzheimer's disease and was living with his daughter Anita who was taking care of him. After arranging a time with Anita so that she could prepare him, I called Sneaky, and we had a nice conversation about playing together again some time. At the end of the call he said, "Thanks for driving up to see me today." He didn't realize that I was at my home in Ventura, while he was in San Francisco. It was hard and really sad to talk to my old friend that day, realizing how the disease had devastated his way of life. He soon moved to a skilled nursing facility, where he remained until his death a few months later.

A few years later, we lost Chris Ethridge. I was blessed to speak with him while he was in a hospital in Meridian, Mississippi, before he died of pancreatic cancer in 2012. Chris was an amazing bass player and song-writer, having co-written three classics with Gram Parsons: "Hot Burrito #1," "Hot Burrito #2," and "She." He went on to play in Willie Nelson's band for many years. Of course, Gram, Michael, and Sneaky were already gone. With Chris's passing, I became the last surviving member of The Flying Burrito Brothers. I've tried my best to keep the legacy alive and to keep it honest.

Legacy is a funny thing. Sometimes you have opportunities to revisit the music of the past, and it just feels "right." The impromptu reunion with David and Roger at Fred Walecki's benefit concert was a great example. Other times, it can be tricky to capture the right spirit. In 2008, we played a couple of Desert Rose Band reunion shows at the Hardly Strictly Blue-grass Festival in San Francisco's Golden Gate Park and at Copper Country, a festival held at Copper Mountain, about three hours outside of Denver, Colorado. John Jorgenson, working closely with our former Desert Rose Band manager, Bob Burwell, brings in the acts for Copper Country each year. John wanted to put together a show at the festival that would pay tribute to The Byrds. He asked me to play bass. I was confused. "Let me get this straight," I said to John. "You want me to be a part of a tribute to a band that I was an original member of? I'm paying tribute to myself?" Very odd. I should have listened to my inner voice telling me not to do it. Just as we were getting through the second song, a huge thunder storm came upon us, which stopped the show. The sky was crying, to quote the great Elmore James. Perhaps God was angry at us for messing with The Byrds' glorious legacy.

While The Byrds will always be a treasured and important part of my musical identity, it's interesting to look back on the ways that I've personally changed since my time in that band. In those days, I was so shy that I would secure a place at the back of the stage when we played a show. Over time, I'd become much more comfortable being in front of a crowd. In 2009, I was invited to give a lecture at the Library of Congress in Washington, DC. I had never attempted something like that before, and it was all very new for me. I prepared for three weeks, and it went very well. In fact, speaking in front of the Library of Congress audience that day opened up a whole new world for me. I was asked to do speaking engagements at various venues over the next few years, including the Grammy Museum, the Getty Museum, the Museum of Ventura County, Point Loma Nazarene University, and John Hartman's UCLA music course. What frightened me as a young man, in terms of addressing a crowd, had become almost second nature.

Life is all about change and growth. We never fully "arrive," and as long as we're on this earth, we can allow ourselves to be shaped, molded, and chiseled by our Creator. I have faced a number of challenges in my personal life, and while shyness was something I overcame, there were still lingering places of anger inside that would get the better of me from time to time. One of those times happened before a show at Edwards Barn in Nipomo, California, that was going to be recorded for a live album for Rounder Records in 2010. Herb and I had already played two benefit shows at the Barn to raise money for the Annunciation Church, a Russian Orthodox congregation in Santa Maria. We loved the sound at the venue, so when I approached Ken Irwin of Rounder Records about Herb and me recording a live duo record there, he was enthusiastic. I hadn't done a live record since *Last of the Red Hot Burritos* in 1972, so I wanted it to be just right. We brought in our old friends Bill Bryson and Larry Park, as well as David Mansfield—whom I'd worked with in the Ever Call Ready days—to play fiddle. We had everything in place for a fantastic evening. Then, during the afternoon sound check, I lost my voice. Not only did I lose my voice, but I lost my focus and then lost my temper. I got so upset with myself—as in *Hillman mad!*

I was finally able to calm down with the help of my father confessor, the priest of the Annunciation Church, Fr. Laurence Russell, by my side in heavy prayer. Jeff Cowan, our wonderful engineer, reminded me that we could fix any vocal problems in his studio. The album was released to great reviews and great sales—plus a wonderful cover story in *Bluegrass Unlimited.* To be featured on the cover of that magazine was like getting a big stamp of approval from our peers in the genre we loved so much. My angry outburst was a moment of weakness, but the result, *Chris Hillman and Herb Pedersen at Edwards Barn,* turned out to be yet another highlight of making music with my good friend.

I've been honest about the fact that some of my struggles with anger were rooted in my father's death when I was still a young man. An unexpected breakthrough happened, however, during an interview in 2010 with Scott Ross. Scott was a New York-based DJ who married Nedra Talley, a member of The Ronettes. They became born-again Christians in the 1970s, and Scott was instrumental in Bob Dylan's spiritual awakening in that period. Roger and Camilla McGuinn were close with Scott and Nedra, so when a friend of mine in Texas asked if I would be willing to have Scott interview me for a televised segment on *The 700 Club* television program, I agreed. Scott was a terrific interviewer, and he brought out some of the emotions about my father that I had previously kept very private. It was such a moving moment for me, Connie, Scott, Nedra, and everyone else who was there, as Scott and I spoke at my dining room table. I had already forgiven my father for committing suicide, but being able to talk about that forgiveness in a public way was like opening the shutters and letting the sunlight in. Those last remnants of anger were swept out into the light as I let out years of pent-up emotions in a way that others could see. Everyone in the room was crying and could feel the pain I'd locked away for all those years. It was a moment when I truly felt the presence and power of Jesus once again as He continued to work in my life. Now the world would know what happened with my dad, but sharing my struggles in an open and honest way made me feel like a free man.

Soon after, Connie and I had the opportunity to visit the Holy Land with our good friends Father Jon Magoulias and Father Peter Salmas, along with their wives Georgia and Nikki. I had met Father Jon some years earlier when he was visiting our parish, St. Barbara's, in Santa Barbara, California. I was helping in the church when I heard a loud voice across the room say, "You kept me sane in the seminary." I looked up to see a very large man with long hair and a very long beard who looked like the leader of a biker gang. I was taken aback. He came over and gave me one of the warmest hugs I'd ever received. "I'm Father Jon," he said, "and if it wasn't for The Byrds, I might never have made it through seminary." I learned that Father Jon had started out as a bassist in a rock band in the Midwest before becoming a priest. From that day on, we became close friends.

During the first leg of our trip we stayed in Jerusalem, which served as our home base. We had so many unforgettable experiences, including boarding a boat on the Sea of Galilee, where many miracles had taken place. To walk where Jesus and His apostles walked was eye-opening. On the day of our wedding anniversary, Connie and I visited Cana, the site of Jesus's first miracle—turning water into wine at a wedding feast. In the Church at Cana, Father Jon and Father Peter read the account from the scriptures and announced that we were celebrating our special day together. There were many highlights on that trip to Israel, but to have such reverence surrounding us in that holy place was beyond beautiful.

We also had the opportunity to visit Egypt and Saint Catherine's Monastery at the foot of Mount Sinai. We had the option to attend liturgy at the monastery or to hike up to the top of Mount Sinai. Connie went to the liturgy, while I opted for the hike, leaving our hotel at 1:30 a.m. with my fellow travelers. Halfway up the mountain, I ended up hiring one of the Bedouin tribesmen whose camel I rode for the rest of the journey. I will never forget how dark the night was and how bright the stars were. I could hear the bells on the other camels coming up the mountain, and I was struck by the realization that the scene was likely very similar during the time that Moses was on this very mountain. Yes, God is at work in our lives. To be in that part of the world with my precious Connie and my close friends, knowing that I'd accomplished all I'd ever dreamed with my music and had been blessed with two amazing children, I felt peace. I'd overcome challenges, unforgiveness, anger, disease, and so much more. Once again, I felt like I was home.

# CHAPTER EIGHTEEN
# BIDIN' MY TIME

In 2013 Nicky was living in Australia, attending classes at the University of Adelaide to qualify for his graduate degree in viticulture. Meanwhile, Catherine, after earning two master's degrees, had begun her career in education. Connie and I couldn't have been prouder of our two children and all they had achieved so far in their young lives. With all that Connie and I had accomplished in our respective careers, there was no comparison to raising a healthy, happy, and loving family. That truth was never more in focus than when Catherine and her husband Nick welcomed their first child, our granddaughter, in late 2016. To see my son-in-law holding this tiny child in his arms right after my daughter had given birth was one of the most beautiful sights we had ever witnessed. Another reminder of what's important.

Of course, even when you have your priorities in order, it *is* still nice to be recognized for your music. On October 12, 2013, I received an award from the Far-West Folk Alliance, which was a real honor for me, having started in folk music in 1963 and now having come full circle. Knowing that Roger McGuinn had received the accolade a few years before made it even more special. I was overwhelmed and surprised at all the wonderful letters that were written to me from old friends like Roger, David, Emmylou, John McEuen, Scott Goldman of the Grammy Foundation, and so many other dear friends. I was so grateful that Russ and Julie Paris nominated me, and it was fun to share the night's award with such a character as Ed Pearl, the former owner of the famed Ash Grove, where it all began.

One of the letters I received that was read aloud at the Folk Alliance event was from Tom Petty. Tom had always been a vocal champion of The Byrds, but I admired his music as much as he admired mine. That's why I didn't mind one bit when Herb Pedersen took some time off from our performing schedule as a duo to go on tour with Tom. In the spring of 2016, Herb had been hired to play banjo and sing background vocals on Tom's newest record with his original band, Mudcrutch. Tom loved Herb's singing in the studio so much that he offered him a job on the road. I encouraged Herb to accept the offer. While home from the tour for a brief time off, Herb was out with his friend Pete DeCoste. Pete casually said, "You and Tom should produce an album on Chris." Upon rejoining the tour, Herb brought it up to Tom, who loved the idea and wanted to explore it further.

After the Mudcrutch tour ended, Herb called me up and told me about the concept, but I was a bit skeptical. "At least give Tom a call and talk it over," Herb urged me. I knew Tom briefly from way back in 1978 when the Heartbreakers were just starting to break big around the world, but I hadn't spoken with him since he sat in with us at the Byrds reunion show in Ventura, California, in January of 1989. Since it seemed important to Herb, I called Tom the next day. We talked for about twenty-five minutes, which mostly consisted of me saying, "Are you *sure* you want to do this?" Tom would answer, "Well, do you *want* me to?" We kept going back and forth like that, which was pretty funny. Finally, I said, "I would love to work with you in the studio!"

It was settled. We would start recording in January 2017 at Tom's two studios, The Clubhouse and Shoreline Recorders. I hadn't made a studio album in over twelve years, and I honestly hadn't really given much thought to making another record. Working with Tom, however, was just the stimulus for creativity that I needed. Originally, I thought about making an acoustic album, but that gradually changed as we started to incorporate electric guitars, drums, and keyboards. Bill Bryson was unable to record with us due to major health issues he was dealing with. Sadly, my dear friend passed away a few months later after a long period of hospitalization due to emphysema and lung damage. It was the first of my records in over twenty-five years that he wasn't a part of. It was impossible to *replace* Bill, but we had to figure out someone who was equally talented in their own way. We called Mark Fain in from Nashville—a skilled acoustic and electric bass player who had been with Ricky Skaggs's band Kentucky Thunder for almost seventeen years. We recorded everything around Herb on acoustic rhythm guitar, Mark on upright and electric bass, and John Jorgenson on electric and acoustic guitar. I mostly sang live with the tracks while we were recording, which I loved. Herb ran the studio band, while Tom was in the booth guiding us—especially me. Tom's great personal engineer, Ryan Ulyate, ran the board and mixed the album.

In addition to our core group, we had a number of guests join us to make the record really special. My two old bandmates, David Crosby and Roger McGuinn, were kind enough to contribute to the album. David came to the studio and sang on "The Bells of Rhymney," one of my favorite songs from The Byrds' first album. Roger overdubbed twelve-string guitar on "Here She Comes Again," the song we'd written together in 1979. I actually played bass on the song—the first time I'd played bass in the studio in a very long time. Tom brought in the Heartbreakers to play on the track. I loved playing bass alongside drummer Steve Ferrone, as well as keyboardist Benmont Tench. Tom played electric guitar on "Here She Comes Again" and harmonica on "Given All I Can See." Such a great band! Mike Campbell played a great solo on "Restless," another song I wrote with Steve Hill.

One day, while setting up in the studio to record, Herb and I started singing the old Everly Brothers song "Walk Right Back." We were just goofing around, but Tom, who was in the booth listening to us sing, ran out and said, "That sounds so good! We *have* to record it right now!" And that's exactly what we did. We recorded the track, sang it, and John Jorgenson played an incredible solo on acoustic guitar. It was magical, once again highlighting Tom's genius as a musician and producer. Another Hillman-Hill song we dusted off and recorded was "Different Rivers," a song we wrote back in the late '80s when my kids were very young. It told the story of Catherine and Nicky and how each of them had such a distinct personality. I'd stashed it away, just waiting for the right time to record it. After adding a reference to Nicky's future wife, Annie, I knew the time was right.

Everything ran so smoothly with the recording process that, before we knew it, we were almost finished. It only took about five or six weeks in all. We brought in Jay Dee Maness to overdub some steel guitar and Gabe Witcher to play some fiddle parts before finishing all the other overdubs and harmony vocal parts at Tom's home studio. Tom was an incredible producer, loving all kinds of music and having the wisdom to know where to go with my songs. It was one of the most enjoyable times I've ever had making an album, and I was very happy with the finished product.

While we were making the record, Herb and I were invited by Tom's manager, Tony Dimitriades, to perform at MusiCares, the annual event put on by the Grammy Foundation. Tom was the honoree that year and got to pick who he wanted on the show to perform his songs. Everyone from George Straight to Don Henley was scheduled for the show. Herb and I decided to perform "Wildflowers," one of Tom's songs that I had recorded on the new album. We had Benmont Tench from The Heartbreakers on piano and Gabe Witcher from The Punch Brothers sit in with us on fiddle. It was a special night honoring Tom Petty and all the charitable work he had done over his career.

After having done such a great job on the album, I wanted to let Tom know how much I appreciated all he'd done for me. I wanted to give him a gift that would serve as a small expression of my gratitude. I knew just the thing, but getting my hands on it proved to be challenging. Back when The Byrds began, I was playing a Fender Precision bass, but on one of our early trips to New Your City, I managed to locate the Guild factory in New Jersey. On a day off, I took a cab over to the factory, where I tried out a Starfire bass. I loved the hollow body and the double cut-away body style, so after some careful wrangling, I left the Guild factory with my new Starfire and headed back to the hotel in Manhattan. Expensive cab ride, but great bass. I used it on a lot of our successful songs, including "Turn! Turn! Turn!" and "Eight Miles High," but I lost it a year later when someone broke into our van and stole a bunch of equipment—a common-enough story for bands that spend time out on the road. I never got that bass back but ended up borrowing another one until I finally gave in and went back to playing a Fender.

In 2015, a gentleman named Chris Middaugh, who worked at Guild, came up with the idea of creating a Guild Byrds Starfire bass with the help of John Jorgenson and Tracy Longo, a very talented luthier. It was completed and offered for sale as the Chris Hillman Signature Byrds Bass. The company manufactured a limited run of only seventy-five basses, which sold out very quickly. They were great instruments, and some well-known players bought them. I thought it would be the perfect thing to give Tom, but the rapid sales kept me from being able to find one anywhere in the US. Connie actually ended up locating one in a music store in Germany and had it shipped over. Tom loved it. I only wish Guild would have made seventy-five more. I was as honored by Guild creating that instrument as I was in 2008 when the Martin guitar company put out the Chris Hillman OM-28 model acoustic guitar. To have Guild, Martin, and Tom Petty eager to celebrate my musical legacy was deeply meaningful and truly humbling. When I gave Tom the bass, I thanked him for all his guidance and help. I mentioned that what we created together would probably be my last album, and that it was a wonderful way to end my six decades of recording. Tom just looked at me. "What are you talking about? I'm not done with you yet," he said. "We need to start thinking about the next record—something with a lot of drums and electric guitars." To hear that Tom wanted to continue to work with me was good medicine for the soul.

The album, *Bidin' My Time,* was released in September of 2017 on Rounder Records. It was great to be back on Rounder, and the entire team was committed to making the record a success at retail and radio. My agent at the time, Paul Lohr, booked a promotional tour, starting on the East Coast, then on to the South and Midwest, and ending on the West Coast. Herb, John, and I performed as a trio on those dates, and everything went extremely well, with great reviews coming in and great feedback from the fans. We arrived in Nashville to play the *Grand Ole Opry* on Saturday, September 30, and then a show at the City Winery on October 1. Those performances came off really well, but I was shocked the next morning, October 2, when Connie and I turned on the news in our hotel room to learn that Tom Petty had been hospitalized. Some channels were even reporting that he had died. Of course I couldn't believe it. I was sure there must have been some mistake. Then the phone rang. It was David Crosby calling to ask if I knew what was going on. We talked for a short time, both feeling sad and refusing to believe that Tom could be gone. I hung up the phone, still unsure if my friend had died or not.

By that point, I just wanted to go home. There were four more shows to play in the Midwest before we were to return to perform at the Troubadour on October 16. I didn't want to do any of it anymore. I was supposed to do a live radio interview in Nashville later that day, but we had our promotions director at Rounder Records cancel it, and we began making plans to return home. The phone rang again. It was Roger McGuinn. I knew then that Tom had really passed. Roger and Tom had been very close over the years, and we were both devastated. I told Roger I was canceling the next four shows, as I was too heartbroken over our friend's passing to complete the tour. "No," Roger responded, "you shouldn't do that! Tom wouldn't have liked to see you cancel shows. Go out and play the four shows, and all the rest you have booked, as a celebration honoring Tom, his music, and all he has done for you." True words of wisdom from one of my oldest friends. I took Roger's advice and we soldiered on, finishing the four gigs in the Midwest. Since Tom's funeral and memorial were on the sixteenth, we moved the Troubadour show to the twenty-third instead. We played the Troubadour, but we did it for Tom, not for me.

There aren't enough pages to contain the words I could write about Tom Petty—a kind and very humble man who took me under his wing for that brief time in early 2017 to produce the best solo record of my career. I got to know Tom very well during our time in the studio, where we sometimes talked for hours about music, our families, our grandkids, and musicians we both knew and had worked with over the years. He was very insightful and extremely intelligent. We hit it off from day one and would have become great pals on the strength of his sense of humor alone. Tom created such a legacy and was such an inspiration to so many. But he also cared about shining the spotlight on others. At the time I worked with him, he had recently produced a wonderful band called The Shelters, guiding them as if they were his younger brothers. If there was anyone who could have ever gotten The Byrds back together in the studio it would have been Tom Petty.

It seems that, with each passing year, loss becomes more and more a part of life. Buck was gone. Michael and Gene were gone. Gram, Chris, and Sneaky were gone. Tom Petty was gone. Even before we lost Tom, I'd had to say goodbye to so many of my compatriots. Tom Brumley passed away from a heart attack in 2009, after relocating his family down to San Antonio, Texas. Tom was always so active and healthy that it seemed he'd live forever. On some of those long Desert Rose Band bus rides, he would keep us laughing and marveling at his incredible stories about playing with Buck Owens and in Rick Nelson's Stone Canyon Band. I miss him. Less than three months after Tom Brumley passed, Vern Gosdin died of complications from a stroke. Vern was like a big brother to me when I was in The Golden State Boys—always watching out for me, especially when we played some of the more sketchy bars. Vern and I stayed in touch his entire life. He always had the worst jokes. He'd say, "Chris, your career would take off if you just got rid of that banjo player." Then he'd call Herb the same day and tell him, "Herb, if you'd just get rid of that mandolin player, your career would take off." We both loved him, and when he sang, it could bring you to tears.

Another dear friend, Joe Lala—my bandmate in Manassas and the best man at my wedding—died in March of 2014. He was living in Florida, where he had been battling stage four lung cancer. I was on tour with Herb and John Jorgenson at the time, and we were booked to play a show in Tampa. I had asked Joe to come play with us, but he said he wasn't feeling well enough to leave his house. As it turned out, the show was canceled. I called Joe and asked if I could visit him. John drove me over and dropped me off. I sent Joe's caregiver home so I could spend some time alone with him. We talked for hours, and I could see how terribly uncomfortable he was. I was watching Joe slip away right before my eyes.

Out of nowhere, I suddenly asked Joe if he had ever been baptized. He said he wasn't sure, but said he might have been during his brief time in the Catholic Church growing up. We talked about death, and I tried to explain that true life begins as we pass from our old life to the heavenly realm, where we'll see all our loved ones who have already crossed over. I felt such a strong calling from the Lord that night to reach out to Joe and draw him closer to God. "I don't want to pressure you or make you feel uncomfortable in any way," I told Joe, "but how would you feel if I baptized you tonight?" After thirty minutes had gone by, he looked at me and said, "Would you baptize me?" I took a pitcher from his shelf, filled it with warm water, and stood over him. "You know I'm just a convert to the Orthodox Faith," I told him candidly, "but I think I can remember enough of the sacrament to recite the baptismal prayer." I gently poured water over Joe's head and recited the prayer: "Do you renounce Satan and all his works?" Joe answered "yes" as I continued to ask him two more times, just as the priests do. "Do you accept Jesus Christ as your Lord and Savior?" He enthusiastically replied, "Yes."

When our time together drew to a close that night and John returned to pick me up, I looked at Joe before walking out the door and told him I'd see him again. I knew it wouldn't be in this realm, but I knew we would be reunited. The next morning, Joe's stepbrother called me. Right after I'd left, Joe was rushed to the hospital. That's where he quietly passed away in the early morning hours. I've asked many priests about my reciting the baptismal prayers to my friend, and all have told me that, while a more formal baptism would usually be required, given the circumstances, it was the right thing to do. I believe the cancellation of my show that night was meant to be, and that it was God's will for me and Joe to be together.

The most difficult loss for me in recent years, however, came with the passing of my sister Susan. She was already battling health issues at the time she lost her son Hillman Curtis to cancer. She never quite recovered, becoming a bit of a recluse in the retirement community where she lived in Grass Valley, California. Not long before she died, Connie and I had a strong feeling that we needed to fly up to visit her. On our drive from the Sacramento airport up to Grass Valley, Susan's daughter Rebecca called to let me know Susan had suffered a stroke that morning. We continued on our way, hoping for the best. When we finally arrived, my sister was in bed, unable to speak and in great discomfort. We spent a few hours with her, Rebecca, and Susan's other daughter Madeline. As I spoke and sang to Susan, I knew she could hear me through her pain and confusion. I was praying she would survive, but I knew in my heart it was not meant to be. After landing back at the airport in Burbank, I got a call from Rebecca that my beautiful sister had gone to be with God. I had held up pretty well until that moment, but after I heard my niece's words, I hung up the phone and the tears began to fall. I loved Susan so much, and we were very close. She was the one person in our family who inspired me to follow my dreams of exploring music, literature, art, and all good things in this world. I miss her terribly, but I'm grateful for the ways she shaped me. I feel blessed to have gotten to spend what time we had together.

As 2018 dawned, I'd lost my sister, I'd lost Tom, and I'd nearly lost my house in the Thomas Fire that ravaged Ventura and Santa Barbara Counties in December of 2017. Connie and I were displaced, still living in a hotel. I'd released what I figured was my last album and, though I had a couple of shows booked nearby, it was difficult to wrap my head around performing in the immediate aftermath of a fire that upended everyone's life. The first show was in January at the Scherr Theater in Thousand Oaks. I was struggling before the performance, but our priest, Father Gary Kyriacou, came down to the theater and prayed with me before the show. As we huddled together, I remembered Roger's words the day Tom died. I shouldn't cancel. I should make music in tribute to those who are lost or suffering. Music can be a healing force in a broken world. Thanks to Roger's wisdom and Father Gary's prayers, we had a great show. It was followed in February by a performance at the Lobero Theater in Santa Barbara that became a benefit to help so many who had lost everything they owned in the Thomas Fire.

Just before the show at the Lobero, I was getting settled into the rented house that Connie and I would call home for many months while our own place was being restored in the aftermath of the fire. My phone rang. It was Roger calling from South America. "Chris," he said, "this August marks fifty years since the release of *Sweetheart of the Rodeo*. I've been talking with Marty Stuart about the three of us, along with Marty's band The Fabulous Superlatives, playing some concerts to celebrate the anniversary." What a fantastic idea! I was totally on board before Roger had even finished talking. With all that had happened in recent months, I was not feeling particularly motivated to play music and really had no desire to accept any more offers of live shows. But the thought of a tour with Roger and Marty was just what I needed to move beyond my apathy. Roger was always a consummate professional and a pleasure to work with since the early days of The Byrds, and I greatly admired Marty Stuart as a musician, singer, and songwriter. I knew what they were proposing would be the antidote to the preceding months of chaos and confusion.

Many phone calls, emails, and text messages followed as Roger and I laid out our plans for the tour. We both agreed that it should be a scripted show—like a Broadway presentation—with thoroughly rehearsed dialogue interwoven between the performances. Marty had a busy touring schedule booked for the summer and fall, so Roger's agent, Andrea Sabata, took over booking the Sweetheart tour around Marty's commitments. The first show was set for the Theatre at Ace Hotel in downtown Los Angeles on July 24, 2018. It sold out on the first day after it was announced, so Andrea added a second show. That one sold out too. David Crosby caught wind of the tour early on and thought we were doing a Byrds reunion without him. He wasn't happy. Roger and I reminded David that The Byrds were already in his rearview mirror before the *Sweetheart of the Rodeo* recording sessions even began, and we assured him that we would never entertain the thought of a Byrds reunion without all the surviving original members.

Prior to our first full band rehearsal with Marty and The Fabulous Superlatives, Roger and I got together at our friend Randall Wixen's house in Calabasas, California. Randall administered both our song publishing catalogs, as well as those of many other great writers. We carefully worked out our stories about the songs and the making of the album. We decided to add all the country songs we had recorded on earlier Byrds albums to the give the audience some insight into where we were headed as early as our second album when we recorded "Satisfied Mind." By the time we got together with the band, we were ready. And so were they! The Superlatives were all huge Byrds fans, and they'd already mastered the songs before we rehearsed with them. We couldn't have possibly found a better group of musicians to work with for this special tour: Kenny Vaughn, fantastic guitar player, fantastic singer; Harry Stinson on drums and vocals, one of the most sought-after background singers in country music; and Chris Scruggs on vocals, upright and electric bass, steel guitar, and just about anything with strings. And, of course, Marty, the brilliant bandleader who put together the perfect group of singers and players to make up the Fabulous Superlatives. Marty's approach to music is so pure and honest, and he is my favorite mandolin player—plus an amazing guitar player on both acoustic and electric. Some years back, Marty bought my old friend Clarence White's custom-built pull-string B-bender Telecaster from Clarence's widow Suzy. The things Marty can do with that guitar are simply brilliant, and it was great to have a piece of Clarence's legacy as part of our shows.

The opening night at the Ace was an emotional one for me. We could really feel the love from the audience, and Mike Campbell from the Heartbreakers joined us onstage to play "American Girl" in tribute to Tom. After those first two nights, we played a show in Saratoga, California, before picking the tour up again in Kansas City and working on and off through the fall until wrapping up in December in Fort Lauderdale. There was a very dramatic opening to the show, as Roger would walk on stage playing "My Back Pages" on his Rickenbacker twelve-string, while I came in from the other side, playing bass, as the band joined us on the downbeat of the first verse. We then proceeded to tell the story of The Byrds' early explorations in country music, from way back in 1965, and then how it developed into the *Sweetheart of the Rodeo* project in 1968. Roger and I scripted the story. We remembered every little nuance and anecdote in the making of the album. It was so much fun revisiting the music and having a conversation with each other on stage, as if we were guests in someone's living room, relaying this fantastic story of making a record in Nashville. It was one of, if not *the* best tour I had ever been a part of in my almost six decades playing music. Not only were The Fabulous Superlatives one of the best bands I had ever played with, but they were all wonderful people. The bond of faith ran strong through all of us and created such a loving and respectful atmosphere—something I rarely experienced in many of my past endeavors.

Perhaps the highlight of the Sweetheart tour was the many wonderful hours Connie and I shared with Roger and Camilla. We traveled in a caravan, with the McGuinns as the lead vehicle, and used Roger's walkie talkies to begin each new day with a rousing chorus of the Rawhide TV theme: "Rollin,' rollin,' rollin' . . . ." When the show was over each night the four of us would gather around a pitcher of martinis in the hotel bar or up in the McGuinns' room where Roger would unleash his impressive bartending skills. Roger McGuinn can whip up a mean martini! He and I would reminisce about The Byrds and the ensuing years. There'd been a lot of water under the bridge and a lot of highs and lows, but our conversations never turned negative. We found ourselves laughing at the many funny memories while our poor wives endured having to listen to the same stories over and over every night. Such a great time of friendship, fellowship, music, and memories with our wonderful roadies, Camilla and Connie, who took care of us both with such patience and love.

It wasn't until the second month of the tour that I found out what was really behind the concept to begin with. Early on, while he was still in South America, Roger called Marty. "We have to get Chris going again," he said. "It's been a hard year for him with Tom's passing and then his house fire." My good friends rescued me, and for that I will always hold them close to my heart. In the end, I think the fiftieth anniversary tour was the perfect medicine for all of us. It was the healing power of music once again.

I had such a passion for the music when I was in my late teens; I lived it and breathed it twenty-four hours a day. I never thought about the money, the future, or chasing down stardom. It was always *all* about the music. I met and worked with some wonderful people over the years. Many have passed on, and many fell where I couldn't pick them up, but I'll always cherish the best and brightest memories of everyone I worked with. Perhaps if I'd not chosen a career in music, I never would have found the most important relationship—the one with Connie. When I look at her, our son Nicky and his wife Annie, my daughter Catherine and her husband Nick, and our beautiful grandchildren, I know I am a blessed man. I'm grateful for all those who have supported me over all these years, and I know what I was put on this earth to do. I will continue to use the gifts God has given me for as long as possible.

# EPILOGUE

I don't know what got into my head to start writing my story seven years ago. Looking back, it began to bother me that so many books had come out about The Byrds and The Flying Burrito Brothers that were filled with inaccuracies and mistruths. This needed to be addressed by someone who was an eyewitness to all that happened, someone who could retell the story honestly and succinctly. I was there, and I remember it all.

It became almost cathartic as I got deeper in with the story—sometimes even opening up old doors I thought I had locked down decades ago. But it wasn't just the music that propelled me on; it was the gradual growth from who I was to who I became—through heartache and triumph, things we all have to deal with in life. Now, at 76 years old, I have met so many interesting people through the years, and those who I've written about in this book have left a lasting impression on me.

I've been happily married to Connie for over 40 years. To this day, I truly believe she was divinely brought into my life. She is my angel, my saving grace, and my true love. Our children, Nicky and Catherine, are firmly settled in their lives. My daughter and her husband Nick have two beautiful children, and my son Nicky and his wife Annie are on a true pathway of happiness in their marriage. This is my blessing.

Life is truly grand, and I thank God for every waking moment.

# ACKNOWLEDGMENTS

There are many people who contributed, in one way or another, to making this book a reality. Thank you to the staff at BMG, including Will Kennedy, David Hirshland, and Patrick Cleary for his vision to bring me into the BMG family.

Many people assisted with the research, including John Delgatto, Matthew Fowler, Regina Jaskow, Adam Jones, Roger and Camilla McGuinn, Sarah McMullen, Ashley Moyer, Al Perkins, Ron Rainey, Andrea Sabata, Ron Stone, Willheim Van Wagen, and Randall and Sharon Wixen.

Everyone who assisted with the photography went above and beyond. Thanks to Brenda Colladay at the Country Music Hall of Fame and Museum; Gary Strobl at the Henry Diltz Studio; Judith and Jacob Jamison with the Estate of Barry Feinstein; Christopher Santacroce with the Hopper Art Trust; the Tom Petty Estate and family; Joel Peresman, Shelby Morrison, Greg Hall, Justin Seidler and Jennie Thomas at the Rock & Roll Hall of Fame; Pace Romel, Diana LaPointe, and Paula Erikson at Sony Music; and Thomas Tierney and Toby Silver for their assistance with the Sony Music Archives.

Thank you to Scott B. Bomar, my incredible editor and guide on this project. Having someone working with you who knows the music, and is also a musician himself, makes for a great team. I could not have done this without Scott's insightful guidance and direction. A great literary editor is someone who can see where the author is going with the story and assemble the parts in a cohesive manner from an entirely objective viewpoint. It has been a huge blessing getting to know Scott and his talented wife Melanie.

To Dwight Yoakam for his beautiful foreword to this book. Always honest and forthcoming, his words set the tone for my story. I love this guy, and hold him in a very special place, both as a friend and as a talented artist—on the screen and on the turntable. Thank you, Dwight, you are an amazing and eloquent man.

To all my former musician friends and bandmates, thank you for your encouragement and for helping me remember all those great adventures. And thanks to all the interesting managers, road managers and other assorted characters whose paths I've crossed over the last sixty years. To Doug Johnson, thank you for all your wonderful designs and fabulous artwork, and for managing the "Bar None Bunkhouse" so well.

To my very creative co-songwriters: Roger McGuinn, David Crosby, Gram Parsons, Stephen Stills, Rick Roberts, Peter Knobler, Michael Woody, Bill Wildes, Herb Pedersen, John Jorgenson, Catherine Hillman, Jack Tempchin, Connie Smith, and most importantly, my dear friend Steve Hill who has been writing with me for over thirty-five years. Together, we have had great success with The Desert Rose Band and all that followed.

To my family and friends: Hillman, Pappas, Hough, Clark, Garver, Bouzeos, Brault, Pekras, McCormick, Thompson, Phillips, Bather, Darras, Farmakis, Barkoulies, McConnell, Colombus, Curtis, Edsall, Stathis-Langel, Zozos, Cassacia, Russell, and Perfit.

To my spiritual Orthodox Christian Fathers: Magoulias, Salmas, Russell, Kyriacou, Fox, Parthenos, Thomas, Stanculescu, Adams, and Paris.

To my beloved wife Connie, whose faith in me never wavered and who kept me focused and on track throughout this entire project. And to my wonderful, beautiful family who patiently helped me along. I love you all so much!

# SELECT DISCOGRAPHY

===

## THE SCOTTSVILLE SQUIRREL BARKERS

| | | |
|---|---|---|
| *Bluegrass Favorites* | Crown Records | 1962 |
| | Ace/Big Beat | 2003 |

## THE HILLMEN (AKA THE GOLDEN STATE BOYS)

| | | |
|---|---|---|
| *The Hillmen* | Together Records | 1969 |
| | Sugar Hill Records | 1981 |

## THE BYRDS

| | | |
|---|---|---|
| *Mr. Tambourine Man* | Columbia Records | 1965 |
| *Turn! Turn! Turn!* | Columbia Records | 1965 |
| *Fifth Dimension* | Columbia Records | 1966 |
| *Younger Than Yesterday* | Columbia Records | 1967 |
| *The Notorious Byrd Brothers* | Columbia Records | 1968 |
| *Sweetheart of the Rodeo* | Columbia Records | 1968 |
| *Byrds* | Asylum Records | 1973 |

## THE BYRDS (CONTINUED)
### SELECT COMPILATIONS

| | | |
|---|---|---|
| *Greatest Hits* | Columbia Records | 1967 |
| *Preflyte* | Together Records | 1969 |
| | Columbia Records | 1973 |
| | Sundazed Records | 2006 |
| *Never Before* | Re-Flyte Records | 1987 |
| *In the Beginning* | Rhino Records | 1988 |
| *The Byrds (boxed set)* | Columbia/Legacy | 1990 |
| *20 Essential Tracks from the Boxed Set* | Columbia/Legacy | 1991 |
| *Free Flyte* | Sony Music | 1991 |
| *Definitive Collection* | Columbia Records | 1995 |
| *The Preflyte Sessions* | Sundazed Music | 2001 |
| *The Essential Byrds* | Columbia/Legacy | 2003 |
| *There Is a Season* | Columbia/Legacy | 2006 |
| *Preflyte Plus* | Floating World | 2012 |

## THE FLYING BURRITO BROTHERS

| | | |
|---|---|---|
| *The Gilded Palace of Sin* | A&M Records | 1969 |
| *Burrito Deluxe* | A&M Records | 1970 |
| *The Flying Burrito Bros.* | A&M Records | 1971 |
| *Last of the Red Hot Burritos* | A&M Records | 1972 |
| *Authorized Bootleg: Fillmore East New York, NY—Late Show, November 7, 1970* | Hip-O Select/UMG | 2011 |

## SELECT COMPILATIONS

| | | |
|---|---|---|
| *Close Up the Honky Tonks* | A&M Records | 1976 |
| *Sleepless Nights* | A&M Records | 1976 |
| *The Best of The Flying Burrito Brothers—Farther Along* | A&M Records | 1988 |
| *Hot Burritos! The Flying Burrito Bros. Anthology 1969–1972* | A&M Records | 2000 |
| *The Definitive Collection* | A&M Records | 2002 |

## MANASSAS

| | | |
|---|---|---|
| *Manassas* | Atlantic Records | 1972 |
| *Down the Road* | Atlantic Records | 1973 |
| *Pieces* | Rhino Records | 2009 |

## SOUTHER-HILLMAN-FURAY

| | | |
|---|---|---|
| *The Souther-Hillman-Furay Band* | Asylum Records | 1974 |
| *Trouble in Paradise* | Asylum Records | 1975 |

## MCGUINN, CLARK & HILLMAN

| | | |
|---|---|---|
| *McGuinn, Clark & Hillman* | Capitol Records | 1979 |
| *The Capitol Collection* | Capitol Records | 2007 |

## ROGER MCGUINN & CHRIS HILLMAN FEATURING GENE CLARK

| | | |
|---|---|---|
| *City* | Capitol Records | 1980 |

## MCGUINN-HILLMAN

| | | |
|---|---|---|
| *McGuinn-Hillman* | Capitol Records | 1980 |

## EVER CALL READY

| | | |
|---|---|---|
| *Ever Call Ready* | Maranatha! Music | 1985 |

## THE DESERT ROSE BAND

| | | |
|---|---|---|
| *The Desert Rose Band* | Curb/MCA Records | 1987 |
| *Running* | Curb/MCA Records | 1988 |
| *Pages of Life* | Curb/MCA Records | 1990 |
| *A Dozen Roses-Greatest Hits* | Curb/MCA Records | 1991 |
| *True Love* | Curb/MCA Records | 1991 |
| *Traditional* | Curb/MCA Records | 1993 |
| *Life Goes On* | Curb Records | 1993 |

## RICE, RICE, HILLMAN & PEDERSEN

| | | |
|---|---|---|
| *Out of the Woodwork* | Rounder Records | 1997 |
| *Rice, Rice, Hillman & Pedersen* | Rounder Records | 1999 |
| *Running Wild* | Rounder Records | 2001 |

## CHRIS HILLMAN & HERB PEDERSEN

| | | |
|---|---|---|
| *Bakersfield Bound* | Sugar Hill Records | 1996 |
| *Way Out West* | Back Porch Records | 2002 |
| *At Edwards Barn* | Rounder Records | 2010 |

## SOLO ALBUMS

| | | |
|---|---|---|
| *Slippin' Away* | Asylum Records | 1976 |
| *Clear Sailin'* | Asylum Records | 1977 |
| *Morning Sky* | Sugar Hill Records | 1982 |
| *Desert Rose* | Sugar Hill Records | 1984 |
| *Like A Hurricane* | Sugar Hill Records | 1998 |
| *The Other Side* | Sovereign Artists | 2005 |
| *Bidin' My Time* | Rounder Records | 2017 |

## FEATURED GUEST ARTIST APPEARANCES

| | | |
|---|---|---|
| *God Loves Country Music*<br>"Create in Me Clean Heart" | Maranantha! Music | 1981 |
| *Down Home Praise*<br>"Dancing with the Angles"<br>"On the Sea of Life"<br>"Where Could I Go" | Maranantha! Music | 1983 |
| *Will the Circle Be Unbroken Vol. 2*<br>"You Ain't Going Nowhere"<br>with Roger McGuinn | Universal Records | 1989 |
| *Classic Country Duets*<br>"Price I Pay"<br>Desert Rose Band with<br>Emmylou Harris | Curb Records | 1991 |
| *Country Music for Kids*<br>"Little Birdie" | Walt Disney Records | 1992 |
| *Daddies Sing Goodnight*<br>"Lullaby Time in the Desert | Sugar Hill Records | 1994 |
| *Tinsel Tunes*<br>"Blue Christmas Lights" | Sugar Hill Records | 1996 |
| *Rock and Roll Doctor*<br>(Lowell George Tribute)<br>"Straight from the Heart"<br>with Jennifer Warnes | CMC International | 1997 |
| *Return of the Grievous Angel*<br>"High Fashion Queen"<br>with Steve Earle | Almo Sounds | 1999 |
| *Folk Scene Collection Vol. 2*<br>"Mr. Tambourine Man" | Red House Records | 1999 |
| *The I-10 Chronicles/2*<br>"The Window Up Above"<br>with Herb Pedersen | Back Porch Records | 2001 |
| *The Gift (A Tribute to Ian Tyson)*<br>"What Does She See" | Stony Plain Records | 2007 |

## SELECTION OF ARTISTS WHO HAVE RECORDED CHRIS'S SONGS

| | |
|---|---|
| Beck | Roger McGuinn |
| Billy Bragg | Rose Maddox |
| Gene Clark | The Mekons |
| David Crosby | The Move |
| The Black Crowes | Nazareth |
| Black Oak Arkansas | The Nice |
| Jeff Bridges | No Strings Attached |
| Cherryholmes | The Oak Ridge Boys |
| Country Gazette | Gram Parsons |
| Marshall Crenshaw | Pearl Jam |
| Sheryl Crow | Tom Petty & The Heartbreakers |
| Crowded House | Larry Rice |
| J.D. Crowe & the New South | Tony Rice |
| The Dillards | Rocking Birds |
| Steve Earle | Roxette |
| Bill Emerson | Roy Rogers |
| Firefall | The Royal Guardsmen |
| Dan Fogelberg | The Seldom Scene |
| Emmylou Harris | Patti Smith |
| The Hollies | Stephen Stills |
| Hookfoot | Marty Stuart |
| Jimmy Ibbotson | Jack Tempchin |
| John Jorgenson Bluegrass Band | Teenage Fan Club |
| The Kennedys | Uncle Tupelo |
| Alison Krauss | Ron Wood |
| k.d. lang | Dwight Yoakam |
| Laurel Canyon Ramblers | Pete Yorn |